W9-BSR-746

Jet Lag

Jet Lag

The Running Commentary of a Bicoastal Reporter

Richard Reeves

Andrews and McMeel, Inc.
A Universal Press Syndicate Company
Kansas City • New York • Washington

Library of Congress Cataloging in Publication Data

Reeves, Richard.
  Jet lag.

  1. United States—Politics and government—1977–1981—Addresses,
essays, lectures.   I. Title.
E872.R43   973.926   81-12715
ISBN 0-8362-6207-7   AACR2

Articles beginning on pages 5 and 16 originally appeared in slightly different form in the *New Yorker*. Articles beginning on pages 31, 38, 73, 76, 109,
113, 116, 141, 169, 198, and 233 originally appeared in slightly different form
in *Esquire*. The article beginning on page 103 originally appeared in slightly
different form in *New York*. The article beginning on page 127 originally
appeared in slightly different form in *Panorama*. Used by permission.

This book is for
Cynthia Reeves
Jeffrey Reeves
and for
Colin O'Neill
Conor O'Neill

Contents

Part 1

California, There I Came!

"This was going to be our first weekend alone together. The big romantic weekend. We decided to sneak off to the Ventana Inn in Big Sur and just look at the ocean and drink wine, go into the hot tubs. . . ."

A warm evening in California. It was in the spring of 1978 and I was sitting on a deck in Pacific Palisades being washed by a light perfume of orange blossoms. There was a constant and faint sound out there somewhere as the ocean, the Pacific, surged in and out. Ciji Ware, a writer and television reporter in Los Angeles, was continuing her story about the first weekend alone with the man who was now her husband, another writer, Tony Cook.

". . . . We walked through the hills and along the beach all day. Then we had a wonderful dinner and drank champagne and we went to go into the big hot tub, the one overlooking the ocean. You go in through separate sides, a men's side and a women's side, and I did and I slipped out of my clothes and I was in the water. You know how it feels. . . ."

Actually, I didn't. I had never been in a hot tub. But I was enjoying the story and the evening and the friendship, thinking, I suppose, that someone *could* live here. Not me, but . . .

". . . . I was sort of bobbing and treading water along. My toes just touched the bottom. I was coming around this corner from the women's pool to the main tub. It was all steamy and I could hear little splashing on the other side. 'Tony, Tony . . . Tony, here I am. . . .'

" 'Mr. Rosenblatt!' "

" 'Miss Ware!' "

"I came around the corner and there was my first boss from New York. We were treading water naked in front of each other. He said my name—I was his secretary ten years ago—and then he couldn't speak. . . ."

I don't think I could have, either. I identified with Mr. Rosenblatt. I was the New Yorker in the tub—or, at least, on the redwood deck that pleasant evening. And I had already taken plenty of kidding that day. A couple of months before, I had written a cover story for *Esquire* magazine with the title: "California vs. the U.S.A."

"The real action in the United States, on one level," I wrote then, "is a tug-of-war, cultural war, between East and West—in shorthand, between Los Angeles and New York City. . . . The new values against the old, Spaceship Earth against the Puritan Ethic, California against the rest of us and our stuffy history."

It was a piece about Los Angeles as a giant Xerox machine duplicating California values—the determined pursuit of happiness—and delivering them hourly throughout the country via prime-time television and the other sirens of American entertainment. I tried to show that it was a mistake to think that California was becoming just like the rest of America—rather, I said, America was becoming more and more like California. And who needed that?

I ended the article, which was widely reprinted, especially in the East, with some scenes from a futuristic novel about the secession of West Coast states to form a new country, "Ecotopia." A fast-talking New York reporter visits Ecotopia in 1999 and in the misty sweetness of communal hot springs decides never to go back East. The little book was required reading that year in the office of Governor

Jerry Brown, so I took it seriously enough to finish with a flourish, writing: "You ready for that? Not me."

Within six months of that sweet evening in Pacific Palisades, I was living in California. Most of the time. I was, according to *Los Angeles* magazine, a "bicoastal."

"Reeves and O'Neill," the magazine said in an article about people with work and homes on both coasts, "are a prime example of two-career couples whose work, separated as it is geographically, demands that they be bicoastal in order to see each other."

O'Neill is Catherine O'Neill, my wife. We had gotten married in July of 1979, then spent a couple of days in a friend's isolated cabin up the coast at Big Sur—the hot tub was great.

There I was: My mail came to Pacific Palisades. My wife's work—she was editorial director of a local radio station, KFWB—kept us, quite happily, in Los Angeles, overlooking thirty spectacular miles of Pacific coastline. Often, though, I wasn't. Much of my work as a fast-talking reporter was still in New York, where we had a small apartment on the West Side of Manhattan, or in Washington or, most of all, on the road.

In the air, really. I was national editor of *Esquire* magazine, which meant I spent a lot of time in an office overlooking thirty blocks of midtown Manhattan or just hanging around the White House. Then in 1979—which was quite a year for me—I began writing a syndicated column for newspapers around the country. And that column, I had decided, was not going to be a Washington column. It was going to be about and from New York and California and everyplace in between. Even if I had to spend my time in a state of permanent jet lag. Often, I did just that, with my body, having started on one coast, stopping for awhile at a couple of places in the middle of the continent, and ending up on the other coast—only to begin the process over again. But my mind seemed to be working pretty well. There is something wonderful, for me, in the twenty-seven-hour day you live by flying west and grabbing the dream of the ages—cheating time.

In 1980, a presidential campaign kept me moving on—candidates, too, like to travel from east to west as many days as possible to get those extra two or three hours a working day. And, during both years, I was traveling America doing the reporting and the research for another book I was doing, this one on Alexis de Tocqueville, the young French aristocrat who explored, geographically and intellectually, the new United States in the early nineteenth century before writing his classic, *Democracy in America*.

There were weeks! . . . I was a panelist on a national public television show, "We Interrupt This Week . . . " that was taped on Friday afternoons in New York. I would leave Los Angeles after dinner on Thursday, fly overnight—the dread "Red-eye" flights— catch a couple of hours sleep at my apartment, tape the show, and fly back home to watch it with the kids before Friday night dinner. Once, I was doing a documentary film for ABC News and I got a call from my producer, Ann Black, who said, "We need you, you'll have to come over to the office today." I came over—some "over"—from Mount Holyoke Avenue in Pacific Palisades to Broadway and Sixty-fourth Street in New York.

I recommend it. Like all bicoastals, I memorized the departure times of all airline flights numbered from one to six—those are the New York–Los Angeles flights. Better than that, I saw a lot of America and a lot of Americans as the 1970s became the 1980s. In one year—104 newspaper columns—I reported from fifty-six different cities. The largest number of them—who would have guessed?—were from California. I noticed that I just called the state "home" a minute ago. Well, it was my home and that is what this section is about.

"Why don't you just write about California as you see it?" William Shawn, the editor of the *New Yorker*, was sitting in his office on West Forty-third Street, and we had been talking about possible articles on politics or government, on the press or television, the things I had been writing about for years.

Why not, indeed? It was one-tenth of the nation—one out of ten Americans lived in California—and they were still arriving at a rate of five hundred per day. And whatever concerns I had about the effect its perfumed messages might have on my children and great-grandchildren, I was charmed by it. There were moments, some of them in hot tubs, when I could have written, as Henry James did in a letter to his sister in 1905: "The charming sweetness and comfort of this spot have completely bowled me over—such a delicious differ-

4

ence to the rest of the United States do I find in it."

The first article that I wrote about my new home was published in the *New Yorker* on November 5, 1979. It was titled, "Vulnerable":

It was midafternoon when I arrived at Los Angeles International Airport on October 23, 1978, but the sky was already dark. Driving home along the Pacific Ocean, I could see black to the north and west—boiling clouds of smoke coming off the Santa Monica Mountains. By six o'clock, I was standing in front of my house, in Pacific Palisades, watching waves of orange flame break over the mountains. Houses in the path of the waves exploded silently just before the flames reached them. I counted eight—puffs of bright gas, and then the houses were gone. By seven o'clock, I was packing the car—family photograph albums and insurance policies first—and listening to a radio report of tires melting as people tried to escape the fire in automobiles. At eight o'clock, the winds—the fierce desert winds called Santa Anas—suddenly died down, and the waves of fire spent themselves north of Sunset Boulevard, five blocks away. In places, the fire had been moving at fifty miles an hour.

My first earthquake was on New Year's Day of 1979. A friend and I were having a late lunch in a little place called the Inn of the Seventh Ray, in Topanga Canyon. There was a heavy jolt, and the floor vibrated. I thought a truck had hit the building. But the floor did not stop vibrating, as it would have if the building had been struck. I was confused. Actions seemed to be taking place in slow motion. People pushed chairs and tables aside, stood up, and began running toward the door. I realized that there was a sound—a steady roaring, as if a freight train were coming into the room. Outside, I still heard the sound and felt the vibration. Stones were clattering down a hillside into the roadway. The next day's *Los Angeles Times* reported that the quake was "small"—4.6 on the Richter scale. It had lasted less than ten seconds, and there were twenty smaller aftershocks. While it was happening, there was no way of knowing that this thing would be judged small by instruments at the California Institute of Technology.

I had already begun to wonder whether God intended for people to live in Los Angeles. Certainly He never meant for millions of them to live there. One of the first Europeans who saw the place—Father Juan Crespi, a Spanish missionary who passed through in August of 1769—wrote that the area was beautiful and a perfect place for a mission settlement. But he also noticed the signs of alternating drought and "great floods," and felt earthquake after earthquake, "which astonishes us." The men who followed Crespi defied God, defied nature, living in air they regularly poisoned, rerouting the rivers, levelling the hills, filling the canyons, building thousands and thousands of homes among the gnarled little trees and bushes—the "brush" in brushfires—that burn periodically and so make room for new growth, on slopes that continually slide back into canyons, above earthquake fault lines veined deep into the earth. Now I knew: Nature wanted Los Angeles back.

"There would be very few people in Los Angeles if they had to live with the energy, the wood, and the water that are naturally here," Richard Lillard, a retired professor of American studies and English at California State University, Los Angeles, told me not long ago. "Everything is imported. Four-fifths of the water in Los Angeles comes from other places—from as far away as 444 miles to the north. Nature has been pushed further here—a long way indeed—than almost anyplace on earth." Lillard has spent a professional lifetime thinking and writing about the ecology of Southern California, and in 1966 he put his thoughts together in a book titled *Eden in Jeopardy*. He wrote then, "Southern California speeds from one brilliant improvisation to another, valuing means, neglecting ends . . . the sun never rises and sets twice on the same landscape."

We sat talking last summer on the deck of Lillard's house, in the Hollywood Hills, overlooking, on a rare clear day, thirty miles of Los Angeles and the Pacific Ocean. "The city is a triumph of American genius and greed," he said. "What we're looking at was once a grassy plain. There were deer and antelope out there, and the Los Angeles River flowed through. It's been rerouted, of course, but it flowed through there"—he pointed to West Hollywood—"and nature remembers. There was a big rain in 1969, the spring of '69, and water began coming up near houses on Melrose and La Cienega. The original springs under La Cienega had begun to rise again."

West Hollywood is on the "City" side of Los Angeles, between the Pacific and forty miles of the Santa Monica Mountains. The Hollywood Hills are part of the southern slope of the Santa Monicas, a range with peaks that reach up to three thousand feet. To the north of the Santa Monicas is "the Valley"—the San Fernando Valley, flatland that stretches more than ten miles to the San Gabriel Mountains and was desert before water was pumped to it from farther north. When we talked about Los Angeles, we were talking about the basin of the Los Angeles River—roughly a thousand square miles between the San Gabriels and the sea, from Malibu in the north to Long Beach in the south. Politically, the area is a collage of cities—the City of Los Angeles, Santa Monica, Beverly Hills, and others—and communities scattered through the southern part of Los Angeles County. Perhaps six million people live in that basin.

"This is a city built by Yankee ingenuity," Lillard said. "The mud flats at the end of the continent were turned into harbors, marinas were dredged, the hills were levelled and nicked, and the canyons filled in. The water is imported. Even the air is imported, by the Santa Anas from the desert. Otherwise, no one could breathe the air that civilization has brought to the basin. The changes in nature have made us all vulnerable. The '61 fire, the Bel Air fire, almost got me in Beverly Glen—my deck furniture was smoldering from the heat—but the flames stopped about twenty feet from the house. Up there"—he pointed to the hills—"that's been bulldozed and filled; it's held up by cement pylons, but the earth still has a tendency to obey the law of gravity. We haven't had 'the storm of the century' yet—that's a geologists' term. The last one was in the 1880s. A lot of water will come—twelve inches in twenty-four hours, say. It would tear out half of what you and I are looking at right now."

John D. Weaver is also a Los Angeles writer, the author of a book on the city titled *El Pueblo Grande*. He and his wife, Harriett, are active in the Federation of Hillside and Canyon Associations, a conglomeration of citizen groups that monitors hillside development in thirty-one communities. Standing behind his house, in Sherman Oaks, recently, Weaver pointed to the west and said, "That ridge over there is above Stone Canyon. That's where the Bel Air fire started in 1961. They think a bulldozer backfired or struck a spark. There were—let's see if I can remember. Harriett, how many acres burned in the Bel Air fire?"

Harriett Weaver is considered one of Los Angeles's experts on brushfires. She has many titles, among them chairperson of the Mayor's Brush Clearance Committee. "Six thousand and ninety acres burned," she said. "Four hundred and eighty-four homes were destroyed, and the total property loss was about twenty-five million dollars." She continued, "The fires are a natural part of the ecological system. Dead growth has to burn off to continue the life cycle of the chaparral on these hills. The problem came with urbanization in the middle of the brush. A third of the city is in brush. In Los Angeles County, they joke that they don't need fire maps, because the whole thing would be red—'extremely hazardous.' We are just asking for it. The deadwood underneath the green that you see out there is soaked with resin and oils. It literally explodes. An acre of brush is the fuel equivalent of fifteen gallons of gasoline. Ernie Hanson, a fire chief in Los Angeles, got a lot of attention a few years ago by calculating that a hundred acres of brush five feet high can produce the same amount of heat as the atomic bomb that was dropped on Hiroshima."

I asked Mrs. Weaver about the fire I had seen in Mandeville Canyon, in the Santa Monicas, on October 23, 1978.

She said that it had burned sixty-one hundred acres. Another fire that day, fifteen miles to the north, had burned twenty-five thousand acres between Agoura and Malibu. The two fires together damaged or destroyed 270 houses and caused $40 million worth of property damage. Two persons were killed in the Agoura fire. "The thing that was remarkable about October 23 was the speed with which the fires moved," Mrs. Weaver said. "It all happened within twenty-four hours, and the Santa Anas were above thirty-five miles an hour. If the winds hadn't died down, there wouldn't have been a prayer of keeping the Mandeville fire from jumping Sunset Boulevard." I had been standing on the other side, the south side, on Sunset. "Someday there will be a holocaust in this town," she added.

John Weaver said, "Not too far from our house, they built some houses that sold for around two hundred thousand dollars." He pointed again to the ridge west of us. "That view was a selling point. They didn't tell the buyers that they're planning to cut the top off the ridge and use the dirt to fill that little canyon—that they want to flatten out the view to build more houses. They're taking fifty feet off the top of the ridge and putting a hundred and sixty-five feet of fill in the canyon." He pointed to a slope and said, "Those homes down there will be flooded out unless the area gets adequate drainage. That's how it works."

"Floods and landslides are a real problem in the hills," Mrs. Weaver said. "A house half a block down the street lost its front yard in the last rain, and the whole thing is likely to go anytime. The brush is important—you need to leave enough to hold the hills against erosion but not enough to form a fire canopy. Worst of all, the developers cut out the toe of hills to get in that extra house. Much of the soil here is clay, and sooner or later, usually when they're wet, the geological planes slide out like cards from a deck. People aren't aware of the dangers—particularly people from the East. That's who they sell these houses to."

The Weavers talked on about the danger of slides, showing me clippings from the *Los Angeles Times*. In one story, about slides in Tarzana during April of 1978, John O. Robb, chief of the city's Grading Division, the section of the Department of Building and Safety that regulates the preparation of land for development, was quoted as saying that homeowners might be responsible for much of their own trouble. "One problem is educating hillside homeowners to maintain their property," Robb said. "Many mudslides have been caused by stopped drains and the overwatering of plants and other kinds of neglect."

"Overwatering of plants?" I said. "Are the hills that unstable?"

"They can be," John Weaver said. "You have to be careful of gopher holes, too."

He showed me some Polaroid snapshots a neighbor had taken of a house in a nearby canyon that had been caved in by a mudslide in March of 1978. "They've put the house back together now," he said. "You'd come out from New York and buy that house tomorrow. It looks fine. What you wouldn't know is that Los Angeles is not at peace with nature—that's why we get these periodic punishments. It's a man-made city, a tribute to rapacity and tenacity. There were people who could make money by putting a city here—the last place there should have been one. Hell, most of Los Angeles was just a swath of desert between great harbors in San Francisco and San Diego."

The next day, I went over to Tarzana, four miles west of Sherman Oaks, to meet a friend of the Weavers, Irma Dobbyn, who is also active in the Federation of Hillside and Canyon Associations. "They're building in steeper and steeper territory," Mrs. Dobbyn said. "Let me show you something." She took me out to her patio and pointed. We were looking at a bare beige pyramid that was flat-topped and terraced. "They've scraped that down to put in fifty-five houses," she said.

"How long will it look like that?" I asked.

"Probably only about three years," she said. "Plants can be slapped on, and they grow very quickly, with our twelve-month season. These pine trees"—she pointed at thirty-foot-high Aleppo and Montery pines behind her house—"were planted when we came here, fifteen years ago."

We got into my car and drove around the corner to Conchita Way, a street of two-hundred-thousand-dollar homes. "You see the cracks in the streets," she said. "The city would come out to patch them when we complained that something was very wrong out here. They said everything was fine, and let the building continue. Then heavy rains came in the spring of 1978, and houses started coming down in April. Mudslides. The Smith house, up there, broke in half and started down the hill. That empty lot a little lower down was a rabbi's house; it just toppled on its front into the street. The Palmers there are suing for the damages to their house. Two men owned that vacant one next door. I think they just walked away from it when the cracks started appearing. That one"—she pointed to another vacant lot—"went in an earlier slide, eight or ten years ago. They're building there again now. See the foundation?"

The rabbi's name, I found out, was Michael Roth. "It looked like a normal house to us," Roth told me when I called on him. "There was a little hill behind us, but it's not there anymore. I was in Philadelphia when it happened, and my daughter called me and said, 'I don't want you to be shocked. If you watch the news on television tonight, you might see a house in the street. It's yours.' " The Roths are suing. "We're suing them all," he said. "The developer, the city, everybody."

Mrs. Dobbyn, like the Weavers, had pointed out earthmovers clanking along on the ridge that forms the base of Mulholland Drive, the long, winding road dividing the City and the Valley. Lil Melograno, who is an assistant to the area's city councilman and also a realtor, took me along the ridge, which is the peak line of the Santa Monicas. "There are 126 acres in this tract," she said as we walked along terraces carved in the crumbly beige clay. "It's a pretty steep slope—parts of it might be as much as 50 percent—and the city is allowing ninety-three houses. The developers originally wanted 438 houses, but we cut them down. That's what the Federation and people like me do. The lots start at three hundred thousand dollars apiece, so, with houses, the cost of most of the properties will be well over a million dollars. The developers cut fifty feet from the mountaintop over there and about a hundred feet here. The fill dumped in the canyon will eventually be 285 feet deep. The city says it'll be a safe development, but no one knows for sure. No one has enough knowledge of control over the elements, the geology. We can't keep up with the technology of earthmoving and building. In the last fifteen years, the developers have learned to carve the mountains up into flatlands. These are just flatland developments with a view." The view was truly spectacular. In places, we were overlooking both the City and the Valley—Beverly Hills to the south, Studio City to the north.

"That's called Benedict Hills," Mrs. Melograno said after we had driven a few miles west along Mulholland. We were gazing out over hundreds of pseudo-Tudor homes. "Prices start at four hundred and fifty thousand dollars. The developer wanted to build 550 houses, but we got him down to 340. They're still building."

"It's a nice setting," I said, and she looked at me strangely.

"It used to be a lot nicer," she said. "They moved six million cubic yards of earth here beginning in 1970. There was a mountain there." She pointed into the air above a cluster of thirty houses. "They cut off 165 feet of it to get more houses in. That's when the mudslides began. I spent one Christmas Eve shoveling mud out of the house of a friend. There's not much that the city can do. We don't do any testing work ourselves. We evaluate the reports of private geologists. We have to take their word, and, of course, most of them are hired by the developers. The only way to stop this would be for the city to buy the land, and it doesn't have the money."

"Is there corruption involved?" I asked. "Is somebody making enormous amounts of money here?"

"No," she said. "I don't think there's much of that. Basically, it's the American way—the attitude that a man has a right to do whatever he pleases with his own property. Even if it's dangerous for him and for everybody else. And it *is* dangerous. Anyone who wants to live on a hillside here faces the same hazards—fire, water, and earth. People are willing to take the chance because there's peace and quiet, they're still closer to nature, and the air is cleaner up here. They accept the chance that something will happen. They live with danger."

"Are you one of them?" I asked.

"Yes."

The flight to the hills was no doubt another attempt to outwit nature. The air is cleaner because many of the hillside homes are above the smog that sometimes blankets the flatlands of both the City and the Valley. The day Mrs. Melograno and I stood on Mulholland Drive—September 12—was one of the worst days for breathing in Los Angeles history. The city was alive with "Stage 2" smog alerts. The day was one of eight consecutive Stage 2 days—a record unmatched since 1955—and admissions to local hospitals because of chronic lung disorders were increasing by 50 percent a day. The basin is routinely in a state of inversion; that is, a pool of stagnant,

11

humid air is trapped above the city by a lid of warmer, drier air that forms north of Hawaii and drifts eastward until it is trapped by the Santa Monicas and the San Gabriels. Pollution, particularly from automobiles, pumps into the stagnant mass until ocean breezes or Santa Anas wash away the whiskey-colored gases. The hills, however, are usually above the inversion level, which often reaches only three hundred feet above sea level.

As I drove west along Mulholland Drive after talking to Mrs. Melograno, I watched helicopters chattering toward Sepulveda Pass, a cut through the Santa Monicas. They dropped, quite accurately, columns of water on a brushfire climbing up the hills along the San Diego Freeway. The fire was stopped after it had covered ten acres. Los Angeles is very good at that sort of thing. It has to be. Disaster—"holocaust," Harriett Weaver had said—is always near. "Disaster control" has real meaning here, and the city office charged with that function is the Office of Civil Defense, in City Hall East— or, rather, under City Hall East. I drove down four levels below the ground, parked my car, and then took an elevator down another level before being admitted—by buzzer—through eight-foot-high steel vault doors that lead to the office of the director, Michael J. Regan. He is a pudgy Irishman, sixty-two years old, who was a patrolman in the Los Angeles Police Department for twenty-one years and then police chief of a small town called Arvin. In 1970, he came to his present job. He told me that he had been the first police officer at the scene of a "killer slide" in Pacific Palisades, down the street from my house. That was in 1956, when part of the palisade overlooking the Pacific Coast Highway had slid over the road-way—something like that happens every couple of weeks in the winter, with houses and patios hanging over the highway—and pushed a small foreign car almost into the Pacific. "You never saw two people as scared or muddy as the two men in that car," Regan said. "The next day, a highway inspector was on the slope. He was signaling that everything was OK when a second slide came and buried him. Killed him."

As we talked, two women carrying rolled maps under their arms walked through Regan's office.

"We're really talking about ongoing preparations for an earthquake," one said.

"It's like a bomb," the other said. "If it drops, everything is gone. If we predict it and it doesn't happen, no one will pay attention the next time."

"Earthquake," Regan said, shaking his head. "That's what the public worries about. But for us it's not so bad. There's nothing you can do about the first shock. But then you can race in and save people before the aftershocks hit. Floods are the thing we worry about most—they're the scariest. There's not a heck of a lot you can do about flash floods, and there's no warning. The ones we get push around boulders the size of vans. And a lot of people are living in certain flood paths."

He paused and continued, "I'm not sure it makes a big difference. Darned near everybody living in Los Angeles is vulnerable to something. Flood, fire, slides, earthquake. If you live in Bel Air or Brentwood, you could be living in a firestorm canyon. People living in houses on stilts—I just shake my head. People in Tujunga, Sunland—they're in a natural flood path."

"What about you?" I asked.

"Me, too," he said. "I live in Verdugo Hills. A flood would wash me off. An earthquake would flip me off. You can't think about it too much. You'd shudder all the time, because you know these things are going to happen again."

Earthquakes are certainly going to happen again. There were four around Los Angeles in June of 1979. What the city is worried about is a big one, and that is what the women I saw were working on that day, with the city's Task Force on Earthquake Prediction. No one is yet sure whether there actually is a science of earthquake prediction—the Chinese reportedly predicted a large earthquake in 1976 and evacuated hundreds of citizens from the threatened area before tremors began—but the need for such capability is obvious. The "General Background" section of the Task Force's October 1978 Consensus Report began:

> In mid-February 1976 the U.S. Geological Survey announced the discovery of a major uplift of the earth covering a large area that is centered approximately on the San Andreas fault in Southern California. Because of its large size and its alignment along a segment of the San Andreas fault that is known to have been "locked" since Southern California's last great earthquake, in 1857, scientists expressed the concern that the "Palmdale Bulge," or "Southern California Uplift" may foreshadow the next great earthquake in the region. . . .

> In mid-March 1976 the U.S. Geological Survey noted the potential significance of the Southern California Up-

lift, and issued a warning: "If an earthquake similar to that in 1857 occurred today in the region about thirty miles north of Los Angeles, the probable losses in Orange and Los Angeles Counties alone are estimated as follows: 40,000 buildings would collapse or be seriously damaged. 3,000 to 12,000 people would be killed. 12,000 to 48,000 people would be hospitalized. $15 billion to $25 billion in damage would occur. Failure of one of the larger dams could leave 100,000 homeless, and tens of thousands dead."

If such a disaster occurred, Los Angeles might be run from a complex of rooms visible through a glass wall behind Michael Regan's desk. The emergency-operations center is encased in concrete, and it contains food, water, generators, and dormitories designed to sustain three hundred people for two weeks. "This is supposed to withstand a war," Regan said. It looked as if it could. The heart of the center is a cross-shaped "war room." One arm of the cross (Regan's office) would be the working area of the mayor and the chiefs of the police and fire departments and their staffs. The other arm, interestingly, is reserved for the press, on the theory that what is most important—the operations center has already been used for fire and rain emergencies—is providing a panicked public with quick, accurate information. The main room, twenty-eight by fifty feet, lined with glass walls, maps, charts, and blackboards marked "Status" and "Deployment," is essentially a communications center, filled with twenty-button telephones and radio consoles, including a setup to commandeer every municipal radio frequency.

The Fire Department's Operations Control Division headquarters is down a long hall. It is an even more impressive room, two stories high, looking very much like the set of the television series "Star Trek." Under a flashing "Quiet" light, men wearing white shirts, black pants, and black ties sit in five-foot-high rust-colored leather swivel chairs before peach-and-cream-colored keyboards, screens, and microphone consoles. Towering over them are two huge maps and display panels with flashing, moving colored lights that monitor equipment and personnel deployment. It was one of the most extraordinary rooms I have ever seen, but several people told me it does not work very well—the equipment, they said, is always breaking down.

Aboveground, the manipulation of the landscape was proceeding as usual. KFWB, an all-news radio station, was reporting that North Hollywood homeowners were protesting plans by MCA, to level three hills to provide flatland for parking and movie sets at its Universal City Studios. The company wanted to level sixty-seven acres, providing enough fill to cover a football field to a depth of 1,125 feet. MCA, it was reported, was willing to give each of the homeowners six thousand dollars for their acquiescence. But one resident, identified as Billie Varga, was quoted as saying, "The hill we're on is going to go if they take down that one over there." Billie Varga said she was worried about "slide creep"—the geological phenomenon that Harriett Weaver had likened to cards sliding out of a deck.

A month later, I was driving north along the Pacific Coast Highway to visit Helen Funkhouser, a seventy-six-year-old woman who had moved back into the Santa Monica Mountains after losing her home in the Agoura fire of October 23, 1978. KFWB was reporting that twenty-seven hundred acres were burning near Pasadena. I passed a steel wall being constructed in what used to be one lane of the highway. The wall is supposed to hold back the crumbling, sliding palisades above Malibu. Then I turned into Kanan-Dume Road, past a sign that said:

> KANAN-DUME ROAD
> SLIDE REMOVAL AREA
> UP TO 20 MIN. DELAYS
> 8:30 A.M. TO 4 P.M.
> WEEKDAYS

Mrs. Funkhouser is an impressive woman. She was a state legislator in New Hampshire before coming to California, in 1961, with her husband, James, a chemistry professor. They were reading in the ten-foot-wide mobile-home units they had bought to replace their house—two were attached, to give them twenty feet of width—when I arrived at their isolated homesite, just north of Malibu, almost at the point where the Santa Monicas meet the Pacific. "We beat the fire by five minutes," Mrs. Funkhouser said. "We lost everything. Paintings, books, antiques. But Jim did manage to get his cello. We thought we would be safe, because we had built a system literally pouring water on every bit of the house and property, but they say the temperature of the fire was between twenty-five hundred and three thousand degrees. Here. This was my chicken-cooking pot." Jim Funkhouser handed me a flattened blob of aluminum. "It takes a certain kind of person to live here,"

15

she said. "We came back. We all came back. We're damn fools, but the trees come back, and so do we. It's a constant battle. Nature keeps trying to take over here. But it's beautiful, and it's where we want to be."

Whatever else you could say about the hills of Los Angeles, they were worth a fortune. People really can't spend a lot of time talking about the weather,in that part of the world—most days there is no weather, just the usual perfection. When I moved in what they were talking about was real estate.

At my own wedding, they were talking about real estate. After the ceremony, two friends, Steve Meyers and Tony Cook—the same Tony Cook last heard from in a hot tub—came up to me and congratulated me for marrying a good house. They were kidding. But each of us had married a woman who owned a home in West Los Angeles—and each of those homes, not mansions, just pleasant houses, had increased in value five or six times in the truly phenomenal years between 1973 and 1979.

I got to write about it, too. I knew a woman named Joyce Rey who had once worked for Governor Edmund G. Brown—the first one, "Pat" Brown, father of "Jerry." I asked her what she was doing these days and she said she had gone into real estate.

"That's nice," I said, with visions of poor Joyce hammering flags into lawns on Sunday afternoons. That's what LA real estate ladies do—they sit through "open houses" from 1:00 P.M. to 4:00 P.M. behind colored flags signaling buyers and a breed of Sunday wanderers known as "Lookie Lous." "Yes, it is nice," she said. "I handle only properties selling for a million dollars or more."

Oh! Readers back East might be interested in this. "Boom" was the title of the piece I wrote for the *New Yorker* of December 24, 1979:

In August of this year, a Los Angeles real-estate firm sent out more than a thousand engraved announcements that said:
The Harleigh Sandler Company is proud to present a brand new concept in the marketing of residential properties from One Million Dollars
RODEO REALTY

16

This Division will provide you expert and confidential counsel for your special requirements.

The "brand new concept" was a real-estate office dealing only in million-dollar-plus homes. There were twenty-nine of them—priced from $1.1 million to $4.2 million—in Rodeo Realty's first classified advertisement, in the *Los Angeles Times*. Rodeo Realty—a division of the Harleigh Sandler Company, which does about half a billion dollars in business annually—also sent out a news release quoting Mrs. Joyce Rey, a vice-president of Rodeo, as saying, "The influx of the international 'Super' dollar has greatly affected the market. We have witnessed not only a tremendous influx of wealth from the oil-producing nations of the world but also from Europe and the Far East. Most people want to reside in West Los Angeles. Owners of homes in this prime area are realizing that their home is worth as much as a buyer is willing to pay. This has created a unique market, requiring the full-time efforts of a specialized real-estate firm."

Rodeo Realty was an idea whose time had come. Or, perhaps, a million dollars was a price that had become routine. Something, at any rate, had "greatly affected" the Los Angeles real-estate market. Fred Case, a professor of urban-land economics at the Graduate School of Management of the University of California at Los Angeles, has compiled a "Single-Family Home Price Index" for Los Angeles County going back to 1900. Plotted on graph paper, the curve of the index looks like half of a postcard photograph of the Eiffel Tower. There is a more or less flat line, like the ground, from 1900 to 1940, a period in which the index began at $2,000 and rose, almost imperceptibly, to $4,500. From 1940 to 1973, the line approximates the base of the tower, rising from that $4,500 to $37,000. In 1973, the line begins to shoot almost straight up, rising in five years from $37,000 to $105,000—an average annual rate of increase of about 37 percent.

At the top of this market are the unadvertised sales of mansions in the city's Bel Air section for fifteen million dollars. The advertised sales for other highly desirable neighborhoods—taken from the listings of one agency, the George Elkins Company, in the classified section of the *Los Angeles Times* of November 4 of this year—include such offerings as these:

BEVERLY HILLS . . . 2 bds, 2 bas . . . Lots of potential & charm. Bring your own decorator or do-it-yourself, perfect for small family or couple . . . $330,000.

HOLMBY HILLS . . . Magnificent rambling ranch on ap-
prox. 2 acres . . . Plans for tennis court . . . Reduced to
$1,900,000.

"Potential" and "charm," of course, are usually code words for
"wreck." "Reduced" means that the sellers had thought they could
get even more, but things had slowed down a bit as the interest on
mortgage rates climbed toward 15 percent, after the Federal Reserve
Board moved to tighten credit on October 6.

I decided to answer an ad for a charmer in the Pacific Palisades
section: "3 BR. 2 bas." The style was "California Cottage." The
house, which I saw in the company of several other house hunters,
turned out to be a thirty-three-year-old one-story bungalow—1,400
square feet of basementless, atticless house on a 50-by-110-foot lot.
It had seen better days, and they were a long time ago. Mrs. Gerti
Brunner, the agent showing the house, was able to do so without
leaving the little living room. What you saw was what you got,
including the third bedroom, created by a plasterboard wall dividing
the garage—in effect a bundling board between an automobile and
sleeping children.

"My God," said a woman looking into a closet-size bathroom.
"This doesn't even compare with the worst house in Levittown."

"Now, now," another prospective buyer said. "That's not the
right attitude. This is California."

The price was $259,000.

This was California—or, at least, the west side of Los Angeles,
where, as Mrs. Rey of Rodeo Realty had said, "most people want to
reside." Those people include Omar (Albert-Bernard) Bongo, who
is the president of Gabon. President Bongo, according to the real-
estate pages of the Los Angeles Times, paid $2.2 million in cash for a
six-bedroom house in "the flats" of Beverly Hills—that city's less
desirable section. The house, with furnishings, was listed for sale at
$2 million, but President Bongo, arriving in one of a pair of matched
white limousines, paid the owners $200,000 extra on the condition
that they vacate the premises within forty-eight hours.

Limousines are far from unusual in the neighborhood. An actress
who lives near the Bongo house says that real-estate agents have
come to her door and pointed to the shaded rear windows of a
limousine parked in the street and said something like, "Madam,
inside that car is a genuine Arab who has authorized me to offer you
cash for your house." But, then, everyone has a story. A Saudi
Arabian businessman I know told me that half of his country's

ministers of state owned houses in or around Beverly Hills and that some of them lived there most of the time. Or the one—true—about a movie producer who bought a Beverly Hills house, then changed his mind before moving in and made a half a million dollars on the resale. Or the head of a department at UCLA who told me that he sought out homosexuals when recruiting new instructors, because "people with families can't afford to come here anymore, and gays are willing to live in tiny apartments in West Hollywood."

Almost as common as the limousines are the "caravans." I arranged to meet Mrs. Rey, and she invited me to my first caravan. She drove me, in her Mercedes, up the winding roads of "the hills" of Beverly Hills to the end of Cabrillo Drive and parked in a small cul-de-sac. We were alone for a short time, and then I heard the sound of screeching tires. Within a minute or two, four Cadillac Sevilles, two more Mercedes, and a BMW were in the little circle. Women burst out of the cars—perhaps twenty women, with long hair and smiles, glints of jewelry—and swirled toward the house, shouting quick greetings.

"Four and a maid's"—four bedrooms and quarters for a maid.

"One point two"—the price was $1.2 million.

"A Persian. Definitely a Persian," said Dorothy Singer, one of Harleigh Sandler's five hundred salespeople. She was showing the house; that is, she had obtained the listing for the company, and she would get a share of the commission, which was 6 percent, no matter who actually closed the deal with a buyer.

"A Persian?" I said.

"Iranians," Mrs. Singer said. "They like all this gilt, the mirrors. Fancy stuff. It's their style."

In ten minutes, the showing was over, and all eight cars were moving down the hill, caravanning toward another new listing. Everything we saw that day was listed exclusively with Harleigh Sandler. The agency would get half of the 6 percent commission paid by the buyer, and the other half would go to the agent or agents involved in the sale. "They get no salary," Mrs. Rey said. "It's all commission. I made four thousand dollars my first year, 1975. Now I need a tax lawyer to figure out how much I'm making."

The rest of the afternoon was a blur. Mrs. Rey did the driving and most of the talking. At one house, she said, "This is North Hillcrest—the less expensive side of Beverly Hills. They're asking one point eight five. Four bedrooms. Someone bought this a year ago—for speculation, I'm pretty sure—at six hundred and fifty thousand. They did a lot of work. See the double baths and dressing rooms? That's a requirement when you get over a million. The tennis court is undersized, but any court adds a hundred or two hundred thousand dollars to the price in Bev Hills. Too bad it's not north of Sunset—it'd be well over two million."

Driving along Sunset Boulevard, Mrs. Rey said, "I sold that gray Tudor there for two million dollars in January. I could get two point five now." As we were passing through the intersection of North Roxbury Drive and Benedict Canyon Drive, she said, "This is a good area. That one just went for one point two. Freddie Fields, the Hollywood agent, sold that one for one point four. Peter Falk bought there for one point two, I think it was. Vidal Sassoon bought that one for one point two five. He got a good buy—it was a divorce situation. A lot of them are."

We stopped at a house on Benedict Canyon Drive. Two million with tennis court, steam showers, and a Betamax system piped into every room. Walls of bookshelves—very unusual. "This house caused one of the first fights I had when I got married," she said. Her husband is Alejandro Rey, an actor featured in the "Flying Nun" TV series. "I wanted to buy it for a hundred and ten thousand dollars— that was in 1969—but Alejandro didn't."

The next house we looked at was listed as being on Oak Pass Road, Beverly Hills PO. "It's not exactly in Beverly Hills," Mrs. Rey said. "The Beverly Hills Post Office addresses are actually in the city of Los Angeles. But the address adds a hundred thousand dollars, sometimes more, to the price. Houses in Beverly Hills proper are sometimes worth double what the same house would bring in LA. The schools and the police are better in Bev Hills, but mainly it's image." The house—"four and a maid's"—was priced at a million dollars. The brochure listing read, "A rich man's country comfort above the city's woes." The owner, an actor named Reid Smith, said hello to the caravanners and then went back to supervising three workmen who were laying tile and carpet in one of the three bathrooms. "Reid's a speculator," Mrs. Rey said. "He buys houses like this and renovates them. Rebuilds them, really. He's quite good. This bedroom"—a master bedroom overlooking a canyon—"is completely new. Reid knows how to tear down and build on to push a house past the million mark. He lives in the house while he's doing the work, and then moves on to the next one."

After our tour, Mrs. Rey drove me to the offices of Harleigh Sandler, at 420 North Camden Drive—a block west of Rodeo Drive, which prides itself on being the most expensive shopping strip in the United States. Rodeo Realty is on the second floor, away from the noise and tension of Harleigh Sandler's ground-floor headquarters. The back walls of the ground floor are covered with blue posters in the shape of diamonds and a large honor roll of names under a sign that says, "Million Dollar Club." There were more than a hundred names under the sign, each that of an agent who had sold more than a million dollars' worth of property in the first ten months of 1979.

"What do the blue diamonds mean?" I asked.

"Those are for people who have sold more than three million," Mrs. Rey said.

There were more than fifty diamonds. Half of the 6 percent commission on those sales, I figured, was ninety thousand dollars for each of those fifty people. A woman I know who works for another agency buys a real diamond every time she makes a million-dollar sale. She has eight diamonds now.

Before going upstairs, Mrs. Rey, who is also a vice-president of Harleigh Sandler, wanted to check "the action." And there was action—shouts across the cubicles covering the floor, and women running for telephones. It all reminded me of the headquarters of a well-financed political campaign. "Joyce!" a woman said, peering over one of the shoulder-high partitions of a five-by-five-foot office. "The house on Roxbury has gone on. Three point five million."

"Who got it?" Mrs. Rey asked.

The woman pointed to the next cubicle and said, "Shane."

"Congrats," Mrs. Rey said. "I used to knock on that door myself to see if they'd sell." She then introduced the woman, saying, "This is one of our stars, Marcia Bro."

"What's the secret?" I asked Miss Bro.

"Hard work," she answered.

"How did you get into this?"

"The usual," she said. "I was a housewife, and I bought three houses through Harleigh Sandler. Drove them crazy. Then my husband and I separated, and I drove them crazy to get a chance here. All you have to do is work twenty-four hours a day. When it was really hot, you had to be at the door with a buyer when they put up the 'For Sale' sign. It's crazy. My father had a house in Indiana that looked like Tara, and he couldn't sell it for seventy thousand dollars. He can't believe that I bought into a duplex with the roof falling in on my head for two hundred thousand dollars. Now you

21

wouldn't live in what they're selling for two and three hundred thousand. We've got the influx. This is where people want to live."

"The whole world wants to live here," Mrs. Rey said.

Upstairs in her office, Mrs. Rey, who is thirty-six years old, said she had taken the California realtor's examination in 1973—preparation courses for the exam usually last six weeks—after working as a city schoolteacher and as a part-time stewardess for Western Airlines. "But I didn't really get into it until 1975," she continued. "After I had worked in Jerry Brown's 1974 campaign for governor. I love the excitement of selling, but I sometimes feel that I'm not really doing anything worthwhile. I used to teach black children at Dorsey High, and I thought that was worthwhile. Oh, well."

"Who buys these houses?" I asked.

"Almost half the sales are to foreigners," she said. "Not as many of them are Arabs as you might think. European flight capital is the big thing—English, French, Italian. They pay cash. They have a hard time understanding the concept of installment buying, of financing. Then, there are the Persians, the Saudis, the Syrians, people from Hong Kong—everywhere. Then, celebrities in all professions—people making a lot of money. The investors and the speculators, the people betting on inflation. Then, there are just people who got into the Los Angeles market and kept trading up."

I thought of a friend, a writer, who said that she hated to have friends in the East know that her house was worth more than a million dollars, because to her it was just a twenty-thousand-dollar house traded up over fifteen years.

A couple of weeks later, I went to see Reid Smith, the speculator-renovator. He had sold the Oak Pass Road house the day before—for, in his cautious words, "close to the million I wanted." The sale, he said, was the fifteenth he had made since becoming a speculator, by accident, in 1974. "I was in a Jack Webb television series called 'Chase,' " said Smith. "I'm sure you never heard of 'Chase.' It was on the air only one season. I saved seven thousand dollars and used it for the down payment on a small house in Benedict Canyon. I paid forty-eight thousand dollars for the house and did some renovation myself. I spent six hundred and fifty dollars. A couple of months later, a friend told me that he thought I could get sixty thousand dollars for the house—so I put it on the market, and I did get sixty for it. I took the profit and bought another house, for fifty-five thousand dollars, held it for six months, put four thousand dollars into it, and sold it for eighty thousand dollars. That one's worth four hundred thousand now. That was the end of 1974, and I was in business. I made some mistakes and was ripped off a few times by workers I hired, but the mistakes were always covered by the inflation in the market. I have good people now, and when you get older"—Smith is thirty—"you know more about what you're doing."

"How many houses do you have now?" I asked.

"I have seven," he said. "They're all in this area, and I'm going to move into one of them—on top of a ridge over there. If I feel like it, I can get a telescope and see most of my property from there."

"What are they worth?" I asked.

"Ten million dollars total."

"You turned seven thousand dollars into ten million in five years?" I asked.

"Yes."

I asked for details.

"Say I bought this house for three hundred and thirty thousand dollars a year ago, putting sixty-six thousand dollars down and getting a two-hundred-and-sixty-four-thousand-dollar mortgage at 10 percent interest for thirty years," he said. "By now, I have a reputation for doing a certain kind—a certain quality—of work, so I can get it appraised at six hundred thousand dollars. That means I can get a second mortgage, a home-improvement loan, up to 80 percent of the appraisal—that's four hundred and eighty thousand minus the two-hundred-and-sixty-four-thousand first mortgage. Two hundred and sixteen thousand dollars. That covers the down payment—the sixty-six thousand—and leaves a hundred and fifty thousand dollars for renovation, with no money out of my pocket. With that kind of renovation, the house is worth a million dollars."

Playing with those numbers and figuring that Smith's carrying costs—payments on the first and second mortgages, property taxes of 1 percent of the purchase price, and insurance—would total something like eight thousand dollars a month, I estimated that, conservatively, Smith could hope for a profit of six hundred thousand dollars for a year's work. And he would have a year's free living—even if it was noisy living, with workmen banging through his house.

"I was lucky," he said. "I got in at the right time. People were buying emotionally. They would pay two hundred thousand dollars extra for a tennis court, but I could put a court in, with lights, on flat ground for twenty thousand dollars. It's the easiest living in the world here, and people kept coming in, bringing money with them."

23

The foreigners came—although I think that that can be overrated. Half the sales to Arabs never go through. I got burned a couple of times. They travel around, and if they see something they like they say, 'Buy it.' But then they go someplace else and forget where they've been. If you don't get the money up front, you may never hear from them again. I was riding a wave and it was great, but it's starting to slow down now."

The slowdown began in California the same time it began everywhere else—in the fall of 1979, when interest rates began climbing. Home-mortgage rates in California now average about 13 percent and could keep rising, because the state has no usury laws putting an interest ceiling on loans secured by real property. But "slowdown" is a relative term, and the demand for housing in all price ranges in Southern California is still such that real-estate agents, bankers, and academics seem to agree that any leveling of prices or reduction in sales volume will be temporary. "Plateau" is the word favored to describe what may happen to home prices, and "the spring or sometime next year" are the words used to predict when the upward spiral may start again.

"I think we'll see a leveling in prices, even a drop in some," Clark E. Wallace, the president of the California Association of Realtors, told the *Los Angeles Times* in November of 1979. "But the gap between supply and demand for homes is so great that we're going to be bouncing right back in the spring and summer."

"There are factors that preclude a real drop in prices," said William Popejoy, the president of the American Savings & Loan Association, which is the third-largest savings-and-loan association in the United States. "There just is not enough housing being built in Southern California to meet the minimal demands, even at high mortgage-interest rates."

California needs two hundred and ninety thousand new houses each year to provide for current growth and immigration, according to the Construction Industry Research Board. But in 1979 only two hundred and five thousand building permits were expected to be issued statewide, and next year's total is expected to be less than a hundred and eighty thousand. The state's fastest-growing region, the south, is, of course, the one that feels the shortfall most acutely. One state official from Los Angeles—Assemblyman Michael Roos, who is the chairman of a California Assembly subcommittee on housing production—has said that he believes the government must consider turning abandoned factories into low-cost housing.

One reason there *are* abandoned factories in "booming" California, however, is—according to Clinton Hoch, who is the executive vice-president of the Fantus Company, the nation's leading industrial-relocation firm—that engineers and other technical personnel are leaving the state or refusing to move there, because they can't afford suitable housing for their families.

"There's a limited pipeline for housing to flow through in California, because of no-growth policies, zoning restrictions, more and more regulations, and a bit of overkill on environmentalism," Popejoy told me. "There is a tremendous migration to this part of the world, and we are feeling the effects of the baby boom. All those babies of the late forties and the fifties are coming of home-buying age; our average buyers are still a couple in their early thirties with one wage-earner making nineteen thousand dollars a year. They buy a house that costs about a hundred and ten thousand dollars, with a down payment of 24 percent. Unless they stop coming to California or decide to live in tents, they're going to keep buying those damned houses, and prices will keep going up."

Popejoy and his family came to Los Angeles in late 1974 from McLean, Virginia—he had been in Washington, D.C., as president of the Federal Home Loan Mortgage Corporation. "To show you what's happened, when we came here prices were lower than in the Washington suburbs," he said. "You could buy more house for the same amount of money. That's all changed. We bought a four-bedroom house with a pool in Benedict Canyon for a hundred and sixty-five thousand dollars. If we sold it now, we'd get over six hundred thousand. Five years."

There could be a slowdown because of high interest rates, Popejoy said, but it would have "zero effect" on houses in the top ranges of the Los Angeles market, and also on houses in the lower ranges. A lower-range house, he said, might be a ninety-thousand-dollar tract house in a place like La Verne—a community fifty miles east of his office, on Wilshire Boulevard in Beverly Hills. "At the top, many people pay cash or they make huge down payments," he said. "Most of those people also have independent financing resources—you get in that class and you should have a banker somewhere. At the bottom, many of the big developers have arrangements with lending institutions, and the demand is so great that something has to be worked out. You're talking about a major social crisis. Across the board, a lot of people are financing home sales themselves. Sellers are taking mortgages for two years or five

25

years to give buyers the time to get conventional financing."

Something has already been worked out over the past couple of years to keep mortgage money moving in California: The state has granted savings-and-loan associations the right to offer "variable rate" mortgages. The lenders have the power, within certain limits, to raise or lower rates during the life of a mortgage. American Savings & Loan, for instance, has been granted three-quarter-point increases on certain mortgages over the past two and a half years. Popejoy thinks that something else is coming one of these days: an American version of the Canadian mortgage system. In Canada, mortgages are given for periods of from two to five years and are then renegotiated, with the lender obligated to offer a renewal, though not necessarily at the same rate, while the borrower is free to shop around for a better deal. Certainly, American bankers are pushing for a system in which they won't be bound by 10 percent, thirty-year mortgages if interest rates stay at the heights they have reached this year.

It is a long, dreary drive to La Verne to search for the ninety-thousand-dollar house: across the Santa Monica Mountains and beyond Burbank, Pasadena, Covina, Glendora, and San Dimas. But the house is there, behind red and yellow flags that say "Hughes Home." There are a lot of flags—different colors for different developers—at the foot of the San Gabriel Mountains. And the place is not so bad if you look toward the mountains. If you look back toward the city, the landscape is gray—gray, scrubby desert. The sky is gray, too, as smog creeps out from the center of Los Angeles at the end of the day. The horizon is defined by lines of cars, whose exhausts color the sky. The housing tracts—dropped, it seems, at random from above—are surrounded by low walls of tan cement block to keep the desert sand out. I was inside a wall, in Hughes Tract 32780, looking at a house identified as "Plan 515"—1,515 square feet. It had three bedrooms and two baths, and was priced from $89,950 to $91,700.

The house—almost half of it was a three-car garage—did not bring the word "substantial" to my mind. I supposed that you could get used to houses without foundations or basements. In Southern California, in part because of earthquakes and the tendency of the adobe soil to expand when it's wet and contract when it's dry, many houses are built on cement slabs dropped onto a base of sand filling a rectangular pit. But no one, I thought, could get used to walls that seemed to be cardboard; I was sure I could punch through from one room to another with the knuckle of my forefinger. There were a lot of mirrors. I remembered that Fred Case, at UCLA, had told me that developers used mirrors so that when prospective customers looked through a house they would like what they saw, because they would be seeing themselves.

"These houses are selling real well," Norm Renner, the Hughes salesman, told me. "I've sold ten this month, and there are two other salesmen. We have our own financing arrangements with banks."

Driving back toward the city along Base Line Road, I realized that many of the houses I was seeing were not really houses. Casitas La Verne Mobile Home Park, which looked like any other development behind cement-block walls, was a tightly packed cluster of twenty-by-sixty-foot prefabricated houses, such as are made in factories throughout California. One manufacturer—Golden West Homes, of Santa Ana—has nine factories, each stamping out five hundred houses a year. The landscaping and the clever alignment of the prefabricated units were impressive; it took me a few moments to comprehend that I was looking at dozens of identical units on tiny lots, often with only six feet between units, or pairs of units— usually two make up a house. Each unit has to be no more than twelve feet wide (to travel on highways) and no more than fourteen feet high (to pass under freeway bridges). Later, I made a phone call to find out about the development.

"It's the coming thing," said Alice Marshall, a saleswoman at Blue Carpet Mobile Homes, which handles many sales in Casitas La Verne. "The houses there begin at twenty thousand five hundred dollars and go up to sixty thousand. The space fee is two hundred and seven dollars a month. You can count on appreciation of about 10 percent a year—that's how much mobile homes have been going up. By the way, that's a pet area. You can have pets if they don't disturb anyone."

The manufactured house may be California's answer to the grown children of the baby boom. In November of 1979, the *Los Angeles Herald-Examiner*—in a series that began with the headline "Can Anyone Afford a Home in Los Angeles?"—followed a young couple, Chuck and Joanne Tucker, as they tried to find a modest house in Los Angeles County. They couldn't. The Tuckers finally moved seventy-five miles away—to Palmdale, in the desert country beyond the San Gabriel Mountains, where they found a house for forty-eight thousand dollars. Chuck Tucker said that in Los

Angeles, "I told brokers I wanted to buy a fifty-thousand-dollar house, and they didn't want to waste their time with me."

"The inexpensive house, as we understand the term, doesn't exist here anymore," said Case, who specializes in Los Angeles housing trends and is a former member of the city's planning commission. "My projections show that the average home price in the county will be a hundred and twenty-three thousand dollars in 1980. The price explosion really began in 1975. It's hard to find a full explanation for what's happened, and, believe me, we've tried. The imbalance between supply and demand is part of it, but that has been the rule rather than the exception in Southern California. And there were other obvious factors—no-growth sentiment, environmentalism, social-good requirements, like smoke alarms, burglarproof locks, and solar heating, and government regulation of all kinds, requiring builders to put in green belts and shopping centers, together with the fact that real estate has become a major area of financial speculation. It's being pumped up by money that used to go into the stock market."

I was exposed to some speculative fever myself when I attended a UCLA extension course called Real Estate Perspective: 1980. More than a hundred people spent fifty-five dollars each to listen to a day of lectures organized by Sanford Goodkin, the president of the Sanford R. Goodkin Research Corporation, which is a national company that provides advice and financing help to people investing in real estate. Most of my classmates for the day identified themselves in conversation as speculators—usually, they owned a house or a condominium or two and were trying to turn them over, on a scale somewhat more modest than that of Reid Smith—and the message they got was clear: Buy! "California is still one-seventh of America's new-housing market," said George Smith, who runs a real-estate consulting service. "There is going to be no real-estate recession in California, because so much money wants in. The best thing that can happen to you is high construction costs and increased inflation. And this is where it's happening. I saw an old friend of mine in France, and he and his wife had put away five hundred thousand dollars in a Swiss account. They were thinking of putting it in Los Angeles real estate. I had to tell him, 'For half a million, maybe I can get you a fixer-upper on the west side.' "

Goodkin himself had the same message: "The prices will continue to go up. Even if they appear to stabilize, that will only be temporary. There is just a limited amount of land in California. . . . We really want inflation. The problem is that while it's kind to real-estate people it destroys the rest of the country." A couple of people began to applaud on that last line.

"Fear. Fever," Case said when we talked about the Goodkin courses. "There's no other way to account for what has happened here. All my charts and the factors we talked about are not enough to explain what has happened to real-estate prices in Los Angeles. You can't talk to people. They just answer, 'How can prices ever go down?' A lot of it has to be hype. There is an unspoken conspiracy among suppliers, builders, real-estate people, and government to drive the prices up—they all benefit from higher housing prices—and there's no resistance on the demand side to stop it. The newspapers are part of it. They don't realize that when they're doing real-estate surveys they're interviewing only the people who want to drive prices up—realtors and the rest."

"Well," I said, "do *you* think prices will go down?"

"It's possible," Case answered. "If there were 17 percent inflation, some people wouldn't be able to buy things like clothing, and they might start saying, 'It's this damned house.' There could be more houses going on the market, for a while, than there would be buyers. There would at least be a slower turnover. But I have to admit I've been saying that for a long time, and even my students have been going out and making money in this thing. Maybe I should have done that, too. But, hell, I'm just a teacher, and teaching is what I like to do." Case smiled, and said, "Rationally, this shouldn't have happened. But it did. I know people back East keep saying that it can't happen—that prices can't go any higher in Georgetown or on Long Island. But the evidence here is that they can—and that people will find some way to pay them. You know, I usually make it a practice not to talk to people in the East about these things. The numbers are unbelievable, and you can feel that people don't believe you when you tell them what has happened here."

The great California real-estate boom finally slowed to almost a dead stop in 1980. Mortgage interest rates in California went above 16 percent. Housing prices didn't go down—or they didn't go down very much—but suddenly the prices made no difference because people stopped buying. At least in California. Ironically, the next place that real estate values began escalating by 30 percent and more a year was . . . back East, in Manhattan.

By then, I was back on my old beat: national politics. I was having a late and loud dinner with other reporters in the barroom of the Pontchatrain Hotel in Detroit during the Republican National Convention, when Robert Scheer of the *Los Angeles Times* began complaining that national coverage was biased against the West— against Western states, Western interests, Western politicians. "Do you know," he said, "that only one national columnist in the whole country is based in the West?"

I was not paying the closest attention, but I said: "Who's that?"

"You," Scheer said.

I had never thought about it. And I didn't think that I could really be counted, by wild stretches of imagination, as a Westerner. I had certainly come to love California and other parts of the West that I saw, but I was still an outsider and I was still spending large hunks of time on the road—which now stretched east for me most of the time.

Back there, friends kidded me about being "on assignment behind enemy lines." I went along with the joke but I didn't think of it that way anymore. I would still stand by the things I wrote in early 1978 and I continued to write about current and coming power struggles on several levels between Americans East and Americans West. What had changed for me, I thought, was that I knew a great deal more about the West in general and California in particular—I saw it as much more diverse than it once seemed to a sometimes visitor from three thousand miles away.

I was walking along the beach in Venice one Sunday morning with my wife, who, like me, was born in New York City, watching and being watched in the passing parade. And it was quite a parade: The people were white and black, slim and gross, fashionable and tacky. There were all kinds—the group I remember best was four Orthodox Jews in black coats and hats, and hanging braids, riding bicycles along the beach pathway, weaving through the roller skaters, the skateboarders, the surfers. "You know I feel like an idiot," I said. "I didn't know there were this many different kinds of people in California."

One of the kinds of people I didn't know anything about was Chicanos. Mexican-Americans. I don't think many Easterners do. If Bob Scheer was right, and I think he was—there is a need for more national writing from the West and the middle of the country—then I did serve a useful purpose just by living in Los Angeles. Inevitably, I began to write in national publications about complicated subjects that almost seemed foreign back in New York and Washington. This column, "Mexican America," was published in *Esquire* magazine on January 2, 1979:

On the day Vilma Martinez moved into Hancock Park, one of Los Angeles's best neighborhoods, she stopped to chat with a new neighbor. He was quite nice, even offering a compliment: "You speak wonderful English." She should; she's a graduate of Columbia Law School.

Being mistaken for a maid is part of her life. Ms. Martinez is one of at least 12 million people of Mexican descent in the United States, legally and illegally—that number is probably much higher, no one knows. She is also, as president of the Mexican American Legal Defense and Educational Fund, an important part of a hidden American revolution—or maybe just the ironic end of the wars in which the Anglos took California and the Southwest from the Mexicanos.

Remember the Alamo? One hundred forty years later Mexico has oil, and we need it; we have Chicanos, and they're tired of being pushed around. The combination is volatile. It's as if millions of angry Saudi Americans were clustered in, say, Georgia and the Carolinas, and their rich home country, Saudi Arabia, was where Florida is. "We all understand," said Ms. Martinez, "that Washington will finally have to listen to us because of Mexico."

First the numbers. The United States government now knows that Mexico has proved oil reserves of 50 billion barrels, probable reserves of 157 billion more, and possible reserves of another 100 billion or so—that is potentially more than Saudi Arabia—and could supply all U.S. energy needs for forty years at current rates of consumption. Mexico also has 65 million people—with 17 percent of the adults living on less than seventy-five dollars a year—and a population growth rate even higher than India's. Projections indicate Mexico could be a bigger nation than the U.S. in forty-five years. The country's unemployment is so high—over 50 percent in some places—that illegal immigration, to work across the 1,900-mile border with California, Arizona, New Mexico, and Texas, may be essential to Mexico's economy and political stability. And those Mexicans—there may be 6 million or 12 million here illegally now—

are absorbed into, usually welcomed into, the Mexican-American community. That community—quite legal—now numbers 7 million, the largest part of an American Latino community, which itself is growing at a rate of 20 percent a year, compared with white America's rate of 4 percent and black America's rate of 7 percent. Despite their numbers—and the fact that they are sometimes lumped with the 5 million other Americans of Hispanic origin—Chicanos, native and naturalized American citizens, traditionally have been known as "the invisible minority." Certainly they have been hard to see politically: In Los Angeles, where Chicanos make up 28 percent of the population—and where 45 percent of kindergarten students have Spanish surnames—there is no Mexican American on the city council. With one million registered Chicano voters in California—only 40 percent of the eligible total—there are only four Chicanos in the state legislature. One Democratic politician told me that all liberals have to do to win Chicano votes is "say a couple of nice words about Cesar Chavez, support bilingual education, go to the Mexican Independence Day parade and the Cinco de Mayo festival, and say 'undocumented workers' instead of 'illegal aliens.' "

The "illegals" are the principal Chicano political issue. After spending time in East Los Angeles, I'm convinced that the real Chicano position on undocumented workers is total amnesty, with the choice of American citizenship for the Mexicans now in the country, and a totally open border between the two countries. No one will say that—Chicano activists talk vaguely of a Marshall Plan for Mexico to eliminate the economic causes of illegal immigration—but many people said things like this, from a young film maker named Louis Torres: "We know where the undocumented workers are—they're sleeping on the couches in our living rooms. Everyone—and I mean doctors in Montebello and the guy washing the dishes in this restaurant—has an uncle from Guadalajara on the couch. They're family and they're just trying to feed their families back home."

Every Chicano I talked with felt threatened by real and imagined government drives against illegal aliens, the "wetback" expulsions that seem to start every time the United States is in or near a recession. Felix Gutierrez, a college professor whose family has been in California since 1812, says sometimes his mother carries her naturalization papers with her and his father-in-law carries pictures of his sons in World War II army uniforms—to prove that they are

Americans. And Gutierrez, who has a Ph.D. from the department of communications at Stanford but couldn't get a newspaper or television job in Los Angeles, said something else that every Chicano said to me, no matter how good their middle-class credentials were: "I am very afraid of the Los Angeles police. I can't drive the way you do because I know how they treat Mexicans."

New immigration laws—and they are coming—mean instant power for emerging Chicano politicians. "The issue is, 'Who gets on the citizenship track?' " said Art Torres, a thirty-two-year-old state assemblyman from East Los Angeles. Vilma Martinez's organization is pushing, through lawsuits, for the granting of local voting rights to permanent resident aliens, Mexican citizens living long-term in the United States. The issue they're really talking about is how many Chicanos will be eligible to vote in California—or Texas—in a few years. Enough, say, to make Art Torres governor?

The truth is, it's hard to figure out who's really against un-documented workers. Not the liberals on the west side of Los Angeles who have live-in housekeepers for as little as two hundred fifty dollars a month or gardeners in at twenty-five dollars once a week. There is no servant problem in Los Angeles. And a lot of other problems are solved because the undocumented workers are doing work Americans don't want to do. Besides that, they may be paying for themselves—several studies indicate that the Mexicans usually pay income taxes and Social Security but don't dare collect benefits or welfare because they're afraid of being caught and shipped back over the border.

But as immediate as political issues are—whether official accep-tance of that immigration reality, expanded social programs, or a larger slice of the American economic pie—they are only part of what seems to be on the minds of the activists, the first real genera-tion of Chicano college graduates. (There were only 148 Mexican Americans in the University of California system as recently as 1967.) What they seem to want most is non-political: Chicanos want respect. They don't want to be called, as the Los Angeles Times used to call them, "the little people who have big hearts." That's true on both sides of the long border. In Mexico City, when Jimmy Carter was president of the United States, President Jose Lopez-Portillo complained: "Mexico is neither on the list of United States priorities nor on that of United States respect."

Oil should get Lopez-Portillo respect. His American brothers and sisters are trying to get theirs by writing their own history, words

33

and images to stand beside Anglo history books that glorify English pilgrims stepping on a rock about ten years after there was a city at Santa Fe. No more Chico and Frito Bandito. And, if they can help it, less emphasis on the macho violence that has always defined el barrio—there may be boycotts and demonstrations directed at a spate of films on Chicano gangs, films with titles like *Gang!* and *Boulevard Nights.* (Even when their violence goes national, Chicanos get the short end: The lead in *Gang!* is played by an Anglo actor named Robby Benson who wears dark contact lenses and has dyed-brown hair in the film. "Can you imagine Hollywood having the balls to let a white actor in blackface and kinky hair play a Watts gang leader?" said Carlos Beltran, who works among the gangs in East Los Angeles.)

"We want the right to define ourselves," said Gutierrez, who has authored several studies pretty well documenting that reporting of Chicano affairs is, in his words, "Anglos quoting Anglos about Mexicans." They may or may not get that, judging by the attitude of Otis Chandler, publisher of the *Los Angeles Times,* who went on television this year to say that there's not much reason for his paper to cover minorities: "We could make the editorial commitment, the management commitment to cover these communities. But then how do we get them to read the *Times?* It's not their kind of news-paper: It's too big, it's too stuffy. If you will, it's too complicated."

The most successful attempt at self-definition to date is a play called *Zoot Suit,* by Luis Valdez, a former organizer for Cesar Chavez's farmworkers union.

It ran for months in Los Angeles, telling mostly Chicano audi-ences *their* side of the East Los Angeles riots of 1943, when marines and sailors rampaged through el barrio attacking the pachucos, the zoot-suiters. And the most poignant moment comes during a mur-der trial when an attorney for the accused pachucos yells a cry that still has not been heard very well: "They are Americans!"

By any definition, they are indeed. Every one of the more than twenty Chicanos I interviewed in a week said at some point in our conversation, "Look, I'm an American"—their folks got here long before most of ours. But they did not want to be assimilated Americans—like Anglos. They wanted to keep their ways *Mexicano,* particularly their sense of family and their fierce self-destructive pride. Certainly none of us will live to see them assimilated—Chicanos almost always marry Chicanas, and their heritage, cul-ture, and language are constantly replenished and enriched by the human flow across the border. You have to imagine what the north-eastern states would be like if Italy were where Maryland is.

Because Mexico literally touches Mexican America, the bonds between the two related peoples and their countries are tangled beyond belief—perhaps, more importantly, beyond breaking. Americans will need that oil to maintain their standard of living. Mexicans need jobs: The safety valve of immigration to the north conceivably holds the country back from the brink of the gov-ernmental chaos and bloodshed that infects the rest of Latin America. Many *Norte Americanos* who have never seen a Chicano will find awareness coming with their heating oil and gasoline in a few years. They'll also find Vilma Martinez back raising money for the Mexican American fund. One of the last times she made the trip to New York, a skeptical foundation officer asked her: "Tell me, Miss Martinez, in the cosmic view, where do Mexican Americans fit?"

Right here in the good ol' U.S.A.

Over the next two years, I spent a great deal of time in East Los Angeles, an extraordinary part of the United States, as large geo-graphically as New York City, where generations have lived without speaking a word of English. It is a Spanish-speaking city, a Mexican-American and Mexican city of one to two million people, legal and illegal, sprawling east of the Los Angeles River in the city and county of Los Angeles.

But it is an oddly familiar place to a New Yorker. The main street of what would be downtown East LA is Brooklyn Avenue. And, as much as part of Los Angeles can be, it is somewhat reminiscent of the Brooklyn three thousand miles to the east. The streets are cracked and bumpy, lined with small stores, two-story homes, and low apartment buildings. On commercial streets nearby, the Spanish signs are tacked or painted over Jewish names and Hebrew characters that sometimes still show through. There are people on the streets—a rare thing in Los Angeles—and they are there all hours of the day and night, shopping, walking, talking, lounging, flirting, fighting.

There is great energy there—the immigrant energy that seems to

35

be the fuel of California whether the immigrants are from Brooklyn or Ensenada—and it seemed very American to me. I sometimes followed the route of the Chicanos who came into West LA each morning for work, at the same time I followed the deliberations back in Washington over what should be "done" about illegal immigration. I had been advocating "doing" nothing and was delighted to write this newspaper column, which was published around the country on December 11, 1980:

At seven o'clock each weekday morning, two or three hundred Mexican men line Sawtelle Boulevard between Santa Monica Boulevard and Olympic Boulevard in Los Angeles. They're looking for a day's work and some of them get it as contractors' and gardeners' trucks cruise the street picking up one or two, sometimes a half dozen, for three dollars an hour.

They are "the problem." Silent men holding brown paper bags with a little lunch. They are the illegal aliens.

A distinguished committee—the Select Committee on Immigration and Refugee Policy, chaired by the Reverend Theodore Hesburgh, president of the University of Notre Dame—is now presenting its recommendations to Congress on how to deal with the problem. It's tough—the commission has been meeting, on and off, for more than two years.

So, what have the commissioners, including names like Senator Edward Kennedy and Representative Elizabeth Holtzman, come up with? Nothing—they are suggesting that immigration laws should be enforced more rigidly and amnesty should be granted to some of the illegals. Which is, in effect, about what is happening, unofficially, right now.

The commission, I think, did a good job. "Nothing" is the right "solution" to "the problem" because there is no solution. The problem is that the poorest section of one of the poorest countries on earth, Mexico, has a one-thousand-nine-hundred-mile border with one of the richest countries, the United States. Men and women—the best and brightest of the poor states of northern Mexico—are going to cross that border to feed their families.

And, as far as I can tell after two years, off and on, of interviewing Americans of Mexican descent and their illegal brothers and sisters, the cross-border traffic benefits both countries. Certainly the illegal immigration benefits Mexico because it provides a political safety valve in places like Chihuahua where unemployment is usually more than 50 percent. Some studies indicate that each illegal alien in the United States sends more than one hundred five dollars a month to relatives south of the border. De facto foreign aid, people-to-people.

The United States, with all our complaining, gets a cheap and hardworking labor force and a relatively stable neighbor. Without that safety valve of illegal immigration, Mexico would be prime territory for a very uncomfortable (for us) socialist revolution just twenty miles from San Diego. Seventeen percent of Mexican adults live on less than seventy-five dollars a year and the country has a population growth rate higher than India's—Mexico's population of 65 million could increase to more than the United States' population in just forty-five years.

There is always an argument against illegals—"wetbacks"—when the U.S. economy is not booming. They are taking our jobs, according to some labor unions. They are living off welfare, according to some conservatives.

My own experience living in Southern California indicates that the illegals are probably creating jobs and maintaining some small industries. First, they are, for the most part, doing menial work disdained by many Americans white and black—there aren't many good jobs open to people who can't speak English. Second, many of the small industries, clothing and furniture manufacturers in California and Texas, for instance, would have to close down or move overseas without cheap, unAmerican labor.

As to welfare, government studies so far tend to indicate that we are actually making money on the illegals—or "undocumented workers" as liberals call them. One study, in Orange County, California, reported illegals paid somewhere between $83 million and $145 million in income and sales and Social Security taxes, but received only $2.7 million in government services, mostly medical services. In San Diego, a spot check of Hispanic names on the welfare rolls showed that only 10 of 9,132 were illegal aliens—the rest were American citizens like you and me.

Whatever Congress decides to do about the Hesburgh commission's recommendations—again, probably nothing—the problem won't go away. This is another case where Washington can learn from the locals. The country should do what Americans in the Southwest and Southern California are doing everyday: Live and let live.

It was a long way from the streets of Brooklyn to Brooklyn Avenue—and I was as happy as I was surprised to have made the trip in so short a time. One day I would be on a gas line on Sunset Boulevard in Pacific Palisades and the next, traveling for my Tocqueville book, I would be in downtown Buffalo, New York, stopping by at a press conference being held by New York's junior senator.

There I was, in Buffalo, listening to Pat Moynihan, my senator—I was still a New York voter—and it was obvious that he did not have the vaguest idea of what he was talking about. I knew I was about to complete a personal circle—I was, at least this time, going to be an enthusiastic and public defender of the great state of California. The column that I wrote then—June 19, 1979, in *Esquire*—was called, "Are Californians Crazy?" Like so much of the work I would be doing as I jetted across and around the country over the next couple of years, it focused on the differences and tensions between regions of the country, particularly between East and West:

On May 18, Daniel Patrick Moynihan, the senator from New York, traveled to Buffalo, in the far reaches of his representative domain to explain the ways of the world to anyone who would listen. Nine reporters showed up at a news conference, sitting politely as Moynihan spoke, as one does to children, of many things. He spoke of SALT and the Russians, of looniness and the Californians.

"Yes, there is a gasoline shortage," he said. "And New Yorkers have been acting intelligently and capably. But there's something about the state of California. They're a funny bunch. They've panicked. It's the equivalent of a run on the bank.

"I was talking to Secretary Schlesinger at a reception yesterday; he told me the average sale of gasoline in California has gone *down* from eight gallons to three gallons. People are just topping off their almost full tanks."

Recalling some of James Schlesinger's earlier mathematics—body counts in Vietnam—I offered Moynihan the hyperbolic opinion that Secretary of Energy Schlesinger was either a fool or a liar. "Does he really think," I said, "that people out there are waiting in line for two and a half hours to put three gallons in their tanks?"

The stupidity of politicans in the coming oil crisis is matched only by their cowardice. It's bad enough that people like Moynihan and Schlesinger and many of their peer group don't know what they're talking about. They also seem to feel compelled to make sure that the country will be torn apart by resentment and manipulations over who gets the perfumes of Araby. So Senator Charles Percy of Illinois says that as far as he's concerned, frenzied Californians are creating their own problems, and Congressman Carlos Moorhead of Los Angeles says he doesn't give a damn about heating oil for the Northeast but he wants gas for his Angelenos.

I do care, very much, about heating oil, and production of it obviously has to be the country's first priority; there is a difference between Californians swearing at one another in two-mile lines and little old ladies freezing to death next February in Vermont. But having waited in some of those lines before Moynihan informed me of what was really going on, I had the distinct impression that, all things considered, Californians were behaving very well—indeed, capably.

It's true that a guy named Diton Williams pulled a gun at a service station in West Hollywood and held off a crowd while he filled his tank. And that Johnny Rodgers, a wide receiver for the San Diego Chargers football team, got so annoyed waiting in line to fill up his Rolls-Royce that he bought the gas station. But it's also true that all the people I saw after the shortage hit La La Land last month were pumping ten dollars worth and more into empty tanks. And that Fred Hartley, president of Union Oil, says that the average sale at Union stations is between thirteen and fourteen gallons.

Los Angeles, in fact, looks a bit like a ghost town on weekends. People simply aren't going anywhere unless they have to. That's part of the reason President Carter only saw two thousand people at the city's Cinco de Mayo festival on May 5 instead of the usual crowd of five thousand or so. On weekdays, traffic seems to be down from 50 to 75 percent of what it was in April.

In April, before this began, California had about 10 percent of the nation's population, 10 percent of the nation's drivers, and 10 percent of the nation's automobiles—and was using 9.5 percent of the nation's gasoline. The average monthly gas consumption per California vehicle was 59.7 gallons, compared with 73 gallons in Virginia and Georgia and a national average of 64 gallons. Californians may wash and love their cars more than the rest of us do, but most of them are not guzzling gas. One reason is that the ownership of small cars is much higher in California than anywhere else in the United States.

There was, undoubtedly, some panic on May 3 and a couple of days after. Gas stations were suddenly closed (or open for only two or three hours a day), and there was, in Schlesinger's pet phrase, "topping off." We'll all be panicked the first time we drive thirty miles or so and see the "Closed" or "No Gas" signs on every pump along the way. That's all there was to it, Washington said, claiming that the California gasoline shortfall was only 3 or 5 percent.

That was not true. The real shortfall was apparently close to 15 percent of 1978 allocations. There were, as it turned out, very real reasons that there was less gas around the freeways. "Panic" was a minor factor.

It has become worse than a cliche to say that there is no leadership in Washington. But things are worse when the substitute for some kind of national unity during a national crisis is an unthinking policy of divide and scapegoat. New York did foul up its municipal budgets and was self-indulgent for years, but that was not the city's real problem, which was that it was old and that in many ways it had outlived its usefulness to the new places, to the West. So, a lot of those westerners thought, let the Big Apple rot in its own juices—Jerry Brown said it was "decadent." God knows, California is self-indulgent—God and the California Coastal Commission forbid that oil wells should interfere with any Pacific views!—but its gasoline problems this spring had nothing to do with mellow wackiness. The "mellow" probably prevented big trouble. Gas shortages may be like blackouts: The first one is an adventure; the looting begins with the second one; then come the riots.

Politics, after all, is about dividing up the resources of a society. The president and Congress can take the risks of doing that or they can let states, cities, and individuals fight it out themselves. California could, for instance, try to cut a separate oil deal with Mexico—it might not work, but it would make people such as Pat Moynihan prophets. They could be prophets of sunny funniness and prophets in their own country, which at the moment they foolishly define as not including California.

Part 2

Different Places

Among the many things I never wanted to do was to write a syndicated column. There were some exceptions, but most "Washington Columns" looked and read about the same to me: well-informed and authoritative filler. You could clip the name and the picture off the top of many of them and you couldn't tell who had written it, or when, or why. More and more editors around the country were putting together editorial and op-ed pages emphasizing local talent—college professors, housewives, and anyone else who thought they had something to say—and excerpting provocative books and magazine articles and speeches. That seemed sensible to me. The new stuff had to be as good as interchangeable seven-hundred-word meanderings about what John Foster said to Dean after McGeorge ran into Teddy—or was it Bobby?—when Lyndon and Nelson challenged Henry over cocktail frankfurters at Averill's party for Louis XIV.

So, four or five times over the years, I had accepted sumptuous lunches from syndicate types and then told them, "No, never . . ." But all life is timing and most "nos" are negotiable and there did come a time—it was late in 1978. I was living in Washington and flying back-and-forth to New York because I was national editor of *Esquire* and also was doing two-minute commentaries, three of them a week, for WNBC-TV in New York and NBC's owned-and-operated stations in other cities. It was wearing me down, particularly the television work. It wasn't that the commentary was necessarily superficial. That is a cop-out. You can say a great deal in two minutes if you work at it. I may sometimes say unkind things about them, but television people work like miners—it's tough. I think that what I didn't like was getting into a suit and tie so often and going through the rituals of makeup—often after flying up from D.C. on the damned Eastern Airlines shuttle—just to do two bright minutes and be back on my way down the elevators at 30 Rockefeller Center. Part of me has always thought that a man's success should be judged by how seldom he has to shave. For television you have to shave. For writing it helps not to.

Anyway, I listened when Tom Drape, an editor at Universal Press Syndicate, came along and said I could be the Garry Trudeau of the written word. UPS was then an aggressive little band of men who had gone to Notre Dame—or wished they had—and had become successful by introducing and peddling "Doonesbury" with savvy, sensitivity, and skill. (The company is now much bigger having bought out the Washington Star Syndicate and picking up folks like William F. Buckley and James J. Kilpatrick—"they," do you notice, have middle initials—and Mary McGrory.) "You're going to be rich. You're going to be famous. Children will chant your name in cities and towns you've never heard of," said Drape. At least that's what I think he said, or I heard. "OK," I said, "I'll try it. But I'm afraid I'm going to hate it and . . ."

I loved it. I love it. Like the prospect of hanging, to paraphrase Dr. Johnson, columning has focused my mind wonderfully. I found myself alive and alert to my surroundings, to what I saw and heard, to what it meant; I was desperate, of course. Twice-a-week, rain or shine, sleet or snow, I have to deliver a readable thought. And I have to deliver it on time—if I'm late the syndicate (aptly named) charges me about seventy-five dollars.

Let me try to explain syndication from the creator's point of view. That is what the writers and artists are called, the "creators"—with a very small "c." The syndicate, or its salespeople, go around the country—probably on Trailways buses—and hang around outside editors' doors. If they get a chance, they tell the editor that a new creator, Richard Reeves, is going to start writing a twice-a-week Washington column that won't be from Washington. If that editor is far-sighted, a visionary trusted by statesmen, beloved of children, and adored by the opposite sex, he (rarely she) will say: "Thank God! This is what Crested Butte has been waiting for—finally real insight into America in our time." Then he will offer to pay $2.50 a week for the column, which is what one capital city newspaper in the West pays for mine.

The syndicate and the creator split the take—after the syndicate, which has staff accountants, takes something off the top for production costs. The creator agrees to create—on deadline—and we're in business. My deadlines are Monday and Wednesday. If I'm late and the column has to be sent to smaller clients by special delivery mail rather than the usual first class, we split the additional cost of $150, give or take a buck or two. That's how I lose $75 each time I'm late—these guys are tough.

Expenses, things like airline tickets and expensive lunches for cheap politicians are paid by—who else?—the creator. John McMeel, the president of UPS, once asked me which raincoat in a pile was mine and I told him to look for the one with a roll of stamps in the pocket to send out tomorrow's column. He laughed—why shouldn't he?

It adds up. Much higher rates are paid for columns in those few blessed cities that still have competition among newspapers. A reverent creator bows each afternoon in the directions of Chicago, Philadelphia, Detroit, and a few other places that still have healthy circulation battles. (Sometimes, one of the papers in those cities and a couple of others will buy up a new feature not to use it but just to keep it away from the competition.) Once a month, the creator gets an accounting—and a check—listing the papers carrying the column. I don't know about other writers, but I am endlessly fascinated—as I once was with baseball statistics—by which papers, which places, buy and cancel me. I still mourn Duluth, Minnesota, which canceled me, for reasons I'll probably never know, in February of 1981. Luckily for my sanity, that loss for the people of Duluth has been one of the few. The column began with 32 newspapers and quickly grew to more than 150.

Maybe it grew because I was often writing about different things

43

and from different places than my fellow creators. I wrote the first column on March 11, 1979, and, at that time, I was already traveling the country doing the reporting for the book (to be published in 1982) re-tracing Tocqueville's American journeys of 1831 and 1832. I was trying to see America whole as I crisscrossed it that year from New York to Los Angeles. Then came the political year, the campaign of 1980, and I was on the road again. Jet-lagged again, seeing places I had never seen, trying to figure out something with a longer shelf life than who said what to whom on Air Force One or on Ronald Reagan's campaign plane. That first column, in fact, was about both politics and all of the United States. The focus was on Sen. Edward Kennedy, who was a pretty hot property at that moment, but the column was really about the bicoastal tension I had felt building in my travels. Those differences, it turned out, did keep growing, in both the United States and Canada, and within a few months were the subjects of both magazine cover stories and political debate when the East vs. West confrontation developed with Jimmy Carter of Georgia opposing Ronald Reagan of California for the presidency. And that was the title of that column in March 1979, "East vs. West":

"Do you know Newport Beach?" Sen. Edward Kennedy said, the words beginning to come faster. "Have you seen it? All those boats in a row? The affluence in California is staggering. You see the same kind of thing in the Rocky Mountain states—they're doing fine. But up my way, in Massachusetts, in the mill towns, have you seen that? People can't make it. They can't handle the basic needs anymore—health, heating bills. Do you know what it feels like going to those towns, talking to those people, going back and telling them you're trying to help them? I represent them."

That flash of East-West hostility will be very significant in shaping national campaigns—and to the immediate future of the United States. A political civil war between the coasts, East vs. West—or perhaps California and its satellites vs. everybody else—seems likelier right now than the Frost Belt-vs.-Sun Belt struggle that many people are talking about these days.

It's essentially Old vs. New and it seems more relevant now than it was in 1976 when almost the entire West voted for a candidate from chilly Michigan, Gerald Ford, and the East, warm and cold, voted for a Georgian. Dirt-farmer Jimmy Carter may have had a sunny accent, but he symbolized old, Yankee, puritan, Eastern values and politics. We should have known then that Ford was headed for Palm Springs.

The continental division may be much wider by next year. A writer who lives, fitfully, in both New York and Los Angeles gets a casual feel for coastal indifference and hostility. The California reaction to news that heating oil prices rose 15 to 20 percent from Washington, D.C., to Portland, Maine: None, they couldn't care less. The Eastern (and Southeastern) reaction to massacres and murders in Jonestown, San Francisco, and San Diego: See, they're all crazy out there in La La Land.

A New Yorker in Los Angeles is amazed to hear grouchiness about a lovely, sunny day on New Year's. The reason, I was told several times, was that the cold people "back East" would watch the Rose Bowl on television and, inevitably, a few thousand would decide to move west. And the West is a protectionist society. Westerners want to protect what they have; they are into sharing experiences but not environment or, the ultimate value in California, property. "Their" environment and property is defined to include things like oil under the Pacific Ocean and the foothills of the Santa Monica Mountains. Their aesthetic pleasure is much more real to them than record-low temperatures in Detroit. They are, after all, the spiritual heirs of the men who took out shotguns to turn away Okies from the California border in the 1930s.

The fight over oil and gas in the coming crisis years is going to make all this much worse—and much more important politically. Westerners want their gasoline, they need a lot of it to get around; Easterners want to get warm.

Western politicians see the nation differently. I asked Pete Wilson, the clear-headed mayor of San Diego, whether he believed the federal government should deal with problems caused by the decline of older Eastern cities. He answered "Yes"—he thought Washington should provide additional aid to Western cities that had to absorb fleeing Easterners. Ed Koch answers that question differently in New York.

In Sun Belt theory, Southerners would side with Wilson. I don't think so. Cities like Atlanta, Miami, and Birmingham seem to be developing along classic Northeastern lines—including ghetto cultures that are more like Newark than Los Angeles. Many Southerners will probably stand with traditional Northern enemies in an East-West showdown.

45

———————

Government has always looked a lot different from outside Washington—but like many other reporters I had done most of my coverage from inside the lovely center of that city.

But when I was spending more than half my time on the road, writing from Cincinnati, Ohio, or Flemington, New Jersey, I found myself returning to a single theme, or rather a question: How does government, particularly the federal government, work at the point where it touches the people paying for it and benefiting from it? The answer, it seemed to me, was: not quite the way the people who first put this country together thought it would, and not the way they think it does back in Washington. That was never so obvious to me as it was one morning walking down a street in Cincinnati in October of 1979:

The sign of the decline of American politics is in the window of Batsake's Cleaners on Walnut Street in Cincinnati. It's a poster showing a blank-faced young man holding a telephone. Under his picture are two words: "Luke Listens."

"Luke" is Charles Luken, a Democratic candidate for the city council. He doesn't have to identify himself further because he is the son of Congressman Thomas Luken. Voters, presumably, have a vague idea of who he is because the family name gets some recognition.

The poster reminded me of something said by Wilson Wyatt, the former mayor of Louisville and Adlai Stevenson's campaign manager in the 1956 presidential election. "The sure sign of the decline of politicans," Wyatt told me last winter, "is those slogans that say 'So-and-so Cares' or 'So-and-so Listens.' That's an absolutely meaningless phrase unless it means that so-and-so doesn't intend to do anything in office."

Usually, in fact, so-and-so doesn't intend to do anything. Making decisions, doing something, is what gets voters mad—if a politician just listens and cares, no one will notice him and he might get re-elected forever.

So who governs America? Part of the answer to that question was two blocks up Walnut Street, in Room 822 of the United States

Courthouse. A three-judge panel of the Sixth Circuit, U.S. Court of Appeals—Anthony Celebrezze, Bailey Brown, and Cornelia Kennedy—was ordering the state of Ohio to revise its welfare procedures because of a lawsuit brought by four Franklin County residents. "Go back and tell the legislature," Judge Celebrezze said, "to hire more hearing officers."

Courts rule because elected politicians—the "Lukes" of America—refuse to take stands or actions that might make anybody mad. They just listen and care—like cocker spaniels.

On the same day, Cincinnati newspapers were reporting the latest developments on a state court order to city officials to renovate or close the city's old jail, which was originally built to house Civil War prisoners. And, the federal government was threatening Ohio with court action because state officials have not been able to come up with an effective environmental protection law. Chicago, at the same time, was being threatened with court action because that city's officials have been unwilling to approve a school desegregation plan.

"A lot of the cases that come in here are pushed in because local officials, county commissioners for instance, didn't want to take responsibility for a decision," said U.S. Magistrate J. Vincent Aug in his office in Cincinnati's federal courthouse. "The courts' power is becoming awesome because they're the only place you can find decision making. Judges may not want to make some of those decisions, but they don't shy away. They know that's what they're here for."

The "Lukes" do shy away. And the situation is not healthy—not if you believe in democracy. If elected officials won't move, unelected ones have to move in or take over. In some cases the courts have already taken over—schools in Boston and prisons in Alabama are examples—and that may soon happen with the crumbling old jail in Cincinnati.

Rule by judiciary has become so common, in fact, that J. Skelly Wright, the chief judge of the U.S. Court of Appeals in Washington, has said publicly that judges "must restrain themselves . . . be more hesitant about filling the void, when, in our judgment, the elected branches of government have acted and failed." But it's becoming harder and harder to hesitate while "Luke" does nothing but "listen."

The miscalculations, almost always well-meaning, of government, seemed starkly visible on almost any street in America—any street, that is, where you don't find Capitol Police. Those are the uniformed guards who work around Capitol Hill in Washington. When they see a senator or congressman coming, they jump into the street to stop traffic. Thus, the great men and women of the day are not delayed in making new laws, many of which will create the kind of disasters that I found on Chalmers Street in Detroit. I had gone to that old city to talk to Douglas Fraser, the president of the United Auto Workers, about politics in general and Edward Kennedy in particular, but the story I wrote about in June of 1979 was on a nearby street:

Douglas Fraser, president of the United Auto Workers (UAW), is a proudly unreconstructed New Deal liberal who would very much like to see Edward Kennedy win the presidency. But he doubts that will happen—and the reason may be down the street from Fraser's office on Jefferson Avenue in Detroit.

If you go three miles east along Jefferson you come to Chalmers Street. There are twenty-nine boarded-up houses and twenty vacant lots along the six blocks on either side of Jefferson—on Chalmers, Marlborough, Philip, Manistique, Ashland, and Alter Streets. They were once good houses, solid two-story brick buildings on tree-lined streets a few hundred yards from the wealthy gentility of Grosse Pointe Park.

Those forty-nine houses and more than sixteen thousand others like them were destroyed by the United States government—by well-meaning liberals. Around here it's known as "The HUD Scandal." In its way, the scandal is far worse than Watergate—it robbed the taxpayers of almost a billion dollars and damn near destroyed the city of Detroit.

This is, very briefly, what happened:

The Housing Act of 1968, one of the last achievements of the Johnson administration, established programs under which poor people could buy inner-city homes with down payments as low as two hundred dollars. The Department of Housing and Urban Development, through the Federal Housing Administration, guaranteed the mortgages.

In 1969, the former governor of Michigan, liberal Republican George Romney, became secretary of HUD and he decided to use the program to rebuild his hometown. HUD acquired thousands and thousands of homes in changing neighborhoods, hired local contractors and agencies to fix them up, and then sold them with the FHA mortgages. The troubles began when contractors began bribing HUD inspectors and faking the repair of many of the houses— there have been more than two hundred convictions and indictments in the scandal over the past eight years. Then it turned out that the new owners were unwilling or unable to maintain the houses or pay the mortgages. Banks began foreclosing—with HUD paying the bills and getting the houses back. The government then tried new owners and the same thing happened again. Finally, in embarrassment, HUD began razing the houses by the thousands.

Today, 11 percent of Detroit's former housing stock is vacant lots—and the twenty-nine houses I saw in Jefferson-Chalmers— some of them had to be worth $75,000—are boarded up, waiting for the wreckers.

"We were wrong about a lot of things and we're paying a price," says Doug Fraser, of American liberalism. "The HUD scandal is an example. We just were wrong about government's capability and the ability of poor people to adjust to a modern urban environment even when they were given good homes."

The rise of conservatism, or "the swing to the right," in American politics, is essentially a reaction to these grand mistakes of liberalism—busing, opposing "law and order," blundering attempts to elevate the poor. The evidence of what happened is still visible on Chalmers Street. And it may be some time before America is ready to try more New Deal government.

North of Detroit, in Saginaw, Michigan, the government had tried to do more good works. I thought they were ludicrous, but anyone who thinks there is not a real constituency for these things should have seen my mail after I wrote about Saginaw that same June:

Talk about government in Saginaw and, sooner or later, someone will mention the doors to the indoor courts at the racquet club. They are designed to comply with the Michigan Barrier-Free Design Act of 1976, so you can get on the racquetball courts in a wheelchair.

"You wonder why people think the government has gone too far?" says Dave Rogers, a local player. "They're throwing money away."

Last Monday, the U.S. Supreme Court unanimously ruled that Rogers was right, that government indeed had gone too far in trying to help the handicapped. The court said the government did not have the power to force a small North Carolina college to provide special instruction and facilities to train a deaf woman as a registered nurse.

Life is unfair. It has been unfair to the woman in North Carolina, Frances Davis. But there is only so much government can do—all the power in Washington or Lansing, Michigan, cannot make blind people into air traffic controllers.

Equal opportunity and/or affirmative action for the handicapped is a very difficult issue, and I am not at all that comfortable with my own feelings about it. My feelings are that the government has gone crazy on this thing, that the Department of Health, Education and Welfare has grossly distorted the Rehabilitation Act of 1973.

The 1973 law said that "No otherwise qualified handicapped individual . . . shall, solely by reason of his handicap, be excluded from participation in . . . any program or activity receiving federal financial assistance." Since then, in half the states, including Michigan, new law has been written extending that clause to include all buildings and facilities used by the public—including racquet clubs.

By "going crazy" I mean giving out estimates as the one I got from Larry Allison of HEW's Architectural and Transportation Barriers Compliance Board. He told me that the number of handicapped people in the United States may be as high as 70 million.

That's almost one out of three Americans. I assume I'm one of them because a doctor's forceps slipped when I was being born and the muscles behind my left eye were severed. I was blind in that eye for a long time and it's still not much good. That's what the Air Force told me when they wouldn't let me be a jet pilot—maybe they were just discriminating against me.

Obviously there are people who are really handicapped. Between five hundred thousand and one million Americans are in wheelchairs right now. I agree with HEW that there should be ramps and elevators and lowered telephone booths in many public buildings.

But Larry Allison and I disagreed about whether buses should have hydraulic lifts for wheelchairs. The buses would cost something like four hundred thousand dollars apiece, and I know they wouldn't work right most of the time anyway.

"If you and I are waiting on a corner," Allison said, "I want to get on the same bus as you do."

Larry Allison is in a wheelchair. He was crippled by polio as a child. OK, buses should have entrances wide enough to take wheelchairs—the required width is thirty-two inches—and a large enough space in the front to accommodate a couple of chairs. I'm healthy enough to be able to help lift someone's chair onto the bus—it would do me and a lot of other people good to help that way.

The alternative, which is the government-enforced reality of the moment, is to spend $2 billion to rebuild the New York City subway system to accommodate the truly handicapped. And how many people like that would use all the subways in the country? The Department of Transportation estimates four thousand people. The number using the Washington Metro would be so low that each trip by a handicapped person would require a government subsidy of two thousand dollars.

"There is a backlash, I know, to some of these costs," Larry Allison said. "And to be truthful, I can't understand all the regulations myself. So some of that questioning is healthy."

On that point, we sadly agree. And, I suspect, so would Franklin D. Roosevelt.

The mail, to say the least, was both heavy and angry for a few weeks—and I did hear from two people, a man and a woman, who said they were squash players and they were confined to wheelchairs. I was, I admit, surprised, but I did not change my general view of some of the congenital silliness of government. What I did do was pick less sympathetic targets to make the same points. I picked on rich housewives and hypnotists and at the same time got in a plug for Monsieur Tocqueville in a column titled: "Why They Hate Government":

A friend of mine in Beverly Hills who wants to lose weight had tried everything else, so she went to see a hypnotist. He couldn't put her under and finally he snapped, "Why are you so hostile?" "Wouldn't you be hostile," she snapped back, "if someone were trying to take away your food?"

She now thinks hypnotists are a bunch of frauds. Maybe they are. Many Beverly Hills ladies think so, enough of them so that their man in Sacramento, a state senator named Alan Sieroty, is pushing a bill in the California Legislature giving the state control over hypnosis.

I have no doubt that this is a good thing. I am against hypnotists taking advantage of overweight matrons or anyone else stupid enough to see one without checking out his trance record. I also have no doubt hypnosis inspectors and boards will cost California taxpayers a lot of money.

This story—the names are withheld to protect the plump—is my answer to someone in the White House who argued that public attitudes toward government are irrational. "They hate it, but they want more and more from it," he said.

Perhaps, though it may be only public officials who want to do so much more. I don't want to do anything about hypnotists but keep them out of my sight. I don't hate them and I don't hate government yet, but I hate a lot of things that are going on and I want to pass a couple more stories along to my friend at the White House:

—In Louisville, Byck's, a small chain of women's stores, has had the pension cost for its two hundred employees doubled since the passage of the Federal Employee Retirement Income Security Act of 1974. But those employees now receive less than half the coverage they did before the law was passed. Who gets the extra money? "Lawyers and accountants," said Dann Byck, the president of the company. "We need them to stay in compliance with the new regulations and to deal with the federal inspectors."

—In Los Angeles, attorneys for the city and the U.S. Department of Labor's Office of Federal Contract Compliance Programs have spent more than three years negotiating the employment or non-employment of an assistant tree-trimmer with psychiatric problems. A dozen calls to OFCCP offices in Washington and California did not produce anyone who would or could comment on the two-page press release the Department of Labor sent to every newspaper and radio station in the country. "How much did this all cost?" said one official. "A lot, and it will cost a lot more over the next couple of years, but I'm not going to talk about it. Did those idiots really send out press releases about this mess?" Yes, those idiots have also filed a complaint against the city and have threatened to end federal aid to Los Angeles "for its failure to hire a qualified handicapped person."

—In New York, newspaper publicity forced the city's Department of Health to stop trying to close down a pleasant, reasonably priced day-care center called B.J.'s Kids on West Eighty-fourth Street.

The health inspectors charged that the place had two children too many to comply with a forty-square-foot-per-child regulation. On the day the health department agreed that the newspapers were right, that B.J.'s was in fact a showplace, building department inspectors arrived to try to shut down the center for violation of other regulations.

There was nothing particularly new about all this. It probably happens a thousand times an hour in the land of the free—and it happens because we want to protect fat ladies and retired workers and the handicapped and children. But it also happens because things are out of hand—and a lot of government folk are out of their heads—within bureaucracies. This is a memo the *Washington Star* discovered floating through the U.S. Department of Housing and Urban Development: "Regarding the last point, the secretary stated that all duplicate program processing should be identified and eliminated except in unusual circumstances in which approval by the secretary is required. This was still an open issue. Therefore two task forces were formed to deal with it."

In 1835, Alexis de Tocqueville wrote *Democracy in America*, which many consider the best book ever written about this country, and he said then:

"I have previously made the distinction between two types of centralization, calling one governmental and the other administrative. Only the first exists in America, the second being almost unknown. If the directing power in American society had both these means of government at its disposal and combined the right to command with the faculty and habit to perform everything itself, if having established the general principles of the government, it entered into the details of their application, and having regulated the great interests of the country, it came down to consider even individual interest, then freedom would soon be banished from the New World."

53

State government, it seemed, was more of the same—or less of the same. While I was traveling through the Northeast that summer, I decided to stop by and talk to two young legislators I knew were moving up in the politics of Massachusetts and New York, in Boston and in Albany. I started with a question to an old friend. It was exactly the kind of question that we would bat around for our own amusement and frustration. But it wasn't a "news" question—as in "How's the president's popularity here in . . ."

One of the things I was beginning to love, that summer, about writing the column was getting the chance to write about the things I might talk with my wife about any night. When she asks me what happened during the day, I don't say: "Massachusetts Representative Barney Frank said today that Ronald Reagan is losing popularity among urban ethnics in this liberal state where . . ." I'd say something like: "I was talking to Barney Frank today about being a legislator and he . . ."

Well, column writing was getting closer to the daily conversations around our place, and, I thought, closer to what politics and government were like. What I asked Barney Frank in July of 1979 was:

Who is Barney Frank responsible to? No one, he says. He's a state legislator.

"No one holds us responsible," says Frank, the Democrat who represents part of Boston in the Massachusetts Legislature. "We are literally irresponsible. People think wholesale, but they vote retail. Any incumbent gets re-elected as long as he votes his district on a half-dozen votes a year—things like stopping a building of a prison, or anything else in the district."

William Hoyt, a Democrat who represents Buffalo in the New York Legislature, says he has a tougher job—by a couple of votes. "There are eight to ten votes a year that could affect my re-election. So I spend 90 percent of my time on constituents' service, most of it is for stuff like making sure the branches from an elm tree are picked up after an ice storm. Voting and thinking about issues are worth maybe 10 percent."

Those are the best and the brightest. Both young, both well-educated and dedicated. Both feeling sort of useless—as they should. Legislative government has broken down in the United States. The collapse into retail constituent service, as opposed to wholesale concerns like building roads or prisons or developing an energy program, shows itself every day in Congress and in the sad words of Barney Frank and Bill Hoyt.

"I didn't realize that I was filled with institutional self-loathing," said Frank, "until I taught a seminar at Harvard and had to explain what it was that I actually do for a living."

"I'll tell you this," said Hoyt, "it's a long way from what the Founding Fathers had in mind."

Certainly one of the things those folks had in mind in Philadelphia in 1789 was that the legislature and Congress would debate the issues of the day, representing differing local and regional viewpoints, and, when it was necessary, pass laws acceptable to the entire body politic. Today, there is no real debate—U.S. senators sometimes fill their days arguing to empty chairs—and most legislators avoid legislating at all cost. Making laws makes people angry and our representatives are dedicated to keeping their constituents calm—only angry people come out and vote against officials in power.

"I take care of the district and I'm OK," said Frank. "A lot of it is the voter's own fault. Congress and the legislatures are low in polls, but none of us is in trouble. Why? Incumbents can survive forever just by slopping the hogs. A political fact of my life is that I can get more political credit for slop I bring in to my district than political debit for giving away slop to other districts. So we all trade and we all get re-elected."

It's also the fault of the press—which ignored Frank when he tried to talk seriously about the civil service reform—and of the executive branch of government, which did its job so badly for so long in so many places that legislators could become heroes by acting as nothing more than ombudsmen helping constituents get garbage and Social Security checks picked up.

"It's fun, though," said Hoyt, who used to be a school teacher. "A great game." He hopes to be a congressman someday. So does Frank.

The Massachusetts representative was talking about his ambitions when he got a call from a Boston television station. They needed a quote about the danger of fireworks at Boston Pops concerts—and Barney Frank is one of the fastest quotes in American politics.

"OK," Frank said, pulling on his suit jacket. "I have to go out and denounce fireworks. Another forthright statement by your legislator in action."

Barney Frank got his wish. Now he's our "congressman in action." He was elected to the House of Representatives in 1980. As a freshman in Washington, he was eligible to attend the congressperson classes at Harvard. The university sponsors them for newly elected members and I monitored them to see what the new crop, the latest listening Lukes, looked like. Not so great to me and that's why I called the column, "Why Congress Is a Joke":

The Kennedy Institute of Politics at Harvard sponsors an orientation program each year for newly elected members of the House of Representatives. The freshmen congressmen are invited to the college for a few days of briefing and of just getting to know one another.

At the beginning of this year, twenty-eight of those freshmen—almost equally divided between Democrats and Republicans—filled out fifteen-page questionnaires about their views of Congress, campaigning, and themselves. Their answers, which follow, provide their own commentary—a sad one.

Q. "A recent article in the *New York Times* described congressmen as errand-boys for their districts. Would you agree or disagree with this?"

A. Agree—11; disagree—14.

Q. "Did you learn anything during your campaign that helped you define how you will do your job as a member of Congress? If so, what?"

A. Importance of keeping in touch with district—9; importance of constituent service—5; importance of position on issues—1; importance of experience—1.

Q. "Which one of the following groups and individuals will be most influential in your voting, admitting that they may all have some valuable information and experience, or expertise that might be helpful?"

A. Letters/calls/visits from constituents—17; House leadership—4; party—2; state delegation—2; local lobbying groups—1; White House—0.

Q. "Did you find voters in your district to be:"

A. Well-informed about issues—2; informed about issues—14; somewhat informed about issues—10; not at all informed about issues—2.

In other answers, the new congressmen downplayed debate and party, while emphasizing the importance of spending time in their districts. One of the freshmen said he planned to spend 60 percent of his time back home, but not a single one said that he or she thought party affiliation was the "most important" factor in his or her election. Only one agreed with the statement that stands on issues could "make or break" a candidate for Congress.

The picture I got from the questionnaires was, indeed, of a bunch of errand-boys—and girls. The freshmen said they were elected, usually, because of "my campaign" or "my experience" or "my personality." They showed no loyalty to president, party, or principle—to anything, in fact, except to constituents whom they did not think were particularly well-informed.

The new congressmen are uncontrollable and unaccountable to much besides their own ambitions, which they feel are best served by running those errands. They are responsive, but they don't feel responsible for the country—which is one reason the United States seems almost ungoverned these days.

But, when the Kennedy Institute asked the twenty-eight of them whether the voters in their districts thought that they would "make a difference," twenty-three of the freshmen said, "Yes—my voters think I'll make a difference."

These people make a difference? Either the voters or the new congressmen are kidding themselves.

Although I did not vote for him and probably never would, Ronald Reagan became president of the United States partly because of politicians like those. People didn't seem to hate government as much as they were disgusted by it.

It was time for a change. And on the day after the 1980 presidential election, I wrote: "There are gray, wet winter days in New York when you just want to head out to the airport and, when the ticket agent asks where you want to go, say, 'Anywhere!' Millions of Americans went to the airport on Tuesday. . . . The issue was change. Do anything. Anywhere!"

I remembered that Lyn Nofziger, one of the president's men since the earliest days in California, had once said of Reagan's election as governor of that state: "When we won, the big question was, 'My God, what do we do now!' " There were a lot of questions in the beginning about whether Reagan really knew what he wanted to do. They were answered quickly. He did know. Whether he knew how was quite another question, but Reagan and the conservatives who had supported him through the years did know that they wanted to reverse some of the sloppily drawn directions that American government had been taking since the Great Depression of the 1930s. If you felt that government was out of control and was operating on the momentum of forgotten ideas and plans, but you also still believed it had a fundamental role as an enforcer of fairness in the society, dealing with the early Reagan days was a problem. I listened to the debates in Washington and often found myself siding with Reagan and his people against the tired voices of some pretty aimless liberals. But, at least for me, a few trips to the outposts of the federal government, the little offices in the provinces, were convincing evidence that Reagan and I were always going to be on the opposite side of many, many arguments.

One of the places I went was to a small town in New Jersey to see what was actually being done by the people running and being served by one of the programs Reagan wanted to eliminate. The column was published on March 19, 1981:

A thirty-two-year-old woman, divorced and making what she could as a waitress, came to Steve Lember's law office on Main Street in Flemington, New Jersey, and said her former husband had kidnapped their two children and taken them to California. Lember got a court order, enforceable in California, and the kids are back with their mother.

It happens every day—even here in the pretty hills along the Delaware River. But it might not after October. Lember, a thirty-year-old graduate of Rutgers Law School, is not in private practice. He is the director of the Hunterdon County Legal Aid Service. More than half of his $21,500-a-year salary is paid by the federal government. Steve Lember will get zero if President Reagan succeeds in eliminating the Legal Services Corporation, which he is trying very hard to do by removing its $321 million line from the federal budget. If Reagan wins this one, the office on Main Street, which gets some state and county help, will almost certainly close for good. "I'll get a job someplace," said Lember, who has been with the office for the past six years. "I have plenty of options—I'm a lawyer. The clients? They have no options."

"I don't get it," Lember said. "Reagan thinks we're trying to overthrow the political system. We might love to, but it doesn't matter what we think because we're too busy just talking to people who have never had access to the legal system. This is what I do every day—landlord-tenant cases, help a lady get Social Security she has a right to before she starves."

Reagan and a lot of hard-eyed conservatives know exactly what they think and what they're doing. Legal aid to the poor—civil cases concerning landlord-tenant or employer-employee relations, for instance—may not be the greatest threat to the established American order, but it's in the top ten. The political system and the administrative arms of the government may be ineffective and inept these days, but the courts work. The legal system still functions in areas where politicians and bureaucrats fear to tread: derelicts sometimes beat campaign contributors in court.

So from their viewpoint, the Reagan people are absolutely right in trying to deny poor people access to lawyers—that is, unless they are arrested for crime. The government still will provide criminal legal representation—muggers don't make revolutions. What it wants to get rid of is lawsuits about rent payments and utility rates and working conditions. The damned Legal Services attorneys in Florida have filed a suit claiming that farm workers have a right to know what kind of pesticides are being used in the fields where they work.

"Legal Services developed strategies for changes in public policy," said Howard Phillips, the chairman of the Conservative Caucus, which has been calling for the destruction of Legal Services for years. "In virtually every debate of the past fifteen years, they have been carrying the cudgels of the liberals."

There is some truth in that charge—even if the cudgels usually have been swung for waitresses who can't afford private help—but there is more important truth in something Steve Lember said on Main Street in a small town in New Jersey:

"You know what I love about this country and why I took this job? Fairness. Equal access to the courts is fair, and America, whatever you say about it, tries to be fair. We've never been as fair as we should be, but we've always tried to move forward. This is the first time that I can remember that we're talking about deliberately stepping backward."

Writing about the handicapped is one way to get mail, but the best columns to write if you are also a stamp collector are about . . . God! More specifically, it is like Christmas around my house when the cards and letters come in after any mention of Fundamental Christianity and evangelism in general, and the Moral Majority in particular. No happy holidays; many predictions that I will have no trouble keeping warm through eternity.

The funny thing—I suppose I'm being disingenuous—about those damnings is that I've always felt that I welcomed my moral superiors into the political fray. I disagreed with them—"moral fascists" was one of my descriptions. But I thought they had a perfect right to do what they were doing, which was to try to take over my country. Things seemed to be working pretty well: They had their say and we were having ours. They were winning the early rounds—including a lot of 1980 elections—but I had a hunch we'd finally win on points. We shall see whether you can fool most of the people most of the time.

I began writing about the latest waves of religion in politics early in 1979. Driving through Kentucky, one long day and night, I was a captive listener and I began thinking about the implications of what I was hearing and what I'd been seeing in recent months. The column, which brought me so many regular pen pals, was titled, "And Now a Word from God":

I was lost in a snow storm driving to Louisville from Cincinnati one Sunday night last winter, listening to the car radio, not paying much attention until Pastor Emery caught my attention. He was one of a string of preachers broadcasting over WHAS-AM, the local CBS affiliate. Most of it was pleasant enough: hymns I remembered, sermons that took me back to Old Bergen Dutch Reformed Church.

But Pastor Emery, broadcasting from Phoenix, was something else. He had this idea, based on the biblical book of Acts, that some sort of conspiracy—which he called "Mystery Babylon"—was taking over America. The chief agents of this conspiracy, he explained at length, were Russian Communist dupes controlled by George C. Marshall, Dwight Eisenhower, and Richard Nixon.

Well, you either believe in the First Amendment or you don't. Pastor Emery has as much right to his opinions as I do—and we're both lucky enough to get paid for them. (I assume some people were impressed enough to send Emery money through the post office box number he repeated every couple of minutes.)

The next day, I mentioned Pastor Emery's theories to Barry Bingham, Sr., the retired publisher of the *Louisville Courier-Journal*. He smiled and said he couldn't imagine why people let stuff like that on the air. The day after that, I found out Bingham's family owns WHAS. I figured there was a lot going on in America that neither Barry Bingham nor I knew much about.

Since then, I've become something of a fan of religious broadcasting. And partly because of that interest, I have been stunned to realize just how much peculiar—I don't use the word pejoratively—information flows through, around, and over the country. I began to notice things that were there (or here) all the time. At almost any newsstand or candy store you can choose between two hundred fifty or so magazines and twenty newspapers published for specialized audiences from aspiring small-business men to homosexuals. In Newport, Rhode Island, I checked the AM radio dial and found thirty-eight stations, three of them religious, two programmed for blacks, and one broadcasting in Portuguese. In Los Angeles, a minister named Scott has his own television channel—30 on the UHF dial—and he sits on a kind of throne all day on camera (live and tape) telling the world how to run itself and asking folks for money.

In New York City one morning in March, I tuned in the PTL Club—Praise The Lord or People That Love—and watched panelists call for a revolution, a religious revolution that would send American ayatollahs through Times Square chopping off the hands of pornographers. "God is about to move in a startling way," said one of them, a radio evangelist named Dr. Ward. "God is using instruments that are strange. He is raising the ayatollah. That power is going to say to corporate evil in our nation: 'We have the oil. You are an energy nation. We can close you. Humiliate you. We are tired of your pornography. We are tired of your marriage patterns, your Broadway smut, the rotten filth of your cinema. If you don't stop it, we'll stop the oil.' "

As the studio audience applauded, the show's host, the Reverend Jim Bakker, who learned his electronic trade as a disc jockey, said: "Amen. Those powers that are mocking religion: You won't be laughing in a few months."

PTL Club runs on two hundred fifteen television stations each day in the U.S. and Canada and, on its best days, with reruns, attracts 20 million viewers. And it is only one of its religious kind. There are at least nine hundred Christian radio and television programs separately produced in the country. Thirty-five television stations and twelve hundred radio stations are religiously owned and directed—and that number is growing by one television outlet and four radio stations each month.

The public radio and television people who watch Channel 13 in New York and Channel 28 in Los Angeles clamor for an "alternative" broadcasting system. What they don't seem to realize is that one already exists in the United States—the informal evangelical Christian network that broadcasts its own messages and ideas around the country, around the clock.

The religious programmers, who have recently begun to have trouble with the government over fund-raising methods, have enormous advantages over other people with mass messages because their operations are essentially tax-free. They also are doubly protected by the First Amendment—as broadcasters and clergymen. I would assume other organizations and non-sectarian preachers are studying the evangelical success. As new technology makes more television and radio channels available, political, social, and commercial propagators are sure to try to repeat those successes. The American theory, which I buy, is that the very volume of ideas bombarding the nation is protection against the seeding of the worst of them. I hope I'm not being irreligious by saying I think ayatollahism is a lousy idea. But I would have said Prohibition was a lousy idea, and evangelists only needed tent shows to help put that one over.

I was traveling in Florida early in 1980 when I realized—or, rather, saw for myself—just how serious these folks were about taking care of people like me "in a few months." The title this time was short and direct, "Religion in Politics":

Forty-two new members were elected to the one-hundred-twenty-two-member Alachua County Democratic Executive Committee in Gainesville, Florida, the other day. Nothing unusual about that, except for one thing: All forty-two were members of one church, the Southside Baptist Church.

The pastor of the church, Rev. Gene Keith, is a Democratic candidate for the Florida State Senate from Gainesville. Why? I asked his wife. "God told my husband to run for this seat," said Tuelah Keith. "After twenty-five years of working with people and watching the situation in this country get worse and worse, my husband felt that this was his burden and that God wanted him to do something."

Keith got the idea of running for office when he became involved with Moral Majority, an organization of seventy thousand ministers recruited by a Virginia television preacher, Rev. Jerry Falwell. Moral Majority referred Keith to an affiliated group, the Committee for Survival of a Free Congress, and the Gainesville minister went to Virginia to attend a five-day candidate school.

Back at Southside Baptist, Keith told his congregation he wanted them to take over the Democratic committee. Fifty-three members—nine of them Republicans—registered as candidates for the committee in the March 11 primary elections. Twenty-nine won automatically because there were no other candidates in their precincts. Thirteen of the other twenty-four defeated incumbents.

This is born-again politics, part of an attempt to mobilize more than 30 million Fundamental Christians as a political force. It involves television shows like "The 700 Club," organizations with names like Christian Voice and the Religious Roundtable, and alliances with issue groups, particularly Right-to-Life and gun-owners' groups. And, it involves enemies, including "godless communism" and "godless homosexuals."

What does it mean? So far, not much. Official born-again candidates haven't done very well to date, partly because agreeing on Fundamentalist religion doesn't necessarily produce fundamental agreement on political issues. Fundamentalists like to interpret the Bible for themselves—and to think for themselves.

But the flurry of activity these days—and of the cash the television preachers and friendly direct-mail entrepreneurs seem capable of raising—is probably the beginning of something big. The Falwells and Keiths are opening doors for more plausible politicians, just as George Wallace and Tom Hayden did fifteen years ago.

One sign, to me, that born-again politics is having an impact is the reaction of more establishment-oriented churches. Last month, for instance, the quadrennial General Conference of the United Methodist Church, representing 9.7 million members, approved plans for a $25 million budget to buy at least one television station and to begin doing battle with the Fundamentalists on their own electronic ground.

"What can you do from the pulpit?" Reverend Falwell asks other preachers, then answers himself, "You can register people to vote. You can explain issues to them. And you can endorse candidates, right there in church on Sunday morning."

Then, in Detroit, at the 1980 Republican National Convention, it became clear to me that, even though I was then one of the few people writing regularly about the Moral Majority, I had really underrated them. Falwell's folks were doing their work behind closed doors in committee meetings and caucuses and I came away from that convention convinced that the big eyes of television had really missed the story by focusing on big names and the big hall. My post-convention column was dated July 24, 1980:

"This convention has shown to all America a party united," Ronald Reagan said as he accepted the Republican presidential nomination, "a party ready to build a new consensus with all those across the land who share a community of values embodied in these words: family, work, neighborhood, peace, and freedom."

It all seems so benign—at least if you watched it on television. In Detroit's Joe Louis Arena, among the delegates, it did not seem benign at all. It was, in fact, more than a little scary if you suspected that all those smiling people might not accept you into their "community of values."

Up close, inside state delegations, the Republicans did not seem a party united at all. There were many obvious tensions in Detroit.

There was, predictably, tension between Easterners and Westerners—and the West prevailed with the nomination of Reagan. Another tension line, not so predictable, seemed to be between born-again Christians and almost everyone else.

It is not every day in America that a political event can be analyzed as a split between Fundamentalists and mainline Protestants—Presbyterians and Episcopalians, for instance. But that was what was happening inside many delegations, and born-agains, who made up about a third of the delegates overall, talked openly about taking total control of the Republican party by 1984.

That sounds improbable. But then no one thought they would hear delegates stand up in caucuses, claiming they should be listened to on issues because, "God sent me here to tell you . . ."

There was more than a whiff of moral fascism in Detroit. It is hard to imagine many Americans being against Reagan's consensus of shared values. But . . . who defines the values embodied in catchwords from "family" to "freedom"?

I, for one, am not particularly interested in having my life defined or judged by Jesse Helms or Phyllis Schlafly. Or, by the Reverend Jerry Falwell and his Moral Majority. I suspect that by Falwell's definitions, most of us have already been plunged into the pit of the immoral minority.

Many of the people in Detroit—including Falwell and his organization—give real urgency to a phrase like "a government of laws." It sure beats a government by men of the cloth.

There was a lot of brimstone behind the smiles of the convention—fear and hatred of many things. Almost half the delegates I talked with raged about the Trilateral Commission—which they obviously knew very little about. That is Protocols of Zionism talk, and there is a word for it: paranoia.

Reagan seems to have carefully distanced himself from this particular strain of American conservatism. But he cannot control it, and it will outlive him. This stuff goes way back—into post-Civil War Southern populism, the kind that raged against Wall Street and, occasionally, burned crosses and people.

The fanatics lost in Detroit. They lost when Reagan selected George Bush as his running mate. Bush may not seem particularly noteworthy to many of us, but there were fists slammed and curses thrown when Reagan announced his name. Those angry delegates—and there were many of them—held their peace for now. They expect to be back in four years and eight years—and they expect to win. Perhaps they will, and by then, like most American moral movements, they may have moderated some of their hostility and intolerance to nonbelievers. But, right now, they are fervid—and scary. They sang "God Bless America" at the end of the convention. So did a lot of reporters in the press galleries—the only outsiders in the arena—and more than one of the outsiders watching the delegates turned to another and said: "I wonder if they believe this is our country, too?"

Back in Florida, I found the preachers were already holding little tax-deductible inquisitions of candidates. The date of the column was September 18, 1980:

State and local candidates have been invited to an "open forum" at the Temple Baptist Church in Tallahassee on Monday night. They will then be put through a ritual of the moral fascism that is being passed off as politics by some Evangelical Christians—a demonstration of why some people fear the God-fearing so much.

The forum will be sponsored by the Moral Majority, the group founded by the Reverend Jerry Falwell, the dynamic television preacher from Lynchburg, Virginia. Presiding will be the Reverend Rayburn Blair, the pastor of Temple Baptist and Florida chairman of the Moral Majority.

This will be the second forum held by Rev. Blair. Three thousand people came to the first one on August 28, before Florida's September 9 primary elections. This one is for the primary winners, the general election candidates. Two weeks ago, primary candidates for the United States Senate, state and local offices were called on by Rev. Blair to stand in the front of the church—and the three thousand people. This is what happened, as reported by Ron Cunningham of the *Gainesville Sun*, who was there:

" 'I want each of you to remain standing only so long as you can agree with each of the statements I am about to make,' Rev. Blair instructed the political hopefuls as they stood, shoulder to shoulder.

" 'I do not approve of practicing homosexuals teaching in our schools.'

"No one sat down.

" 'I am opposed to abortion on demand when the health of the mother is not at stake.'

"They continued to stand.

" 'I am opposed to the so-called Equal Rights Amendment,' Blair continued.

"All agreed.

" 'I support stronger laws against drug abuse, marijuana, and pornography.'

"Not a muscle moved.

" 'I can truthfully state that these positions have been my deepest convictions for at least six months,' Blair finished.

"Having gone this far, of course, none of the six was going to blow it now.

" 'All right,' Blair shouted to the approving multitude. 'We can all see where these gentlemen stand. Let's give these men a big hand.'

"And they did.

"And then came the disclaimer. The one that Blair and other Moral Majority officials are compelled to give so long as they wish their organization to continue to enjoy the tax-exempt status that other religious groups claim.

" 'We are not here to endorse any of these men,' Blair said. 'Because Moral Majority is not here to endorse candidates, just moral principles.' "

No one can be sure what all this means—except that the Moral Majority is determined to prove that it can have it both ways, becoming a political force while maintaining tax exempt status. No organization represents or can control millions of Evangelical Christians, and my guess is that the Falwells and Blairs can influence only a tiny minority of American voters. Among other things, many Evangelical Christians are black and there were fewer than a dozen black people inside Temple Baptist that night.

But the Moral Majority folk are a clear and present danger. Not because they are wrong about what they believe, but because they believe that they have the God-given right to judge others wrong, evil, immoral. They don't—under the American system, God himself doesn't have that right, not on this earth.

My rantings—alas!—didn't seem to have much impact. The forces of sanctimony were an important factor in the election of so many senators and congressmen that they probably could have started up a Moral Majority chapter inside the Capitol itself. But watching some of these folks in action, I had no doubt that there would be another day—some of them are going to give good intentions a bad name.

They are not, however, resting on their Bibles. As soon as the election was over, a group affiliated with the Moral Majority and with Phyllis Schlafly began taking on network television. Filth! Garbage! I sort of agreed with them and, yet, I believed they were, to use their word, fundamentally wrong. I tried to deal with my own feelings and ideas about the Righteous Right in a column titled, "Television, Morality, and Me" on February 3, 1981:

A man named Donald Wildmon called a press conference in Washington last Monday to say: "For years concerned citizens have urged, pleaded, and even begged the networks to halt the trend toward increasing amounts of sex, violence, and profanity. Instead of reason, restraint, and responsibility, the networks have rather displayed an arrogance and indifference rarely matched in the history of corporate America."

Right on, Brother Wildmon! I can't argue with those words—even if they did come from one of the leaders of America's new moral fascism.

Wildmon is the chairman of the National Federation for Decency, a group that claims a membership of sixty thousand presumably decent Americans. Those wonderful folks are planning to monitor network television for twelve weeks and will then tell the rest of us which sexy and violent shows (and their advertisers) we should boycott. If they do a half-decent job, we all could be avoiding most of prime-time television and half the cars, beers, lipsticks, and aspirin made in the U.S.A.

We would then watch only approved shows—approved by Wildmon, the Moral Majority, and the rest of the flock trying to make the world safe for God. The Big Three—Wildmon, Jerry Falwell, and Phyllis Schlafly—will tell us what's good for us and for our souls.

They're not only putative totalitarians, these three, they are also fools. First, they should have their heads examined for thinking about turning television over to American advertisers—and that would be the result of effective boycotts. Even Wildmon realizes and charges that many commercials are really little sex shows—and still he wants to turn programming over to the hucksters who pour little girls' behinds into shrunken jeans. Second, and most important, they totally misunderstand the significance and function of free speech in this society.

The decency federation is one of hundreds of pressure groups trying to change television programming. ABC alone has listed two hundred fifty of them—representing evangelical Christians, Jews, Sioux Indians, gays, Puerto Ricans, the Palestine Liberation Organization, and friends and enemies of everything animal, vegetable, and mineral, etc. etc. etc. . . .

The existence of the pressure groups is a tribute to freedom of speech. Donald Wildmon and I and everybody else can say whatever they like about television and about each other, about Ronald Reagan or the Lord. That is what makes America great. It is also what makes America stable.

The morality mob wants law and order—and they obviously prefer the latter. But they don't seem to understand that free speech is the key to American order. The genius of freedom of speech—in a society whose courts have ruled that magazines have the right to publish plans for the H-bomb—is that it is the most effective way to control dissent that democratic man has yet devised. Dissent in the United States is dissipated in the millions of words and images hissing from press conferences, lecture halls, talk shows, and street-corners. These people don't get that.

"These people," said David Wolper, one of television's most distinguished producers, said of the groups that wanted to censor his productions. "These people want to burn the book before it's written."

Wildmon and the rest—on both the political and ecclesiastical right and left—want to stop the writing, the showing, and the telling of ideas and scenes and stories that they don't like. And if they succeeded, the United States would explode from the unvented anger that would quickly stretch the fabric of the nation. Men and women who can't write books and shout slogans go to the streets; men and women who can write and shout go on television. Now, when they go on television, they may offend Mr. Wildmon—or me—but they are no threat to the America both of us love. The revolution will not begin on the "Merv Griffin Show."

So, shout on, Brother Wildmon! I will, too. You're right about one thing: Prime-time television is becoming a national junkyard of gratuitous sex and violence and stupidity. A little public pressure on the networks is called for right now. But boycotts are not, because they will inevitably lead to even worse television and worse problems in the country. Wildmon's idea of television would, I'm sure, reduce the sex and violence—and increase the stupidity. The man understands television; what he doesn't understand is freedom.

The letters after columns like that condemn "atheists," or a word the political evangelicals use with great venom, "humanists." I don't know whether they're right about the humanism; I do know that I am not sure enough of anything to be an atheist. God, just using the word makes me nervous. I am, after all, the descendant of a long line of Protestant ministers. Stern men of the cloth, judging by old photographs, although I did find out fairly recently that there was a certain family tendency toward running off with choir singers. In fact, my brother and I were always told that one of our grandfathers, a Dutch Reformed minister, had died before we were born. Actually, he was living in Newark—with a choir singer, of course.

Newark was seven miles from Jersey City, where we lived. It might as well have been in Borneo. Jersey City was, to say the least, a somewhat insular place. We seemed to be just about the only white Protestant family around Summit Avenue and I grew up thinking that the United States was a predominantly Italian nation run by the Irish—that's the way it was in Jersey City. It was only when I went away to college—three miles away to Hoboken—that I realized America was a Protestant country, that we ran it.

But, before that, I grew up about half-Catholic. You had to do that in Jersey City. I spent a lot of time smelling incense and staring at the Virgin Mary and all that came rushing back to me when Pope John Paul II visited the United States and I visited a couple of Roman Catholic churches in Green Bay, Wisconsin. This column was the result on October 11, 1979:

I went to mass for the first time in twenty years one Sunday this spring. It was in Green Bay, Wisconsin, at St. Agnes'. It was one of the shocks of my life and I thought of that Sunday again and again as

70

millions of Americans cheered Pope John Paul's journey to our country.

I was totally unprepared for St. Agnes. I am not a Catholic, but I grew up in a Catholic city, Jersey City, and had spent my share of time in the smoky semi-darkness of cathedrals, absorbed in the hum of Latin.

St. Agnes is not dark. It reminded me of a high-school gymnasium complete with banners showing happy animals and sunlight bouncing off pale brick walls. The parishioners, a thousand strong, were in polo shirts and shorts. The priest was young, his hair in a kind of blond afro—there was no mystery in his light voice or in the words he chanted in English. Guitars and xylophones backed us in singing, "The spirit is a' movin' all over—all over the world." As the mass ended, the man next to me reached for my arm. I jumped, but he only wanted to say, with a smile, "Have a nice day!"

What had happened in twenty years? Whatever happened to guilt? What kind of church was this? The Presbyterians, for God's sake, would have looked down on this.

I thought St. Agnes, the largest church in an overwhelmingly Catholic city, must be some kind of aberration. I drove to the center of Green Bay's grim downtown, to St. Willebrord's. The church itself was what I remembered, dark and soaring—and crowded. The priest was young and he was talking, colloquially, about "the Spirit," which he said showed itself through "sharing."

"Hey," he said, "I've accepted Christ. . . ."

Hey, I thought, this is an American church. I realized that it was only my own ignorance that caused my surprise. I just hadn't noticed that a new church had evolved since I was growing up, an American Catholic church. Two of the world's greatest institutions, two of the great ideas, "the church" and the United States of America had come together—and the American idea had prevailed. That seemed very important to me, a demonstration of the great coherent strength of our society.

The pope, the man we sincerely cheered, represents another time and another church, the Roman Catholic Church. It is part of the American heritage, we honor it, but it really doesn't have that much to do with us. The enthusiasm, the fondness for John Paul, must be something like that Lafayette saw when he toured the United States after the Revolution and was honored as the symbol of France's aid to the American Colonies in their war against the British.

The pope, too, is a symbol of part of the American past. He is also

71

a marvelously theatrical figure, a star. What he says? Family. Birth control. Divorce. Abortion. Sex. That means almost nothing here today—unless you happen to be working for the church. If you are a bishop or a priest or a nun, then the pope is the boss. For most other Americans, he's a nice man with lovely, old-fashioned ideas.

The trip was a wonderful spectacle. It was also a tribute to America, a nation that has come a long way since, even, 1960, when a pope visiting the White House might have been seen as a threat to the Republic. Viva il Papa! Viva America!

Traveling, for a columnist, is its own reward. It is not necessarily fun—in fact, it is often torture—but with your mind focused on that next deadline, you notice what's happening around you. The flight to Green Bay was, ironically, one of the experiences that led me to write about real estate in California and other places. It was a Sunday and I was flying North Central Airlines from Grand Rapids, Michigan. A stewardess came to my seat and said: "Excuse me, the pilot noticed you were reading the *New York Times* and wanted to know if he could look at the real-estate section after you're finished?"

He's that interested in real estate? I thought there must be something going on. I soon noticed that real estate—deals, prices, contractors, architects—was the principal topic of conversation of a whole class of people. "The next leadership class," I guessed in one column, adding: "Whatever you call it, the class is made up of people who work with their heads instead of their hands and do pretty well at it—managers, lawyers, 'communications' people, teachers who have good enough jobs that they can call themselves educators and people who just have a hard time explaining exactly what it is they do for a living. . . . The class distinction of the 1980s is going to be between those who talk real estate and those who talk sports."

That made as much sense to me as talking about the difference between Republicans and Democrats—which is what political columnists are supposed to do. But the more I traveled, the less the names of political parties were the focus of either my work or my conversation. That is not what I found people talking about—or what I saw around the country. The issues and the trends I saw were not always, not often, related to press releases from the White House or Senate office buildings. An incident in New Orleans made me realize how many security devices and people I was seeing everywhere. What did that mean? A waitress on Long Island focused my thinking about how many Americans were guiltlessly cheating the government. What was going on?

"The Ethic of Fear," published in *Esquire* on March 27, 1979, would never have been written if I hadn't been walking through an airport a long way from my homes on either coast:

The three small boys were lined up against the wall at a Delta Airlines gate in the New Orleans airport. They were frightened and mystified, trying to reassure one another in French. Only the oldest one, about twelve, spoke any English, and he finally understood that security guards wanted his little brother to turn over his plastic flashlight. The thing was shaped like a gun, an old derringer.

"Aren't you overreacting?" asked the pilot of the Delta jet to Birmingham. One guard, a woman, looked up for a moment and said, "We've got rules here!"

So we do. Everywhere. Traveling back and forth across the United States for the past three months would convince any foreigner that the country is a police state—a new kind of police state filled with blank-eyed men and women in uniforms of many colors, guarded by dogs and by devices with names like Razor Ribbon, Rearoscope, and Microlert. The plastic identification cards to get into work, the metal detectors at the doors of the Federal Courthouse in New Orleans, the gate that clangs down in front of the Montgomery newspaper each night at six o'clock, the improved barbed wire from Vietnam strung around the tennis courts in the parks of Tucson— welcome to the New World.

Security World. That's the name of a trade magazine—circulation 36,240. The journal is the sponsor of the International Security Conference, which began its annual tour across the country in Los Angeles, heading for Houston and New York. There were 280 exhibits, most of them spying devices, as well as seminars for officers of private police forces on such topics as "Effective Interrogation Methods" and "Polygraph Versus Voice Analyzer."

"Isn't that illegal?" someone said, pointing to a $1,995 voice stress analyzer in the Law Enforcement Associates, Inc. (LEA) booth in the Los Angeles Convention Center. "Sure," said William Howard

73

Thompson, LEA's West Coast distributor, with a selling smile. "In California, it's against the law to tape another person without their permission. But, hey, everybody's doing it and no one is ever going to be convicted. The police could break in while you're taping and they couldn't do anything. A tape is inadmissable as evidence if you don't identify yourself at the beginning—and you're not going to do that, right?"

The analyzer is designed as a lie detector. You plug it into a telephone and its red gauges are supposed to "reliably evaluate the validity of a person's verbal statements." The quote is from LEA's sales literature, which goes on to list possible uses for the gadget: "Lawyers may evaluate the opposition's true intentions. . . . Negotiators can use the SDS (Stress Decoder System) during complex union negotiations. . . . Businessmen can be assured their partners have genuine confidence in proposed ventures. . . . Purchasing agents can confirm that they are getting the best price from their major suppliers. . . . Journalists can evaluate the validity of information, [which is] sometimes provided anonymously."

Thompson also offered the Surveillance Scope and Starlight Viewer to observe people surreptitiously day and night, to say nothing of the dandy little Rearoscope, a pair of eyeglasses with hidden mirrors to spy on others without looking toward them. And, in the booths around him, there were hundreds and hundreds of alternative hidden-eye and -ear systems—television cameras, electric beams, sound and heat sensors, and a dazzling range of mechanical spies, many of them developed by the government for use in Vietnam.

Thanks to the miracles of modern technology and paranoia, any American can permeate his room with microwaves linked to alarms, wear a Microlert pendant ($300 with gold-filled chain) that can call the police electronically, and buy a key chain ($9.95) that is actually a blinding chemical-spray gun.

Exhibit Hall B of the convention center was a living museum to a nation without trust, a dangerous nation. The private security business, now proudly hauling in billions of dollars, is a testament to a people without faith in their government or one another. New Yorkers, at least, long ago gave up the belief that they would be protected by police, turning instead to private guards, locks, guns, and dogs; the rest of the country seems not far behind. Employers have given up the hope that their employees are basically honest. Most of the devices at the conference were designed to intimidate pilferage-minded workers, and for $13.95 you could get a book titled *Managing Employee Honesty: A Systematic Approach to Accountability*. We need to manage honesty, it seems, because the old systems have broken down. Religion—preached and civil—has lost its disciplining, frightening grip; so has peer pressure, the wagging tongues and pointing fingers of stable communities. We are mobile and alone. Who knows what we are up to?

Who knows the American ethic? What is right and what is wrong in this society where Henry Ford says his company knew it was making cars that killed people and he's sorry—and he's praised for his "openness"? And his employees rip him off, fully believing that they are themselves being ripped off from a hundred directions.

Security, then, is the answer. A new ethic can be defined, or enforced, by the ex-FBI agents and fear hucksters at the International Security Conference. Plastic cards, polygraphs, one-way mirrors, rules and regulations, millions of them, can presumably accomplish the same ends as can any set of ten commandments. The government can regulate Ford and Ford can regulate its employees.

In fact, in some cases the assumptions underlying the commandments of security are almost biblical. One is original sin: We are all crooks waiting to happen—unless *they* protect us from ourselves. "There's nothing that we as security people can do about the moral decay of the present generation," reads one excerpt from *Internal Theft: Investigation and Control*, a book published by *Security World*. "The thing that we can do is increase our security precautions."

"Employers," reads another excerpt, "have a definite moral obligation to safeguard their employees' integrity by doing everything possible to deter them from yielding to the temptation to take dishonest advantage of their positions." It sounds gratifyingly like God's work.

Where does *Security World* end? In Raton, New Mexico. On February 12, an Air Force sergeant named Laurence Chamberlin drove into the town in a snowstorm. He was out of gas and out of cash. The three banks in Raton refused to cash a five dollar check from Chamberlin's California bank—security regulations, *no* out-of-town checks cashed. Chamberlin slept in his car; the temperature dropped to six degrees. Three days later—frostbite—and both his feet were amputated.

Paying a bill in a fancy little French restaurant out on the east end of Long Island also served to calm my deadline tremors. I forget the name of the place and whether the food was any good. What I remembered was what happened when I handed the waitress my American Express card. She came back smiling—which meant, thank God, that the plastic hadn't been rejected by a computer somewhere—handed me the little form you fill out and said: "Please don't put the tip on there."

"Why?"

"That's our policy, sir. We prefer cash."

Who doesn't? Good for her: The restaurant was paying her more by cheating the government, the Internal Revenue Service, out of its share of the tips, which are, after all, income. Good for me: I was going to pay less taxes, too, because the cost of the dinner became deductible when I put the incident together with something that had happened to a friend in California and came up with the idea for another *Esquire* column, this one published on May 22, 1979:

The *New York Times* recently published a guest column by British writer Anthony Sampson that began: "What is one to think about the economic and moral effects of the 'black economy'? One by one the European nations have been discovering, with varying indignation, the growing numbers of people who are paid in cash, avoiding all taxes, and the underground network of the *travail au noir*, the *schwarz arbeit*, or moonlighting."

Sampson continued, with a bit of shock, that it was also happening in Great Britain. Her Majesty's chief tax collector estimated that untaxed cash payments could amount to 7.5 percent of the British economy.

I wondered why the *Times* thought that was a foreign news story. The same thing is happening here. In Hollywood, someone who wanted their house painted a couple of months ago called in a contractor for an estimate. He arrived with his foreman who spoke only Spanish and measured the walls while the boss asked about colors and the rest. The estimate was thirty-five hundred dollars. That night, the foreman returned with a friend who spoke English and offered to do the job for six hundred fifty dollars—in cash.

Guess who got the job? Guess how much of that six hundred fifty dollars the Internal Revenue Service will ever see?

On Long Island, in a fancy little restaurant far out in the Hamptons, the waitresses politely tell you it is their policy not to put the tip on American Express bills. The intent is to cheat the Internal Revenue Service.

Back in Los Angeles, if you know the right phone numbers, you can have your car overhauled by the same people who do the work at your dealer's and for half the price. They come to your home and do the job in your garage or driveway—or right in the street. In New York City, in front of Bloomingdale's or any other store that attracts a crowd, you can buy handbags, gloves, or perfumes from street peddlers for a third of the prices marked on the same things inside the door. You can also settle your bar tab at a discount at some of the more fashionable drinking stops on Second Avenue if you pay in cash. Sometimes bartenders pocket the money, screwing the boss and the IRS, but sometimes the barkeeper is the boss.

In almost any American city, you can get practically anything you need—dental care and clothing are two things I know about—by bartering. People trade their skills or products with someone else for theirs—the trick is finding someone who has what you need and needs what you have, such as a lawyer writing a plumber's will in exchange for fixing that damn sink. In most places, you can find a barter company or exchange to put you in touch with like-minded traders.

All of which is illegal if no taxes are paid on the transactions. The official position of the IRS, of course, as articulated by spokesman Leon Levine, is "Income is income, whether it's cash, goods, or services."

The IRS does not have—or won't reveal—estimates of how much underground economic activity they believe is going on in the United States. Levine and I were talking about the "straight" underground economy as opposed to the traditional criminal economy—garage sales rather than cocaine sales. "We are aware of what's going on," said Levine. "Beyond that, I don't know what to say. If you write a couple of ads for your next door neighbor and he gives you a case of booze, that's awfully hard for us to detect. Obviously we're not looking for more and more publicity about this subject."

What is going on, I suspect, is much more than what used to go on. It is a massive reaction to inflation and rising taxes—and the perception that those escalating prices and levies are corporate and government rip-offs. Not that an underground economy didn't always exist. Gamblers have always been around; so have candy store owners who dipped into their own tills to buy baby shoes and dentists who asked for cash. But *travail au noir* seems to be growing, booming really—barter and work-exchange marts in Oregon have gone to computers to establish their own credit systems—and the England that Sampson described in the *Times* seems to be only a little more advanced than the America I've been seeing.

"You are whisked back into the world of Adam Smith's 'invisible hand,' " Sampson wrote, "in which supply and demand are swiftly matched: Efficient and willing men appear, who actually seem to enjoy working hard; they have friends who can do other jobs, all in return for crisp pound notes. . . . And while we may be shocked to discover how unlaw-abiding we have become, we may also be relieved to discover that we are also rather more hard-working than we thought we were."

I'm not sure how much of it is "we." Many, many of the "efficient and willing men" turning up everywhere are obviously illegal immigrants. The painter's foreman in Hollywood is Mexican. The salesmen outside Bloomingdale's and other stores are from southern Europe and northern Africa. The French waiters are really French. Two days before Sampson's piece appeared, I had walked ten blocks along Lexington Avenue in New York on an eccentric little errand: I had left my pipe home and was looking for an eighty-nine cent corncob. Stopping in a dozen little shops and stores, I could not find anyone who spoke English well enough to deal with "corncob"—Greek, French, Chinese (Hong Kong), and Arabic, but not English. The same thing is often true with cabdrivers.

I doubt that all those hard-working folk are in the U.S. legally. I am convinced that the number of illegal aliens in the country is double the numbers periodically released by the Immigration and Naturalization Service. (One of my small pieces of evidence was a recent *New York Times* article noting that Italy's Christian Democratic party had opened a campaign headquarters in New York because the CDP estimated there were several hundred thousand voting Italian citizens living in the metropolitan area.) And I'm not convinced that that is a bad thing.

My guess is that the United States is benefiting from illegal immigration, that the government is, by accident or design, doing the right thing in its generally lax enforcement of immigration laws. The constant stimulation of new cultures is what has made America thankfully different from England. We need the stimulus of New American dreamers—particularly now when real Americans have bumper stickers that say "I'd Rather Be Sailing" and mean exactly that.

So who cares? Maybe nobody but the IRS and ripped-off contractors should. But it *is* corruption, and there is probably a connection between the kind of underground economy we now have and societies that tolerate tax evasion and bribery as necessary to commerce and government. One response to hidden commerce is depressing and debilitating: spying and security. I remember when large numbers of New York cabdrivers began ripping off their bosses by not turning on their meters and then pocketing the fares. The response of the cab owners was to install electric devices that triggered the meter when weight hit the back seat—and to hire private cops to follow their own employees.

But all the cops and electronic devices and regulations in the world are not going to change the way things are going as long as people believe that they have to cut corners to survive, as long as they believe "the system" is unfair or unmanageable. Americans are very ingenious folk; their consent is essential to the process of government.

In Louisville, a man said: "There is nothing government can do that can help me. It can only hurt me." Politicians, he added, were "a bunch of garbage." Sentiments I've heard a thousand times from cabdrivers and black kids. This time it was from Dann Byck, Jr., president of a chain of women's clothing stores, son of a president of a city council, exactly the kind of educated, thoughtful, and attractive person one would expect to demonstrate civic leadership.

So, Byck puts his spare energies into Louisville's theater groups. Others are simply madder than hell—and they think the laws, the American contract, no longer apply to them. They are beginning to feel just as moral about evading taxes as college students felt about evading the draft during Vietnam.

If so many people believe the country is unfair, the country is going to be changed by them. I don't know the answers. At the moment, all I know are a few good underground phone numbers.

Business, as Calvin Coolidge tried to tell us, is the business of America. The business of journalism has always had a certain amount of trouble with that idea. I remember, when I was still a reporter at the *New York Times* in the early 1970s, discussing a series of articles we were planning on American suburban growth. Someone said: "You know all these years we've been covering politics and thinking that pictures of shopping centers were just free advertisements. Hell, we should have forgotten about the politicians and covered the developers and the shopping centers. That was the real story, destroying an old America and making a new one."

True. Washington is the worst place in America from which to try to figure out something like that. "Business" as a conversational subject in Washington ranked well below the price of each year's Beaujolais—at least until Ronald Reagan and his merry band of Republicans came to town. But they did talk about business—and industry and commerce—in Detroit and San Angelo, Texas, and Houma, Louisiana. Those were the places I was often writing from in 1979 and 1980 and I was beginning to write about how business saw government rather than in the Washington style of seeing business through government's eyes.

One result was a two-part column in October 1980, on the problems—and the future—of the American automobile industry:

"The Ford Motor Company will survive," said Philip E. Benton, Jr., a vice president of the company. "It may be much different than it is now. It may be international, but the company will survive."

Benton, the general manager of the company's Ford Division, the basic domestic car company, spoke affably and rationally in his office high above Detroit's uneasy streets. But, I think we both knew, he was threatening the government and the people of the United States. Support us or else!

Or else, what?

"There are three choices," he said. "The government can support us. The government can take on the Japanese and cut down imports. Or, we can go offshore—we could manufacture cars and trucks for the American market anywhere. Say, South Korea."

The economics of self-exile are clear. It costs an American automobile manufacturer something like seventeen dollars per man-hour to produce a car; it costs a Japanese manufacturer about nine dollars per man-hour. Under a free trade system, the Japanese have the option of delivering a comparable car to an American buyer for less money, or delivering a better car for the same price.

But would the American auto companies really become foreign manufacturers—in, say, ten years?

"We would do what we have to do," said Benton, who headed up Ford's extremely successful European truck operations before coming back home. "We start off disbelieving that we would have to do something like that because of what it would do to the country. The industries that supply us—steel, aluminum, glass—would evidently follow us offshore."

The automobile industry, which with suppliers, dealers, and repair, accounts for one-fifth of the gross national product, will become the test-case for the kind of economic future the nation will have. The foreign vs. domestic car battle—with Japanese imports now accounting for 25 percent of the American market— is very complicated, but the consequences of the decisions made in the next couple of years are not. The United States for the foreseeable future cannot compete with many other industrial nations, particularly industrialized Asian countries.

So, we, the people, as opposed to Ford, have an uncomfortable choice:

1. Take our reduced place in a multi-national free-trade world, knowing that many basic goods will be manufactured offshore and that millions of American workers and thousands of businesses will be dislocated—that means out-of-jobs and out-of-business.

2. Or, begin putting together a complex protectionist structure to keep foreign products out, knowing that we will then lose foreign markets that provide other millions of jobs and support thousands of domestic businesses.

3. Or, finally, "Buy American" knowing that we are not getting the best but are, at least for a while, maintaining the livelihood and standard of living of many fellow Americans.

Patriotism is the last refuge of scoundrels and auto companies. That's what the new car commercials are really about: Buy our cars and save our women and children from the Arabs and Japanese.

Benton and other automobile executives now jet back and forth to

Washington saying all that they need is some time to become competitive again. Keep Toyota and Datsun and Honda out for a few years and we'll take care of everything. My guess is that that is a lie—that they will, in fact, use that time and the money generated by patriotic sales to build and tool-up for offshore manufacture.

The dream of Ford and General Motors, I suspect, is to keep the American market and open the China market—manufacturing the cars and trucks for both where labor is cheaper than it is in Detroit.

There are very tough choices ahead. For Washington and for each of us. The government has to decide what kind of place America will be for the next twenty or fifty years. Many of us have to decide, too—the choice between a Ford Escort and a Toyota Corolla is a political choice. Made in U.S.A. or Made in Japan.

The Ford Escort—base price, $5,069; probable cost with options, $6,100—is a good little car with estimated highway gas mileage as high as forty-four miles a gallon. Ford Motor Company let me drive one and watch the thing being made at Wayne, Michigan, under a sign saying: "Quality Means Business. Business Means Your Job."

Then I went to Hertz and rented a comparable foreign car, a Toyota Corolla, which could be bought for almost one thousand dollars less and has a highway rating as high as thirty-six miles per gallon. To me, the Toyota seemed a better car—more tightly built, better handling, and a little peppier.

Which one would you buy?

If I were buying—I'm not because I am happy with a 1971 Ford Maverick—I think I would buy the American car. I'd do that even though it would burn me to feel manipulated by the new car advertising trying to make me think it is my patriotic duty. I also hate the thought of rewarding Detroit for its own incompetence, for the years of pretending that Americans couldn't really want smaller, more efficient automobiles.

But I was persuaded, reluctantly, by Philip E. Benton, Jr., the general manager of Ford Motor Company's Ford Division. "You know the gates are open to Japan," he said. "We could sell cars there, but the Japanese won't buy them. They're all little economists over there. They know what makes a country tick: providing jobs for its own people."

Jobs, the jobs of the millions of Americans depending on the automobile industry, is the immediate issue in the tricky negotiation and manipulation now going on between the government and the auto companies. You know how tricky things have gotten when someone like Benton says: "Let's face it. Our system of laissez faire private enterprises has run its course. Government, industry, and unions have to work together now. It's what people like me used to condemn as socialism."

Now, the very companies who abused laissez faire are begging for government intervention and threatening both the government and the rest of us. There are three choices, Benton told me: either Washington subsidizes the American automobile companies, or blocks Japanese imports, or the American companies will move overseas, say to South Korea, and become foreign manufacturers themselves.

The idea, of course, would be to take advantage of the cost differential that makes it possible for the Japanese to manufacture cars for nine dollars per man-hour while American costs run at seventeen dollars per man-hour. Ford's better idea might be called blackmail, but it will probably work because it would be insane ten or twenty years from now not to have a healthy American-based and American-owned automobile industry—even if it was manufacturing most of its units offshore.

That's the way the future is going to be—an interdependent multi-national economy. The last thing the United States should do now is to begin putting up trade barriers.

Partly because of the industry's own stupidity and partly because other nations were inevitably going to re-invent the hubcap, the problems of the auto industry have become the problems of all of us. Detroit does need design and experience time to catch up now—and we have to pay for it. My feeling is that we will be better off paying privately by buying American, than publicly with federal subsidies and such. Let the government stay out of this mess awhile longer—this is the Vietnam of the 1980s. Ford calls the Escort a "world car"—they want to compete with the world. If they can't do that, then we won't have to worry about imported cars because Americans won't have the jobs or the money to buy Toyotas.

In that same month, October 1980, I had broken off from a Ronald Reagan campaign trip in Corpus Christi, Texas, to go to San Angelo in the western part of the state. There was something there I wanted to see. Maybe it was the future. At least it was an example of the interdependent global economy that I had been writing about from Detroit. The column was datelined "San Angelo" and was titled "The Japanese Planes: Made in Texas":

I have seen the future and it works in a hangar out by the airport near this west Texas city of seventy-five thousand people. That's where they make the Mitsubishi MU-2, a twin-engine executive airplane.

"They" are five hundred local workers. They work for the Japanese. Twenty or so Japanese executives are rotated in and out of here, two hundred fifty miles west of Dallas, for three- to five-year tours to tell the Americans what to do.

My first impression was that the Japanese, who tend to travel through town in small groups, reminded me of the British at an outpost somewhere in colonial Africa about one hundred years ago. There is some of that—the Japanese are selling those turbo-props to American companies and the money goes back to Tokyo—but the natives around here are mighty happy with the arrangement.

"We welcome them," said James Heath of the local Chamber of Commerce. "The Japanese employ our people, pay our taxes, and put money in our banks. They even add a dimension to our culture. One of the best restaurants in town is serving some Japanese food, the China Gardens.

"We know they are competing against planes made by American companies," he said. "But we also know the future is international—and we want a part of it. We were hoping to get some Japanese textile work in here. A French company just bought Monarch Tile here and they are putting in computerized systems for the first time. We are trying now to make a link-up with the German-American Chamber of Commerce."

Heath, in fact, was hired to aggressively go after foreign industrial development in San Angelo, a raw-boned, Baptist oil and ranch town that, even locals say, is in the middle of no place. For fourteen years before coming here—going back to the time Mitsubishi executives first became temporary Texans—Heath was director of international investments for the Texas Industrial Commission.

What Texas sells here and abroad is a determinedly pro-business climate. No corporate or personal income taxes and a "right-to-work" law. That means no union at Mitsubishi or some other places in town, the Ethicon Division of Johnson and Johnson, and Levi Strauss.

"Give us some promotion. We'll take them here from anyplace," Heath said. He meant industrial or commercial investment. What San Angelo—and the rest of Texas—doesn't want is agricultural investment. "We do our best to stop foreigners from buying ranch land," he said. "That doesn't do us or anybody much good. The foreigners buy it as an investment for tax reasons, and what happens is that some of it is taken out of production and the prices they are willing to pay just drive up everybody else's valuation and property taxes."

The business of America is business, and San Angelo is the real world. The little city turns out five of the planes a month—they cost $1.5 million each—with components and parts made in Japan. American companies are buying MU-2s as fast as the Japanese can build them—I mean, Texans can build them.

I originally ended the San Angelo column by referring to the campaign between Reagan and President Carter and my own view that rosy promises of the "re-industrialization" of America were naive or deliberately misleading. I wrote one column about that in August of 1980, mentioning a study of American productivity that had been published recently by two professors at Harvard Business School. Then I decided that I really should have used more of the study itself, so I did another one. Being a syndicated columnist is never having to say you're sorry you left out something. You can always put it in next week and I did. The first column was called "Re-

Industrialization—The New American Myth" and the second was called "American Business Is Committing Suicide":

"Re-industrialization" is going to be one of the buzzwords of the 1980 presidential campaign. It was popular at both the Democratic and Republican conventions, and Jimmy Carter and Ronald Reagan have each made it part of their standard campaign rhetoric.

It sounds good and no one is quite sure what it means, which is a working definition for most of what politicians say. "Re-industrialization"—the word itself is supposed to create images of modernized factories and happy American workers cheaply and efficiently producing new Chevrolets and RCA televisions that will be so well made that even the Japanese will be waiting in line to buy them.

The word was popularized in the last couple of years by Jack Kemp, the Republican congressman representing the suburbs of a city with broad but tired shoulders, a workingman's city, Buffalo, New York. Kemp defines re-industrialization as government programs designed to promote the formation of capital for new American plants and equipment—federal aid and tax incentives to build new factories and increase American productivity.

It's a nice word and will probably get politicians through the 1980s. But it is no answer—or, at best, a short-term answer—to the country's long-term problems of declining productivity and balance of trade. Whatever our politicians say, the United States is not about to regain the industrial dominance it enjoyed from the end of World War II until a few years ago.

Even if the government adopts a Republican plan—or a Democratic variation—to allow, say, United States Steel to manufacture its products as efficiently as Japanese steelmakers, the American advantage would soon disappear. Whatever small advances in technology we made would be copied quickly by other industrial nations where workers are paid less, where people still accept a lower standard of living and still tolerate working conditions that are part of the American past.

The problems of American industry go deeper than the things businessmen and others like to blame: overpaid or lazy workers, government regulations, or high oil prices. A big part of the problem is American bosses.

Two professors at Harvard Business School, Robert H. Hayes and William J. Abernathy, in the current issue of the *Harvard Business*

Review, write that there is "prime evidence of a broad managerial failure—a failure of both vision and leadership—that over time has eroded both the inclination and the capacity of U.S. companies to innovate . . . responsibility for this competitive listlessness belongs not just to a set of external conditions but also to the attitudes, preoccupations, and practices of American managers."

Lawyers and accountants have taken over American industry, the professors argue, and they do what lawyers and accountants do best—make deals and squeeze companies and workers for short-term profit. The bottom-line folk would rather merge than manufacture. And the last thing they are interested in is new ideas. Invention and conceptual breakthroughs don't show up immediately in quarterly profit statements.

Sadly, the politicians, both Democrats and Republicans, are buying the businessmen's line: Give us tax incentives and we'll produce as we did in the old days. We won't. The future depends on what the incentives are used to finance. If tax breaks underwrite research and innovation, then the United States will get moving again. If the government finances "re-industrialization," then we will just be making ourselves feel better—for about ten years.

Who's killing the American economy? OPEC? The government? Lazy workers?

None of the above, according to two professors at Harvard Business School. American business is commiting suicide in a mindless race for short-term profits, write Robert H. Hayes and William J. Abernathy in the current issue of the *Harvard Business Review*.

The two academics statistically track the decline of American productivity and the rise of financial managers and lawyers to the top ranks of American business—and the fall of production people—and then report foreign observations about diminishing American economic influence.

This is what they heard from Japan:

"Instead of meeting the challenge of the changing world, American business today is making small, short-term adjustments by cutting costs and by turning to the government for temporary relief. . . . Success in trade is the result of patient and meticulous preparations, with a long period of market preparation before the rewards are available. . . . To undertake such commitments is hardly in the interest of a manager who is concerned with his or her next quarterly earnings reports."

And, this from Canada:

"Inventors, scientists, engineers, and academics, in the normal pursuit of scientific knowledge, gave the world in recent times the laser, xerography, instant photography, and the transistor. In contrast, worshipers of the marketing concept have bestowed upon mankind such products as new-fangled potato chips, feminine hygiene deodorants, and the pet rock."

The bottom-line folk, the merger moguls, the profit-center pirates don't know where the hell they're going and they're taking the rest of us with them. They do, however, know they're lost—so they blame oil producers and government taxes and regulations.

Their whining, though, hardly explains why West German productivity is now four times American productivity. The Germans, after all, import all their oil, and German business taxes and regulations are heavier and heavier-handed than American ones.

The difference, to a significant degree, is the myopia of American managers. "When executive suites are dominated by people with financial and legal skills," Hayes and Abernathy write, "it is not surprising that top management should increasingly allocate time and energy to such concerns as cash management and the whole process of corporate acquisitions and mergers."

Joan Didion wrote years ago that the highest art form in Hollywood was "the deal." Now that numbers mania has spread to all of American industry. The bosses, the ones who do the most complaining and finger-pointing, are part of the problem, not part of the solution. The problem is that the United States has more and more trouble selling its products abroad—and, increasingly, at home—because we are not making anything particularly new or well. We're just making deals. That's all many of the new managers know how to do.

The fact that I was finally writing about business did not make me pro-business. Certainly my mail indicated that other people thought

I was anti-business or, at least, anti-corporatism. I greatly prefer the latter description—and I think it is more accurate.

I began my grown-up life working for a large corporation, the Ingersoll-Rand Co., which manufactures pumps and compressors and a lot of heavy and light industrial machinery. The college I went to in Hoboken, you see, was Stevens Institute of Technology. I graduated in 1960 and my degree is ME—Mechanical Engineer.

I-R, as we called it, was not such a bad place and I liked my job well enough. But from day one, I did not like the restrictions or the atmosphere of the corporation. I didn't like the meetings or the memos. I didn't like the unquestioning acceptance of arrogance and stupidity from men—they were all men—who happened to have slightly bigger offices. I didn't like: "That's the way we do it here. . . ." I did not want to be like the men I saw who were ten, twenty, and thirty years older than I—neither the successful ones nor the failures.

Besides I was a lousy engineer. I had been sucked into the world of technology in the science mania of the 1950s. Any reasonably bright public high school student was pushed toward an engineering school in those days. Four years later, my senior civil engineering project was the design of a mill building on the east coast of Florida. The building had to house a great deal of heavy lifting equipment—cranes and hoists—so the strength of the columns and the configuration of space inside the roof were critical. Also, because of hurricane danger, the building had to be capable of withstanding twice the highest winds recorded locally—a safety factor—and those winds had reached 100 miles per hour. So I went to work—five months' work—and designed a roof pitched to handle the hoists and a structure that probably could have taken winds of 500 miles per hour. Unfortunately, I made a bit of a mistake with the columns. My angled roof, it turned out, was actually a wing holding the building up. If the wind dropped below 150 miles per hour, the columns would buckle and the whole damned thing would collapse.

That is why when I saw a chance, I became involved in starting a weekly newspaper in the town, Phillipsburg, New Jersey, where Ingersoll-Rand had its largest plant. I was the first editor of the *Phillipsburg Free Press*—the whole staff, in fact—and I did that anonymously and part-time for six months in 1961 and 1962. When I could afford to pay myself $120-a-week, I quit I-R, engineering, and corporations—at least corporations that did not publish newspapers.

But there is part of me that still lives those endless days in the labs of Stevens Tech. That's the part I was thinking about when the space shuttle *Columbia* was launched on April 12, 1981:

"I've never heard such hype in my life," said Sen. William Proxmire of the noise, amplified through seven thousand reporters, coming from Cape Canaveral and Houston these days.

Big deal, he said, the space shuttle *Columbia* is just a big truck going out into nowhere. And covered wagons crossing the Missouri River were just big carts carrying furniture into a wasteland where there were no houses.

Proxmire, who is one of the brightest members of the United States Senate, has made something of a career of griping that spending money on science, or technology, is like throwing it out into . . . into space. His anti-intellectualism—anti-technical intellectualism—has been institutionalized over the years in his popular Golden Fleece awards.

The awards, usually good for an ironic laugh, commemorate things like taxpayers' money "wasted" on experiments by college professors studying why monkeys in cages grind their teeth around other monkeys. That was a real Golden Fleece award given, rhetorically, to the National Science Foundation a couple of years ago for underwriting such experiments by a professor in Michigan.

Very funny. But, in fact, the professor had been commissioned to study aggressive behavior by crewmen in submarines and space craft. Beginning with monkeys in cages, when you think about it, may not be the worst idea in the world.

Maybe it was even the right idea. Maybe not. That's the problem with research—and a lot of other things: You can't tell the great ideas from the silly ones in advance. Even Proxmire's own business, politics, is like that. In campaigns, only 10 percent of what candidates do works to influence voters, but no one knows which 10 percent.

The space shuttle may not be the right 10 percent. I think it is, but what do I know? We—John Young and Robert Crippen circling the globe, all the engineers and scientists, and all of us who paid for it—are guessing that this will give us some answers to the questions outlined in the National Aeronautics and Space Administration's plan for the years 1981 to 1985:

"Space science deals with the most fundamental questions we can ask about ourselves, our origins, and our destiny. Who are we?

Where did we come from? Where are we going? Are we alone? "What are the size, scope, and structure of the universe? What is our place in it? How did it begin? Is it unchanging or does it evolve; and will it have an end?"

Once philosophers had to deal with those questions. Now scientists can. Unfortunately, scientists are more expensive and it takes more of them to come up with answers that are often less rewarding than those of poetic thinkers. That is the curse of our times.

But why curse the light? We have to try to find out. We have to put space labs and telescopes, carried out there by shuttles, those expensive trucks, to see as far as we can see.

I understand the frustration of friends and senators who think the price is too high for uncertain results, that the money could be better spent on earth. But William Proxmire would not ban the written musings of poets and philosophers. The thoughtless condemnation of the searchings and sometimes painful probings of science—in space, in medicine, in genetics—is just another form of book burning.

The oil companies, which were employing a lot of my college classmates, were a fair target for an anti-corporate, lapsed engineer. And they deserved what they got from columnists and citizens alike—the dislike, fear, and envy due big winners. They beat the government and that was the big political story of the 1970s—so big it really wasn't reported. I wanted to talk about my view of that, and oil and gas country in Louisiana was a good place to start. The column was published on March 27, 1980:

An outsider traveling through the Cajun country around the boomtown of Houma, Louisiana, needs an interpreter. Not because the local language is French, but because oil and gas is spoken here.

Take the "Drilling Report" in last Sunday's *Houma Daily Courier and Terrebone Press*. How many people understand this:

"96—17S—17E; Union Oil of Calif.; A.J. Ellender et al; 1; Loc. . . . 8,700-' RA SUE Calvert & Todd; 11; fishing for tbg."

"—23S—19E; Texaco Inc.; CI LWR 70 B RBBI SU; SL 301; 78; State Potential 3-12-80; oil, LWR 70 R090, GL, 82 BOD, OL CK, GOR 1130,

BS & W 52 percent, Gvty 32.6, TP GL, CP O perf 12925—39."

My interpreter, Roger Kuechler, the editor of the *Daily Courier*, said even he didn't understand it all. But he did know that "Ellender et al" referred to the heirs of the late Louisiana senator, Allen J. Ellender, who, like a lot of local politicians, leased land to oil companies. "Fishing" meant something—a wrench or a piece of tubing—had been dropped into a well and someone was trying to fish it out.

So it goes—a small example of the control of information that makes the United States government and millions of Americans hostages of multinational oil companies. In a more comprehensive piece of reporting in the *New Yorker*, Richard J. Barnet wrote:

"The information on proven reserves is largely in control of the oil companies . . . the power of the oil companies would be quite sufficient in itself to arouse public suspicion, even if they were all run by saints."

Seven years into the great energy crisis and most of us—including most of the highest officials in the land—don't really know what is actually happening. Information is power and the oil companies—based in America but loyal to themselves and their own international profits—have the information about reserves and supplies. Even government reports on how much oil is in those holes in Houma are based on whatever numbers the companies choose to release.

But companies—Exxon, Mobil, Texaco, and the rest—have won a tremendous political victory in those years. They are in charge of our futures. That issue—who controls?—was in doubt for a little while a few years ago. But the battle is over, as Barnet reports:

"For a brief political interval in 1974, the public fury was so intense that the oil companies became populist targets. . . . it was folk wisdom that the crisis was exaggerated, that the 50 percent rise in heating bills and the doubling of gasoline prices were making the companies rich, and that the companies were in league with the sheiks against the consumer—and it was all true. At one point, according to Mobil's Chairman Rawleigh Warner, 'There were three thousand bills in the hopper in the Congress, all of them means of doing something dreadful to the oil industry.' But by 1979, nothing more dreadful than deregulation and profitable price increases had occurred. Indeed, during this period the oil companies' problem was neither nationalization nor divestiture, but what to do with their spare cash."

That was the great political failure of the 1970s. Government was unable or unwilling to win control—or even win real oversight—of the oil industry. The companies beat the rest of us. They will determine what happens in Houma, and the rest of the United States during the 1980s.

Whatever I thought about big businesses as I traveled the country, I was in admiring awe of the energy and the wheeling and dealing of all of us, we the people. Americans, a Harvard professor with a European background told me, were people who thought "dropping out" meant becoming a lawyer in Denver. Taking a day off, she added, meant working like a mule all day fixing up the house.

My own contradictory feelings about business and that awesome American energy—usually materialistic—was a hard thing to write about until it all came together when my own family was hustling for a few dollars. The column also gave me a chance to hit a couple of familiar themes, and explained part of the reason I could afford so much cross-country travel. It was published on June 21, 1979:

"OK folks, this is the moment you've been waiting for," said the flight attendant as the seat belt sign flashed off on United Airlines Flight 755 from Fresno to Los Angeles last Sunday night. Then he began walking down the aisle passing out United's 50 percent discount coupons.

It was a long walk because every seat on the Boeing 737 was filled, and two dozen unhappy people had been left at the gate. Marching right behind the attendant was a smiling middle-aged man waving twenty-dollar bills, offering to buy the coupons on the spot. Then a woman who had been quietly reading, grabbed for her purse, and began following him, trying to outbid him for the precious coupons. Hands were waving all over the plane. Flight 755 was a bazaar.

This was one of the last United flights on June 17, the last day of the airline's three-week giveaway of half-fare coupons for its domestic flights between July 15 and December 15. We had four seats on Flight 755—took two children for a weekend at Yosemite National Park, partly to get eight of the coupons on the $25 flight between Los Angeles and Fresno. We'll use them for $440 round-trip cross-country flights later in the year. The tickets cost us $200; the discounts are worth as much as $1,760. And the weekend was great.

"O beautiful for spacious skies . . ." It's great to be an American. And Flight 755 was an American happening—to say nothing of what happened on the ground. Los Angeles International Airport was a madhouse. The place was filled with entrepreneurs jiggling "We Buy" placards and cash in the noisy air. A twenty-five-year-old waitress named Mary Poche had flown in from Salt Lake City with $17,000 in small bills to buy up coupons, which she hoped to resell at a profit to travel agents and corporations.

The happy craziness of the discounts—it could cost United and American Airlines more than $500 million to redeem these coupons—tells a lot about what kind of people we are. I have been traveling the country for months looking for clues about where the country is going, and some of what I had found out was dramatized by an hour and a half in discountland:

—Given half a chance—at a buck—Americans are anything but the laid-back, lazy people being popularly pictured these days. What foreigners still notice first about us is our demonic commerce—twenty-four-hour supermarkets, advertising, and sell, sell, sell. As obnoxious as much of that is, it rings of freedom when you compare it to places like West Germany, where stores that close at 6:30 P.M. and on weekends effectively force women not to work, keeping them home and busy stocking tiny refrigerators every day.

—"Middle America has discovered the airplane," said Jon Lowell, when I asked him what was the major conclusion of a book he had just finished with Robert G. Kaiser. The two reporters—Lowell from *Newsweek* and Kaiser from the *Washington Post*—have written *Great American Dreams*, and the title tells it all: More and more Americans are traveling farther and farther, more and more frequently. They are seeing America first and loving its pleasanter parts. Experts predicting a slowing of the exodus from the North and East to the South and West are dead wrong. The country is going to tilt into the Pacific and the Gulf of Mexico—and, whether we like that or not, we might as well begin planning for it.

—The nation's "underground economy" is flourishing and growing. Many of the discount entrepreneurs refused to tell me their names or to be specific about how much they were buying and selling. How did they know I wasn't from the government, from the Internal Revenue Service? That growth of cash business, of barter-

94

ing, of work by illegal aliens is going to continue as long as Americans believe their government is unfair and wasteful.

Oh, the guy following the attendant on Flight 755 bought ten discount coupons. The lady behind him got three. Even on Sunday, the business of America is business.

That tilt west, of course, had slid me into Los Angeles. It was there, watching the passing parade and local teams, that I was able to indulge the hidden ambition of most men, once they learn they are not going to be great athletes, to become sports writers.

Judging by my mail, however, neither of these columns, which I thought were important, won me very many fans. Win some. Lose some. The first one was released on January 20, 1980, a day the Los Angeles Rams were playing for the professional football championship of the world, and ran under the title, "The Real Super Bowl: Musical Stadiums":

What follows may be considered un-American and dangerous to your health:

I seriously question whether there aren't better uses for taxpayers' money than bribing professional football and baseball teams to move from city to city.

What prompted this possibly treasonous thought was a vote last week by the Los Angeles County Board of Supervisors to "lend" $5 million to the Oakland Raiders of the National Football League. The owners of the Raiders will get the money if they will move their players four hundred miles south to the Los Angeles Coliseum. That would be added to the $10 million the Raiders' owners say the county and city must put up to renovate the coliseum before they would even consider moving down.

This is a burning issue here on Super Bowl Sunday. The Los Angeles Rams are playing their last game as the home team inside the county limits today against the Pittsburgh Steelers in the Rose Bowl. The Rams, you see, have been enticed to move thirty miles farther south, to Anaheim in Orange County. Except for Disneyland, the Rams' owners are getting almost everything in Anaheim—including millions of dollars in development rights to the property around their new stadium.

Who benefits from musical stadiums?

The fans, everybody says. My answer to that is from Gene Palmer, a farmer in Platte City, Missouri, who was interviewed several years ago by Haynes Johnson of the *Washington Post* and said: "In Kansas City, the residents of Jackson County were asked to approve some municipal revenue bonds to build those sports complexes we have out there. And we've got Mr. Lamar Hunt that's come in from Dallas, Texas, and brought us professional football games. But there's no way for the average person to go to see a football game. The reason is, they have 'em all on season tickets and the tickets are held in very tight hands. The average person is never eligible, or even given a chance, to buy season tickets even if he could afford to. The banks, all the major corporations, the utility companies, everybody in politics from the state level on down— they all have lots of tickets. The county court has one whole side of the stadium. And the public is paying, whether they go or not. Every little guy that's got a three-bedroom house or any goddam thing that's taxable, he's paying for it."

Those damn tickets have become the royal favors of democracy. "This kind of thing is, of course, not restricted to Kansas City," Johnson said. "Nothing shows more clearly the nature of Washington relationships—professional, social, political, and economic—than the scene on any Sunday at Robert F. Kennedy Stadium (built by public funds) when the Redskins play: about fifteen hundred season-ticketholders—newspapers, law firms, advertising agencies, and political offices—control the fifty-five hundred seats. Entertained in the owners' box are presidents, Supreme Court justices, Cabinet officers, members of Congress, editors, columnists, commentators, and wealthy Georgetown hostesses."

Then, eight months later, it was time for another season and on August 31, 1980, I wrote this column under the title, "The Cripples of Autumn":

School's back in and many a young man's fancy will be turning to football. Older men's fancies, too—a lot of heroes of Saturdays and Sundays past will limp over to watch the kids play.

Limping, living as a cripple, is too often the price of the cheers of autumn. Alan Greenberg, a sports writer for the *Los Angeles Times*, noticed, during ceremonies honoring former Los Angeles Rams players last year, that many of the dazzling athletes of yesteryear could barely walk onto the field.

"The scene," Greenberg wrote, "pointed up a seldom remarked-upon legacy for football players—they often pay a lifelong price in pain or loss of mobility for their days of glory."

He then contacted thirty former players for the National Football League team to see what effect years of high school, college, and professional football had had on their bodies and their lives. The group played during the years between 1946 and 1976—some, like quarterback Frank Ryan and defensive tackle Roosevelt Grier were stars—and most of them were living in constant pain from old injuries.

"What do you want to do—kill football?" joked Les Horvath, a running back in the late 1940s. "Have you ever seen an ex-football player who wasn't crippled?" Horvath, a dentist now, had four shoulder separations as a player and his tendonitis has sometimes been so painful that he could not lift his shoulder high enough to put a hand in his pocket.

Ryan, who is forty-three years old, is now the athletic director at Yale University. After several operations, he cannot straighten his right knee. "My ankles are bad," he said. "I can be walking around like a perfectly normal person, and something might shift in them and I literally won't be able to walk. . . . my body is a constant reminder that I sacrificed something playing football, and I'm not sure that what I got is really worth it."

Grier, forty-seven, has a speech impediment from a severed nerve, sometimes cannot straighten up, and is in daily pain. Running back Tommy Mason, forty, has compressed neck vertebrae and a noticeable limp. He is facing another knee operation, his seventh. Tackle Don Simensen, fifty-four, said: "I can pour a cup of coffee, but if I pick it up, I get more on the floor than in the cup."

Wide receiver Pat Studstill can't run, can't straighten his right elbow, and, like many of his teammates, has cronic arthritis. "I've got pain constantly," he said, "and I've got a limp. But it is kind of a stylish thing. . . . I'd do it all over again. I was one of the few people that can say I was one of the best in the world at something."

Many of the old men say that, that they treasure the experience—pain and all. "I ignore the pain," said center Art Hunter, forty-six. "If I thought about it, I could be in bed twenty-four hours a day. It's like background music. I don't dwell on it. Most of the guys just think about the good times."

Football players, great ones, are good at ignoring pain. And if the hurt is too bad, the teams have highly skilled physicians—doctors whose skill with drugs and braces is used for getting an hour's play out of a man even if the price is a lifetime of greater pain.

"I can hardly walk," said center Bob deLauer, fifty-nine. "The doctor says I've got legs of an eighty-year-old man. Everyone gets full of arthritis. But when you spend a career hitting into people, something's got to give."

What was a nice boy like me doing writing about Los Angeles? Actually living in La La Land?

Well, I was enjoying myself and I was, I think, gaining some insight into one of my neighbors in Pacific Palisades, fellow named Reagan up on San Onofre Drive.

On the Sunday after the 1980 election, I wrote about him, then President-elect Ronald W. Reagan. In a way, the column was a sequel to the first one I had written back in March of 1979—"East vs. West." This one, published on November 16, 1980, was called, "The West's Man on a White Horse":

Ronald Reagan spent most of last week resting at his 688-acre ranch in the hills twenty-five miles northwest of Santa Barbara. It's the place he's happiest; the United States has a Westerner for president.

That's an important fact to remember as the Reagan presidency begins. Many of the issues that could divide the country in the 1980s are not the old issues of North vs. South or Frost Belt vs. Sun Belt, but the new ones of East vs. West.

The most obvious of those issues are energy and urban policy. The East consumes energy; the West produces it. California, Reagan's state, is an oil-producing nation. The cities of the East are declining and want federal aid to maintain a shadow of past glories, the cities of the West are growing and they want that federal aid to handle new population and problems.

The conflicts are building. Just as they did in Canada where the prospering, oil producing western provinces are practically in revolt against that country's domination by Ottawa, Toronto, and the rest of the Canadian east. The same thing could happen here—and the West could be very happy to have its own man in the saddle back East.

"A new Mason-Dixon Line is being drawn at the 100th meridian," said Colorado Governor Richard Lamm, who is a Democrat but could find himself agreeing quite often with the Republican president from west of the meridian. "Regional politics are greater than at any time since the Civil War."

The 100th meridian, to Western eyes, is the dividing line of America, slicing the country through the middle of six states, North and South Dakota, Nebraska, Kansas, Oklahoma, and Texas. Forty million people live left of that line—in the West—and 180 million live to the right.

The right—the East—has always had the power. But the West has the oil, the uranium, most of the coal, a lot of the sunshine, and land, lots o' land under starry skies above. And the use of that land is going to be one of the issues dividing the nation. More than 60 percent of it is owned and regulated by the federal government. In California, 45 percent of the land is federally owned. In Nevada, the figure is 87 percent.

The movement to take that land—return it to state control—has been called the "Sagebrush Rebellion." It is a very real thing in places where there is sagebrush, and it almost became part of the Republican platform during the party's national convention last summer in Detroit. Westerners dominated platform committee hearings there, and had voted to endorse the rebellion, which is heavily backed by oil, timber, and mining companies. They were talked out of that by Sen. Paul Laxalt of Nevada, Reagan's campaign chairman, who said he was with them but said that the endorsement would cost Reagan votes in the East.

Western hostility toward the federal government increased significantly while Jimmy Carter has been president—Georgia is just another Eastern state when viewed from the Rockies. Because Western states vote later during primary election season, Carter never really campaigned in them in 1976 or 1980 and is woefully ignorant of their problems. When he was attacking new federal dams as "pork-barrel projects," he was threatening the life blood of the West—water. When he, and other Eastern politicians, discussed heating oil subsidies and imposed a national fifty-five-mile per hour speed limit, those were seen as anti-Western in California and the Southwest and other places where long distances mean high-speed driving.

Land, water, energy, and people, people moving west, are all going to be major issues for at least ten years. And many people already out West cheer each time they see Ronnie Reagan wearing a Stetson and looking over his little spread in the mountains.

Part 3

What We Know and When We Know It

Way back when, in 1973, when I was covering politics almost all the time, I wrote: "If I'm interested in influence, it's influence with other reporters. More than anything, I want the respect of the men and women in my peer group. When a journalism class I taught asked me whom I write for, I found myself answering, 'Other political reporters.' I wish I had said history or something, but that's what I said."

I would not answer that question the same way now. For me, over the years, there has been an evolution that seems to have progressed from writing for the approval of editors, then writing for the respect of peers and now . . . now I might say that I write for myself. Still I care, though, probably too much, what other people think. I have to care about editors because they are the people who basically decide whether I'm going to be published and how much I'm going to be paid for my words. And I soon discovered that one way to have influence with my peer group was not only to write for them, but to write about them.

Maybe that was the reason I found myself writing, and thinking, more and more about the journalism, print and electronic, and then about entertainment in both media. Or, maybe, it was just because I needed a job. I became unemployed in January of 1977.

The story has been told, at some length, by other people and I don't particularly want to dwell on it here. I was the political editor of *New York* magazine when it was taken over in some fancy and secret financial maneuvering by Rupert Murdoch, the Australian publisher who already owned the *New York Post* and has since taken over the *Times* of London. There was great gnashing of teeth, meetings, strikes, and angry statements, some of them by me. But I knew I was finished the moment Murdoch's name came up.

Most of the man's work was garbage—most of his publications added dimension and a professional sheen to sleaze. He was smart and tough and enormously wealthy and he gave us all a little demonstration of how articulate money is in all accents.

Forty of us—that's the number I remember—walked out of *New York*'s office at 755 Second Avenue, a place that was a sort of second home to some of us. It was very sad—writers, artists, everybody needs a place to hang out. *New York* magazine, when it was run by the wild and talented man who founded it, Clay Felker, was a good place to go in the afternoon. That's always the question for writers: What do you do in the afternoons? In the mornings, you write. That's lonely, but the afternoons are lonelier. Anyway, it was gone—the people on the board of directors, the ones who always wanted you to come to their houses to, I guess, impress their friends, had sold us. We brought a pretty good price—nine thousand pounds of writer, editor, and artist.

It was the best place I ever worked and that's saying a lot because I was a reporter for the *New York Herald Tribune*. That had ended, too—as exciting as the *Trib* was, at least for a young reporter, it was badly managed. What days those were. On Sundays, maybe a dozen of us would come into the grimy old building on West Forty-first Street and try to put out a better newspaper than the best, than the *New York Times*—and sometimes we did.

I walked out of the *Trib* for the last time on April 23, 1966, and took the gold-painted plates of the last two front pages from the lobby wall. They are hanging now on the wall behind me.

I had come to the *Trib* from the *Newark Evening News* in New

Jersey. Maurice (Mickey) Carroll, who is now a reporter for the *Times*, was then a *Trib* reporter living in Morristown, New Jersey, and he had noticed a couple of stories I had done roaming northwestern Jersey at night, chasing murders and murderers, accidents, and town meetings. The first time I met him was at a party with some other reporters and he said: "Would you be interested in working for the *Trib?*" I would, I said, be willing to work for nothing and swim to New York each morning.

They paid me $163.60 a week, which was $68.60 more than I was getting at the *Newark News*. The *News*—the Northwest Jersey Bureau in Morristown where I shared night duties with a wonderful reporter named Don Singleton—was where I went from Phillipsburg. The *Free Press*, the little newspaper I had helped found, became quite successful, an "award-winning newspaper," as they say, with a circulation of more than four thousand in a town of eighteen thousand. But I decided to move on when I realized that I didn't enjoy being the boss—and I wasn't particularly good at it. I just wanted to write.

Then, on that sad April 23, I thought I was on my way back to Jersey. But the "enemy," the *New York Times*, came to the rescue. A.M. (Abe) Rosenthal, who was then metropolitan editor and now runs the whole paper, called and I switched my loyalties from West Forty-first Street to 229 West Forty-third Street, my professional home for the next five years. I told Abe I was making $200 a week at the *Trib* and he offered me $230. Years later, he told me he had known all along that I was lying about the $200.

Enough of that. My problem, again, in January of 1977, was that I had no place to write. This time the phone didn't ring very much at all. A friend told me I had the Barbra Streisand problem: "Everyone thinks everyone else is calling, so she ends up going out with her hairdresser." I ended up, for several months, doing a piece here and a piece there—for the *New York Times Magazine* and for the *New Republic*—but my only regular writing turn was as a book columnist for the feisty little *Washington Monthly* magazine. Then Byron Dobell, who had been an editor at *New York* magazine, called and asked whether I was interested in doing a "Media" column for *Esquire*.

I began by trying to give my own overview of prime-time television, which the magazine published in November of 1977:

I have always thought that careful viewing of a single night of

103

prime-time television could tell you almost everything you need to know about America. I did it on a Monday night and found out I was wrong—at least I hope I was wrong. Switching from ABC to NBC to CBS, I took eight pages of notes—mostly weak jokes on the order of the one that has an Italian boy asking a Mexican girl out for "a pizza and a dozen margaritas"—but I found only one sociological pattern: Of the first ten commercials I saw, six were for things that rot your teeth and two were for things designed to help your body absorb the first six. In order, ABC and NBC offered me Bubble Yum, Canada Dry ginger ale, Milky Ways, Kool-Aid, Crest toothpaste, Duncan Hines cakes, and Alka-Seltzer.

Nothing else was clear. I began with "The Primary English Class," an ABC pilot of a possible series about a night-school class for immigrants. The message, I think, was that foreigners are stupid because they don't understand English well enough to come up with double entendres like the one from the teacher who, after seeing the amorous Italian and the Mexican girl locked in the closet, quipped, "Funny how those little things pop up in classrooms." Next came NBC's "Little House on the Prairie," a lovely show that brought tears to my eyes, probably because I realized that I could never be as good a father as Michael Landon. Over to CBS for "Maude," a tasteless package carried by Bea Arthur's comic talent. Something has to be said for a woman who can meet an old college classmate—a stroke victim—who is in a wheelchair and say, "Here you come out in this thing and talk like thish!" What the old classmate then says to Maude is: "This stroke has been bad news and good news. The bad news is I'm paralyzed. The good news is my husband left me." Then, same network, came "All's Fair," a show, of sorts, about Washington. The message, I think, was that Americans are stupid, particularly liberals and conservatives. Sonny and Cher ended the evening, again on CBS, with King Kong (Cher in his palm) visiting Dr. Joyce Brothers for psychiatric help—the skit probably could not have been done better. It was not, however, done as well as the General Motors commercial that followed, in which an engineer said, "I don't think anybody wants to move away from the freedom you get with personal transportation." A stirring reminder of Roosevelt's fifth freedom, freedom from small cars.

Is that what we want? Yes, according to the folks who run one of the television networks. Julian Goodman, chairman of NBC, has issued a call for networks, stations, and advertisers to "stand together" against government and other outsiders who try to "restrict further the networks' ability to provide the kind of program service the public wants . . . a service that is widely enjoyed and endorsed by the public . . . and the evidence is in the fantastic growth in television homes and the hours people spend watching television. . . . The system works." It was Queen Victoria in 1847, I think, or a guy I knew in Jersey City, who first said, "Potatoes are widely enjoyed and endorsed by the Irish. And the evidence is in the fantastic amount of growth in the number of families eating them and in the hours spent digging for them."

Paul Klein, who also works for NBC (he is the network's programs vice-president), once said, "You view television irrespective of the content of the program watched. . . . you take what is fed you because you are compelled to exercise the medium." Like the Irish and eating potatoes. I suspect that he is quite right, and that much criticism and analysis of television—and potatoes—are much too complicated. On the day I chose to watch seriously, as seriously as possible, the United States Commission on Civil Rights issued a 181-page report complaining that television perpetuates sexual and racial stereotypes. The commissioners made much of the fact that Mary Tyler Moore called her boss Mr. Grant while men on her show called him Lou. I'm just not that sophisticated (although I do have an idea of how much money MTM makes compared with those Lou men), and I tend to think television has had only two overriding social effects: (1) It has led to citizen unrest by continuously showing half of us how the other half lives and has programmed us for instant gratification, or at least resolution of financial and other problems, within a half hour, less commercials; (2) it is turning us into zombies. Television, as it exists, is our Soma—and the three networks are the major pushers of Huxley's brave new drug.

That's about all I saw in one night on nineteen inches of color television—really color nothing, merely painless time passing. To try to expand my mind about what was happening to television, for several weeks this summer I read *Broadcasting* and *Variety*, the industry's trade journals, which is how I picked up Mr. Goodman's—Julian's—speech. It was television talking to itself, which sounds like the shoptalk of Inca chiefs. A self-portrait of the staggeringly rich complaining, with a bit of paternal confusion, about reports of a little agitation in the jungles beyond their golden temples. Most of the trade talk was about money, self-congratulatory talk about the division of the spoils (profits of network-owned-and-operated stations have reached an annual rate of 186 percent of their tangible value), and there was also a smattering of indignant concern about the misguided observations of outsiders like the government, schoolteachers and parents. Thus, Goodman went on to say, "The public interest will be better served if they (imperfections) are corrected from the inside, by broadcasters who have the tools of knowledge and experience, than from the outside by those who don't." CBS broadcast group president John A. Schneider dismissed parent-teacher-association complaints of violence on television as "a marvelous hype . . . They are getting more animated PTA meetings than they've had in many years."

The major immediate problems facing the industry, judging from the pages of the businesslike *Broadcasting* and the entertaining *Variety*, are subversive talk about banning television advertising of products containing saccharin and an internal debate about how much sex the networks can get away with during the 1977–78 season.

The saccharin stakes are $52.7 million a year in commercials for diet sodas and such. (That is out of a total of $6.7 billion of annual television advertising revenues, projected to reach $13 billion by 1985.) The trades are filled with talk about the "First Amendment rights of advertisers."

It's not that the industry is not responsive to criticism. Sex, for instance, is its answer to the violence complaints. There is great discussion about how much soft-porn the folks out there are ready for this season. "People in the U.S. basically shy away from talking about sex and permissiveness," said CBS-TV president Robert Wussler. "And yet they don't mind sitting down and watching a bit of it. . . . A little bit of titillation, I think, is what they probably want but never want to say it." In defending a series called "Soap," Fred Silverman, the president of ABC Entertainment, said the show is "socially redeeming" in that "no character in 'Soap' is ever rewarded for immoral behavior. . . . The clear message is not, 'Do what they do,' but, 'Laugh, enjoy, and learn what not to do.' . . . I'm confident that we'll have a winner on our hands." ABC network president James Duffy, asked whether America was ready for explicit sexual stuff at nine-thirty each night, answered, "I would think probably by us putting it on the air . . . America is ready for it, yes." They'll tell us what's good for us—potatoes in bed—and if we don't like it we can always turn to CBS or NBC for their spuds.

They'll also tell us what's good for them. Or what's bad. What's bad, they say, is a Federal Communications Commission proposal to add four new VHF (very high frequency)—channels 2 to 13—stations: one each in Charleston, West Virginia; Johnstown, Pennsylvania; Knoxville, Tennessee; and Salt Lake City, Utah. It seems that the FCC has figured out that the original allocation of channels in the United States, designed to prevent overlapping signals and screen images, was based on the presumption that the country is flat. Because of nearby mountains, it turns out, those four cities can each handle another channel. *Variety's* report on the proposal ended: "The filing is likely to be greeted with more than the usual disdain by broadcasters, since it comes as FCC chairman Richard Wiley prepares to leave office and pass the issue to others."

Sonny and Cher and "Soap"—and disdain—are about all we can get from television as it presently is constituted. The system works, as Goodman said, but because of the limited number of channels, it has to work for the benefit of the three networks that provide the programming for and reap the advertising benefits from all but about thirty of the nation's five hundred fourteen VHF stations—and, quite naturally, the networks and other station owners will oppose adding any profit-diluting stations, even four small ones in places like Johnstown.

In the end, I think, you can't learn very much by watching the prime-time series or even by attacking network programming because you don't happen to like it—many more people, even without choice of fare, like it very much. The questions, and future battles, are not about current programming but about future development of technology.

Over the next ten years or so there will be a series of struggles—extremely important political fights—between those who want to preserve the present system (the networks) and those who want to expand it so that they can make a few bucks (the advocates of new technologies—of cable television, ultra-high-frequency channels, satellite-to-home transmission, and pay television). Although there are very real problems with it, the technology exists, or could be developed, to allow most Americans access to twenty, forty, or perhaps eighty television channels.

The networks will do their damnedest to keep that battle as quiet as possible in the hope that technological questions, or new federal regulations, will be settled by bureaucrats and staffers working unnoticed with data provided by ABC, CBS, NBC, and the National Association of Broadcasters. People not quite satisfied with the status quo (status monopoly) will have to try to make those questions the stuff of a national debate—a loud, angry one. If television access is not expanded—and I can think of no reason why anyone but a network executive would not want it expanded—we are all going to be faced with a Hobson's choice: Leave things as they are, with a very few probably well-meaning people like Goodman, Silverman and Wussler in control of what may be the society's biggest engine—which begs them to become robber barons, making a nation fit their uncertain mold; or have the government, which cannot abide forever such concentration of private power, take the whole thing over—which would probably be worse.

That column, in a way, was only a starting point—both for my thinking and for some of the men quoted. Robert Wussler was soon fired by CBS and Fred Silverman left ABC to become president of NBC, forcing Julian Goodman into retirement in the process. That was all part of hard-eyed musical chairs, a sideshow of the ratings game—none of it meaning much to the rest of us, none of it changing the directions of American television. The people are interchangeable, therefore scared, therefore cautious. But the technology is relentless, it will not let any of the rest of us be as we were.

Television, I realized as I thought more and more about it, may or may not have only two "overriding social effects." It is a complicated and evolving phenomenon, and I now wonder whether anyone of an age to witness its public beginnings will ever have the time and perspective to understand what miracles, good and bad, are actually in the box.

"Television changed what we knew and when we knew it," I said in a documentary—"Lights, Cameras . . . Politics"—that I wrote and hosted for ABC News and which was broadcast on the network on July 11, 1980. (The program won an Emmy from the National Academy of Television Arts and Sciences.) That was the difference: the technology of instantaneous, pervasive, and persuasive communication. The only thing the invention of television could be compared with was the invention of the printing press—each invention changed what people knew and when they knew it. So, each changed how people thought and acted, politically and socially. "Television is more than a medium—it's our environment," I said that night, when, I guess, more people watched me than would ever read what I had written. "It's like the weather. And all that machinery is in private hands. The networks own it and they use it to suit their own purposes—to get the big audience—to sell. They do what they can to try to make the everyday world more interesting and more dramatic. They've made us the most informed people in the world—but not the best informed."

And there is a chance that all the information, the same inputs, will someday make all or most all of the world's people the same. I've watched "The Love Boat" in the mountains of Morocco. I'm not certain of what that means, but I know it means something and I began trying to figure it out in a column I transmitted electronically from the hills of southern France. *Esquire* titled the column, quite accurately, "TV Imperialism":

At night, when the tourists have gone, the village of St.-Paul-de-Vence, perched on a hill above the Mediterranean, is still much as it must have been four hundred thirty years ago when Francois I of France fortified the place with ramparts that still stand. Some of the small houses were built in the twelfth century and the narrow streets between them seem filled with silent history—silence and history punctuated only by electronic gunshots and the familiar theme music of "Police Woman."

Angie Dickinson and Earl Holliman clean up the streets of Los Angeles on Television Francaise I Saturday nights at nine-forty-five. You don't know whether to laugh or cry.

"Media imperialism" (or sometimes "cultural imperialism") is what we are being accused of now. And we, the United States, with some help from England, are certainly guilty. Leaving aside the effect of Telly Savalas on foreigners, consider a few numbers: Thirty-five countries import more than 30 percent of their television programs from the U.S.; 35 percent of the feature films shown in the world's fifty-four largest countries are American; Visnews (from Britain) and United Press International Television News claim that their film is used on newscasts reaching 99 percent of the world's television receivers; Associated Press reports are used in about four thousand major newspapers outside the U.S.; in ten of the world's most important nations, at least three of the five largest advertising agencies have Madison Avenue names, and in twenty more countries, the largest single ad agency is American.

These figures, from the United Nations, trade journals, and European studies, were compiled during recent years and published this summer in *The Media Are American* by Jeremy Tunstall of the City University of London.

Professor Tunstall argues, rather convincingly, that the accepted components of modern media are essentially American innovations, imitated blindly by or imposed on the rest of the world—cheap, multipage daily newspapers, advertising, weekly and monthly news and feature magazines, radio programming, box-in-the-home television, and feature films. After each of these American developments, other nations scooped up U.S. technology and hardware, then had to turn to us for the software—press services, Hollywood films, and canned television half hours—to make use of their new toys. Economically it made sense and still does. The software comes cheap, especially when compared with what original productions would cost, say, in Bolivia. In 1976, a stale half hour of "The Untouchables" could be had for as little as thirty dollars in Haiti, Cyprus, or Kenya, while newer stuff might go for five thousand dollars in England, France, or West Germany.

So what's new? Good neighbors have been grumbling about the Americanization of the world for fifty years. In the 1920s, the Canadians began griping about a brain drain caused by American publications' trumpeting of the States' "unlimited promise, higher wages, better living conditions, and good times." In 1944, William Haley, director general of the British Broadcasting Corporation, warned that "in the entertainment field it is essential that the use of . . . Bob Hope, Jack Benny, and other programs does not become a Frankenstein." And one of Haley's associates added, "If any hundred British troops are invited to choose their own records, 90 percent of the choice will be of American stuff."

That's the dirty little secret: Given a choice, most people pick that American stuff. The British, our sometime partner in spreading our language and popular culture, have a 14 percent quota on American content on their three television channels. The quota in the Soviet Union, of course, is close to zero. And that is part of what's new: The Russians are, in the words of another British observer, "desperately concerned about the explosive effect of widespread satellite broadcasting."

That may well be the next American media assault—TV news and entertainment bouncing off a satellite network into living-room boxes in countries where governments have been able, so far, to keep that stuff out. The Russians and other xenophobes may have no technical defense against us this time. The BBC in World War II and Radio Free Europe have demonstrated that once those waves are in the air over a country, it is very, very difficult to prevent a fairly sophisticated citizenry from finding electronic ways to bring forbidden sounds or pictures into their homes.

The question the Russians must be asking themselves is whether the U.S. and its satellite disc jockeys will be able to sell American values as effectively as they have sold Coca-Cola—and television itself. Already, Tunstall argues, the wide dissemination of the American news product is beginning to impose new professional standards—an American value system—on journalists in the strangest places. He cites surveys and interviews with foreign editors and reporters who sound more and more like *New York Times*-men—demanding objectivity or fairness, stressing presentation techniques and both sides of a story. "The notion of professionalism among journalists, broadcasters, and in other communicator occupations," he writes, ". . . implies autonomy—independence from either political or commercial direction—with the communicator depending upon his 'professional' judgment to make decisions." One example he cites is a strike by television newsmen in Paris demanding the right to report without government interference—an American right previously unknown in French television.

Dangerous stuff, at least to many governments. Third World leaders, with some prodding from Moscow, are now questioning the relevance of Western (Anglo-American) news standards to reporting on their countries and regions. And some of this is more than the ravings of active or aspiring tyrants. There is, for instance, a real question of whether "both-sides" reporting (a value related to our two-party system) translates well into other languages and other political structures. How many sides were there in Angola? Or in France? Perhaps there are stories better covered by a genre of blatantly partisan journalism that long ago disappeared from New York or Washington. For that reason alone, cultural imperialism—the term favored by Marxist analysts—will almost certainly become one of the major political issues of the 1980s.

But whatever the opposition and despite the fact that there may have been somewhat more American television exported ten years ago, when much of the world had no indigenous video software, it is hard to imagine much of an ebb in the Anglo-American word-and-picture tide. (The United States, incidentally, imports only 1 percent of its television, almost all of that from England.) Part of that flow is related to the almost epidemic spread of the English language. In the sixteen countries of western Europe, according to a 1969 survey, 42 percent of respondents under twenty-five said that they could speak English "fairly fluently." In the Netherlands the figure was 62 percent, and even in language-protective France it was 27 percent. The streams of language and media obviously are intermingled, and in Tunstall's words, ". . . the English language is relatively free of separate scholarly 'high' and vulgar 'low' forms . . . [and] has an unusually small gap between its written and spoken forms. . . . All of the great popular American journalists understand the significance of using simple *spoken* English in the press. . . . English is the language best suited to comic strips, headlines, riveting first sentences, photo captions, dubbing, subtitling, pop songs, boardings [billboards], disc-jockey banter, news flashes, sung commercials."

The British professor does not attempt to draw any conclusions from his study but simply observes the internationalization of consumption and a proliferation of hot dogs and Ohio State T-shirts in French villages. The subversion of local culture is sad, but who knows? Perhaps an international cultural umbrella, even a shabby "Made in U.S.A." one, will serve the same goals—mainly, stopping us all from killing one another—that some utopians promised for political umbrellas, planetary governments, or leagues of nations. Armies might be stopped someday by calling in the Beatles or Angie Dickinson.

The future may be plastered on the walls of Paris. Thousands of posters have been put up there showing a lovely green-eyed brunette looking directly and invitingly out. The slogan under her breastbone reads: *"Une vie plus heureuse, c'est votre affaire. Adherez au parti communist."*

I translate that as: "I guess you could call me that Cosmopolitan Girl. Join the party!"

There were rewards, large and small, to writing about my own business. First, the research is easy. Let's face it, I know more about journalism and journalists than I do about politics and politicians. I watch politicians; I am a journalist. And, on very good days, you not only get to vent your outrage, but sometimes something happens because you got angry. That happened with this column in *Esquire*:

On the morning of January 3, 1979, a man from the Southern California Gas Company went to 11926 Orchard Avenue in South-Central Los Angeles to collect a $22.09 gas bill from a thirty-nine-year-old widow named Eulia Love. She chased him off the property. He went to get the cops. She went to a local market and bought a money order to pay the bill. Then she went to the gas company's truck and tried to pay the man, but he refused to take the money order and rolled up the cab window.

Shortly after four o o'clock on that afternoon, the gas man returned with two Los Angeles policemen, Edward Hopson and Lloyd O'Callaghan. Mrs. Love was standing in her yard with two of her children. She was holding an eleven-inch butcher knife—a little longer than an ordinary table knife—in her right hand. She was sort of waving it around, according to police. She walked back toward her house, a distance of thirty feet and the policemen followed her, cornering her. Both officers had already drawn their guns. She turned around and O'Callaghan knocked the knife out of her hand with the one-pound, twenty-six-inch baton that Los Angeles police carry. What happened in the next few minutes is in dispute, but the end of the story is not. Hopson and O'Callaghan each fired six shots, emptying their .38 caliber revolvers. They hit Mrs. Love, who was apparently on the ground, eight times. She died instantly from a bullet in the chest.

The next day's *Los Angeles Times* reported the story in one paragraph beginning, "A thirty-nine-year-old woman was shot to death by Los Angeles police, who said she threw a knife at them during a dispute over her gas bill. . . ." The *Times* next mentioned the story eight days later, on January 12, under a one column headline in the second section: "Police Victim Hit by 8 Shots." That story ended with a quote from Captain Tom Hays, commander of the LAPD's Training Division: "Our policy is to shoot to stop, whether that's one shot or two shots or more. You shoot until your purpose is accomplished."

The January 12 story was published two days after the coroner's report had revealed how many wounds were in Mrs. Love's body and after two black city council members—Mrs. Love was black—had called for an investigation of the shooting. Until then, the story had been kept alive, barely, by Los Angeles' "other" newspaper, the *Herald-Examiner*, which had run, among other things, a twenty-three-paragraph front-page story on the shooting on January 5.

In Los Angeles, barely anyone reads the *Her-Ex*. LA is as close as you can get to a one-newspaper town. The *Times* pretty well controls what Angelenos know, and Angelenos know what the *Times* wants them to know. It did not want them to know about the financial affairs of movie-man David Begelman last year, so it didn't print anything about them for months and then, after he pleaded guilty to fraud charges, went back to reporting what an ornament the Begelmans were to LA's social scene.

The *Times* probably just didn't give a damn about Eulia Love and assumed its readers didn't either. Los Angeles' paper of record ran two more short stories on January 23 and February 3 about City Council questions and a complaint by the city's District Attorney's office that police had not immediately notified that office of the shooting, as required by law. (On January 30, the *Times'* editorial page called for an investigation of the Love case, as the *Herald-Examiner* had done on January 15.) The longest *Times* story came on March 2 under a two-column heading in the second section: "Gates Assails News Media in Death Case."

Gates is Police Chief Daryl F. Gates. Essentially, he was attacking the "hysteria" of the *Herald-Examiner*. Most people seemed to agree with Gates—in LA the cops can do no wrong. At least if they do what they do in the right places. In a nice bit of understatement, Larry Gross, spokesman for the Coalition of Economic Survival, offered this opinion to the *Her-Ex*: "This sort of thing would never happen in Beverly Hills."

I doubt it would even happen in New York City, which is a fairly tough place. In New York, which has more than double the population of Los Angeles, sixty-seven civilians were shot and killed by policemen in 1977 and 1978, compared with fifty-three in LA. New York police officials refused to go on the record about their California brothers' procedures, but one assistant chief said he had recently been told by his Los Angeles counterpart: "Your problem in New York is that you don't have a high enough kill ratio."

Many Californians would agree. Dorothy Chapman of Alhambra felt strongly enough to write the *Herald-Examiner* saying: "What's the use of spending money on policemen if they are not allowed to perform their duties? . . . The Los Angeles police are the neatest, most intelligent, well-mannered group of men you could want to meet."

114

A woman in Mar Vista named Barbara Benom wrote a guest column for the *Times* on March 1 about being pulled over at night on the San Diego Freeway and being forced to kneel on the roadway with her hands clasped behind her head with six pistols and shotguns pointed at her. Later it was explained to her that her car and clothing—which she was sure the highway patrol could not have seen in the dark—matched those of a robbery suspect. She didn't believe that, but her conclusion was: "I accepted their apologies, and said that I understood. . . . The fact that I was pulled over didn't bother me—they were just doing their job. But the fear that any small thing could have gone wrong, and, with six guns pointed at me, well, mistakes happen."

Legislators, for instance, make mistakes. On February 28, the *Times* reported:

"The city attorney's office, in its first interpretation of a new state law that went into effect January 1, said Tuesday the city will be required to withhold all information developed from investigations of officer-related shootings.

"The interpretation was made public during a meeting of the city's police commission and means that findings of the police department's investigation of the shooting death of Mrs. Eulia Love, a woman killed as a result of a dispute over a gas bill, will be kept secret. . . .

"And the interpretation means that anyone who files a complaint alleging officer misconduct never will learn what, if anything, was done about the complaint.

"Members of the police commission took no immediate action, although all present at the meeting expressed concern."

My concern is for one-newspaper towns. What would have happened if there were no *Herald-Examiner*, as weak as it is? Well, there would just be the *Los Angeles Times*, whose publisher, Otis Chandler, I will quote here as he discussed his paper's attitude toward coverage of blacks, Chicanos, and poor people in general: "We could make the editorial commitment, the management commitment to cover these communities. But then how do we get them to read the *Times*? It's not their kind of newspaper. It's too big, it's too stuffy. If you will, it's too complicated."

On the day *Esquire* hit the stands in New York with the Eulia Love column, I received a call from a reporter I knew on the *Los Angeles Times*. "Chandler is going nuts," he said. "Half the staff is being assigned to Eulia Love. He says no one, no one, is ever going to write about him again that way. Our asses are on fire. . . ."

A couple of weeks later, the *Times* ran five pages of stories investigating the killing of Mrs. Love. The police commission did, for about the first time in its history, overrule uniformed officers and required public release of information on officer-related shootings. Whatever actually happened that January morning, civilians began to assert control over the Los Angeles Police Department—because of Eulia Love. And, I was told, the *Times* decided it had to restructure its coverage of the city's huge minority populations—or, rather, really structure such coverage for the first time. (Unfortunately, for me, *Herald-Examiner* editors, who I thought deserved a Pulitzer Prize for their coverage of the story, were mad at me for harping on the paper's low readership and cancelled my syndicated column— then reconsidered a few days later.)

All of that didn't help Eulia Love. Maybe someday it will help someone else.

There are also smaller outrages in the world. For me ghostwriting has always been one and *Esquire* gave me the chance to go after it in this column:

In Jeb Magruder's Watergate book, one line of the acknowledgments reads: "I would also like to thank Patrick Anderson for his invaluable advice and assistance on this book." That was one of the three sentences in the book that Magruder wrote himself.

John Dean, on the other hand, actually did write a manuscript. It wasn't, however, *Blind Ambition*—that was written by Taylor Branch. What Dean wrote was a pile of pages, unpublishable, according to some sources, incoherent, according to others. When last seen, Dean was on the book-promotion trail, telling talk-show hosts about the lonely agonies he endured as a writer.

This is not about Watergate; it is about ghostwriting. It is a reaction to John Dean's bloody-fingers-on-the-typewriter number, which I have been privileged to watch a couple of times and to read about a couple more. I happen to hate Dean. It's fear, of course. If any nice Jewish boy is afraid that, stripped to the core, he is Sammy Glick, I worry that at the center of a well-brought-up WASP is a little John Dean, which is what I thought I would look like when I grew up. In one of my fantasies, the Russians land at Montauk and Dean is there, offering to help them avoid traffic on the Long Island Expressway.

Anyway, ghostwriting seems to be on the ascendancy because celebrity publishing is about as financially sure as any kind of publishing can be. Bottom-line watchers on the East Side of Manhattan can't wait for memoirs anymore; they want today's celebrity today. Which means they must supply a writer, since John Dean or Howard Cosell or William Colby or Dan Rather are just too busy right now to sit down at a typewriter—or they don't have the vaguest idea what to do with those dead keys. But, taped or made-up, their stuff usually sells well—better than mine.

I suppose I'm more jealous than outraged. The books are no more fraudulent than most breakfast cereals. The non-writing "writers" only give the impression that they can do something they can't, that they can marshal the intelligence and discipline to write their own stories. But, after all, I don't go around pretending I know Joe Namath or that I ran the Phoenix program for the CIA.

In talking with several prominent ghosts—a contradiction, I guess—I came away with the impression that they know they are in the business of hard-cover half-truths. Each of them offered some variation on this thought by Mickey Herskowitz, formerly a *Houston Post* sports editor and now a TV personality, who has written in the name of Cosell and Rather, among others: "In the end, honesty is up to them. I will point it out when my own research indicates they are not telling the truth, but if they want to go ahead anyway, I forget about it. It's like being a lawyer: You are paid to believe your client."

Sometimes a ghost has to go further. June Callwood, a Canadian journalist who has patched up books for Barbara Walters and Otto Preminger, has said that she used incidents from her own life and friends' lives to flesh out Walters' autobiography, *How to Talk with Practically Anybody about Practically Anything*.

"It's a matter of financial need," said Pat Anderson, the ghost behind the stories of Magruder, Lawrence O'Brien, and former *New York Times* editor Turner Catledge. (Anderson was also Jimmy Carter's chief speech writer during the 1976 campaign.) "It's a respectable way to make a dollar, to buy the time to work on my novels."

Martin Mayer, who has written eighteen books under his own name and several under names like Rudolf Bing, said that he divides each day into "information-gathering" and "writing" times, and when he is in the researching phase of his own books, he fills the writing time by ghosting.

The pay for ghosts ranges from ten thousand dollars to one hundred thousand dollars per book, which usually, according to my sample, involves about five months' work. Most ghosts, it seems, do not want a percentage of royalties or their name on the cover; many said they did not want to be held responsible for the content of the books.

Herskowitz, whose name is on the cover of one of Rather's books, works from tapes—twenty-five to forty hours of conversation on the average. That seems to be about standard, unless you're dealing with retired spies. Peter Forbath, a novelist and former *Time* correspondent who is doing Colby's book, found that the former CIA chief had trouble talking in rooms wired in any way. "It looks," Forbath said, "as if I'm going to have to do the book walking through parks."

The books are done quickly, partly because publishers prefer it that way—they want the book while the principal is hot. "Sure, it takes less time," Anderson said. "You ask about the five most important things in their childhood and take their word. I couldn't do that with my own childhood because all the incidents are important to me."

Or as Herskowitz put it: "It's a lot easier than figuring things out in your head." He can write ten to twenty-five manuscript pages a day and in just four years has banged out the "autobiographies" of Cosell, Rather, Jimmy "The Greek" Snyder, sports attorney Bob Woolf, astronaut Walter Cunningham, and hockey wife and mother Colleen Howe—those plus Gene Autry's, which he had just about finished up when I talked with him.

"It's really their story," Herskowitz said. "I just do the fine tuning. I did the book Howard would have done if he had the time." Mayer said that differently: "I do the book this guy would write—if he could write a book."

"It's just an extension of the traditional editorial function," Anderson said. "You wouldn't build your own house, would you?" No, I don't think so. But I doubt I'd go on television to talk about the house I'd built if Pat Anderson had done it for me.

There are, according to one publisher, about fifty well-regarded ghosts in the country, ranging from Frances Spatz Leighton, who just added onetime House of Representatives doorkeeper William "Fishbait" Miller to her stable after doing servants and kennel keepers at the White House, to Taylor Branch, an extremely talented young writer who rose to the top of the phantom heap with the success of *Blind Ambition*. Branch, who reportedly earned $20,000 for becoming John Dean's hands and head, moved on to basketball's Bill Russell. His price (and everyone else's) is going up right now—the offers for writing a book for CBS's William Paley were above the traditional ceiling of $100,000. (I don't know what my price is. I've been called twice—by onetime Franklin Roosevelt assistant Thomas "Tommy the Cork" Corcoran and by onetime Howard Hughes assistant Robert Maheu—but neither one called back.)

There is one other thing: When the typing stops, ghosts are expected to disappear back to wherever they came from. "There is a cycle," one said. "In the beginning, the subjects feel guilty. They keep insisting that the ghost should get equal credit. That fades. By the time you get to the publishing party, they don't even know you. They're too busy telling friends how much joy and pain there was in writing *their* book."

The *New York Times*, like most companies dealing with unions, affirmative action, and all the other things that make the United States both great and a mess, has a policy of posting "Job Opening" notices on bulletin boards around the building. The idea is to let each employee know that he or she has an equal opportunity to move up the ladder. The notices are usually put up the day after management has picked someone for the job.

In the late 1960s, when I was the paper's chief political correspondent in New York, I answered one of those notices: "Television Critic." I went to see Abe Rosenthal, then an assistant managing editor, and said something like: "I'd really like to think about it. Television is probably as important as politics. Looking at society through television may be just as valid as looking at it through politics."

I think he thought I was kidding. But I wasn't. When I began writing the syndicated column, there were months in which I wrote about television as often as I wrote about politics or government. Often, of course, I was writing about both, as I did in this column on July 26, 1979:

President Carter's energy speech to the nation the other night was a milestone in the history of American democracy—and its lasting significance had absolutely nothing to do with what the president said.

What was more important was the way NBC covered the president's speech. The network plugged into QUBE, the two-way cable television system in Columbus, Ohio. And eight thousand, one hundred QUBE subscribers, pushing buttons in their living rooms, rated Carter. They voted electronically on whether he had succeeded or failed, on whether he was too tough or too timid.

If you watched NBC after the speech, you saw the future and it worked—for better or for worse. The instant feedback of two-way television is both thrilling and frightening. It could mean pure democracy; it could mean government as the "Gong Show."

What happened was that NBC switched to Columbus and asked QUBE subscribers five questions. They were simple questions: "Does the president's speech leave you optimistic, pessimistic, or confused? . . ." "Are you more confident now about the president's ability to lead the nation?" . . . "Are President Carter's plans to deal with the energy shortage tough enough?"

Well, 61 percent of the QUBE button pushers were optimistic, 33 weren't confident about Carter's leadership, and 40 percent thought he wasn't tough enough. Those numbers aren't particularly important—in a way, the first national use of "two-way," interactive television was just a game.

But the Wright Brothers at Kitty Hawk didn't seem like all that much—at first. Two-way electronic politics—by television or telephone—is going to revolutionize the United States. You have to imagine those little push-button consoles in a hundred million homes. Families will be watching two-hour, prime-time congressional debates structured to meet the dramatic needs of television—say, on Social Security tax increases. Then the viewers, the nation, will vote. Let's say that more than three-quarters say no increases. What do you think Congress will do?

All that, I am reasonably certain, is inevitable. Americans are not a people who resist technology—if we've got it, we flaunt it. The House of Representatives is already on television, and some members are already pushing for debate rules that will make law-making more comprehensible—and more appealing—to viewers.

Around Columbus, QUBE, which is only eighteen months old, is already part of local government. In Upper Arlington, Ohio, new zoning codes were presented to QUBE subscribers for their unofficial approval. Should the boulevard be widened? "Touch now," the screen flashed—and people at home voted "Yes" or "No." Within ten seconds, the zoning board knew what people, or at least a lot of them, really wanted. The Federal Drug Administration has held labeling hearings in Columbus just to get the public feedback of QUBE subscribers.

"Columbus is just the beginning," said Leo Murray of Warner Cable Corporation, which developed QUBE. "This is our research and development department."

It's also R and D for the whole country. The history of American democracy has been of expansion—blacks, women, and younger people were given the right to vote, initiative and referenda were accepted, more and more public questions were decided in open meetings.

Modern pure democracy is next. It will have real dangers. What would have happened in 1967, for instance, if the entire nation could have voted on whether dissenters against the Vietnam War should be held in preventive detention?

There are other arguments against it—and people to make them. Professional politicians hate the idea—their jobs may be at stake. But it's the future, and it started right before our eyes the other night on NBC.

Direct electronic democracy sounds both crazy and farfetched to some, but so did televised trials not so many years ago. Then, the miniaturization of television equipment made it possible for the cameras to come into courtrooms without disrupting the proceedings. The march of technology—where was it taking us? Ever since I had done a television film for the PBS network on cameras in the courtrooms of Dade County, Florida, I had been wondering about that. I wasn't sure that the questions should be about how much space the equipment took up or whether it made a lot of noise. When there were riots after a couple of televised trials—ironically, in Dade County—I wrote a column about my concerns on May 25, 1980:

What was left in Miami were blocks of burned-out buildings and debris, and fifteen dead people. And two names, scrawled and painted on walls: "McDuffie" and "Jones."

Arthur McDuffie was a black man allegedly beaten to death by Miami policemen—officers whose acquittal on murder charges was the immediate trigger for the rioting. The burning, looting, and killing began within an hour of television reports that the accused policemen had been freed by an all-white jury. Parts of their thirty-nine-day trial, in Tampa, had been televised on Miami news shows.

Johnny Jones used to be the superintendent of schools in Dade County, the best-known and most respected black man in south Florida. He lost his job when he was convicted last month of "grand theft" for using school funds to buy things like gold-plated faucets in his vacation home. The Jones trial was televised, nightly, by WPBT, Miami's public television station.

The impact of television in courtrooms has had more study in Florida than in any of the eighteen states that now allow cameras at trials. Two years ago, the state allowed the televising of the trial of a confessed young murderer named Ronnie Zamora. There was even a nationally televised public television film on the trial, which I wrote and hosted after watching hour after videotaped hour of the trial.

After that experiment and studies of the trial, by judges, bar associations, and the state supreme court, Florida began to allow television to be a part of its jurisprudences. The Florida Supreme Court decided that television did not disrupt courtrooms.

I thought then that was the wrong question. The right question, it seemed to me, was whether televised trials would disrupt the society. Television is essentially a dramatic medium that transmits feelings and conflicts better than it transmits information or logical argument. How would the public react to witnessing, dramatically, the conviction of an attractive defendant? Or the televised acquittal of unpopular defendants? Would there be crowds at the courthouse demanding what they perceive as justice?

In Miami, there were mobs. They may have gathered anyway—if television had never been invented—because blacks in Liberty City and other sunny ghettos had real and frustrating grievances.

Jobs—blacks needed them badly, but the city and country were mobilizing to find employment for new Cuban refugees. And, as Miami becomes increasingly a Latin city, the classified advertisements in local newspapers demand bilingual skills—skills Cubans and other Spanish-speaking immigrants have, but that American blacks don't.

Justice—with or without the impact of television, the McDuffie and Jones verdicts were bound to be unpopular among many blacks. But . . . the courts are playing with social dynamite. Television changes everything it touches and there is no guarantee that the courts are any more immune than the National Football League. Once there are television cameras in a courtroom, there is no such thing as a change of venue. The McDuffie trial was held in Tampa; the Jones trial could have been held in Minneapolis. The crowd—the citizenry on which a democratic system of jurisprudence depends—is always where the action is. It's in their living rooms, just off the street.

There is a right of public trial in the United States. But how public, and where, are legitimate questions. We don't have trials in stadiums for obvious reasons. I don't think television caused any riots or deaths. I do think it was a factor in that it is a pervasive and persuasive medium that cannot be accepted anywhere just because cameras are now quiet enough not to disturb judges and juries.

A column, usually, is one idea expanded. That, to me, means having at least two ideas a week, 104 a year. I don't, of course. But I do have several that I feel strongly about and I don't have any compunction about repeating them. Over the years you learn that in a media-bombarded society, you have to repeat and repeat to get through— that's what commercials are about. So, when in one day's edition of one newspaper, the *New York Times*, I find three separate stories dealing with the processes of changing what we know and when we know it, that's a column. And it was my column of February 1, 1981:

Last Tuesday's *New York Times*, as I read it, reported routinely on the inevitable breakdown in the American criminal justice system, the stupidity of education as we know it, a new way of governing ourselves, and the end of public vice.

It was just another day in the revolution—"the Communications Revolution." The phrase is carelessly tossed around a lot these days, but three stories in that morning's paper gave it real meaning for me.

—"High Court Decides States Can Permit Televising of Trials" The front-page headline announced that the nation's highest court had ruled unanimously that courtroom justice could be dispensed on television. The decision was consistent with state rulings that television equipment is now so unobtrusive that it does not disrupt trials.

The technology has improved—that's part of the revolution—so that you can hardly notice the wires and cameras now. But we may notice the results: television justice instead of courtroom justice. The people who bring us "That's Incredible" will decide which trials we'll see; crowds and talk-show offers will be there for popular defendants, judges, and prosecutors. The punishment of public ridicule may be worse than anything a judge and jury can threaten. Televised justice is essentially a return to the stocks and pillory in the village square.

—"Television Blocks the View"

Another story reported that the Annenberg School of Communications at the University of Pennsylvania has concluded that television is the reason that "we have a serious national problem blocking the way of better understanding and support of science."

Blame television, the report states, because the networks depict scientists as older, more dangerous, and shorter than other people—and use them in cartoons. (I didn't make up that part about height—the university looked at fourteen hundred dramas and measured the characters.) The whole thing is a joke, part of a useless attempt to try to change television to meet the needs of education rather than changing education because we now live in a television age.

Television is here to stay. It's our environment. What we need are different kinds of teaching and teachers to deal with children raised comfortably among cameras, screens, computers, and lasers.

—"Almost Half of Sample in a Poll Reports 'Addiction' "

A third story reported that 205 people in Columbus, Ohio, indulged in "an obsessive, compulsive use of a substance or activity to cope with pain of any kind and to produce a high."

The reason that was news was that those people were almost half the 402 Columbus residents who had answered a question about addiction by pushing buttons on QUBE, the city's two-way cable television system. The idea of buttons and computers and percentages makes the whole thing seem valid; it must be true if it's electronic.

Who knows what the percentages really mean? But those same kinds of percentages—recorded someday in two-way systems all over the country—will almost certainly become part of the political process. Interactive television, after all, could replace city councils and Congress. Direct electronic democracy.

The one thing about push-button democracy, though, is that there will still be a turnout problem—because there is a turn-on problem. In Columbus, after three years of use, far and away the highest-rated service QUBE offers is pornographic films. Dirty movies. Vice, as we used to call it, is moving off the streets and into midwestern homes.

It's going to be a brand-new world. It is a genuine revolution, happening so fast that we hardly notice it. And we certainly don't know what all the results of this will be: the consequences of changing what we know and when we know it. The revolution may change democracy itself or it may just keep more of us at home at night and, maybe, produce a few more morning smiles.

Oh, God. When I said that the people who gave us shows like "That's Incredible" would decide which trials would be televised, I had no idea how far they might go. Then, on March 18, 1981, wandering around the annual convention of the National Association of Television Program Executives, I found out. This is the column I wrote:

Television, as we all know, is making it into the courts of America and, as we all might have guessed, one of the first trials to get the full video treatment is about gossip and show business. The cameras have converged on Carol Burnett's libel suit against the *National Enquirer*. The Cable News Network is actually broadcasting the whole thing, gavel to gavel.

It got me to thinking that television should not have to beg to get into courtrooms. Television is big enough and powerful enough and rich enough to set up its own courts. Producers could choose interesting defendants and break for commercials. They could hire their own judges and everything.

A smart producer could open the show with a little musical fanfare and an off-stage announcer saying: "What you are about to witness is real." The doors to the courtroom could be thrown open, and there could be a freeze frame as the voice said: "This is the defendant. . . ." Then: "This is the plaintiff. . . ." Freeze again. Drum roll.

We call this one "The Case of the Cartier Knockoff." The words could be sort of whispered by a pretty star. Maybe Stephanie Edwards—remember, the redhead of "Good Morning, America." During the trial she could break in with interviews of spectators— "Do you think he did it?"—and with defendant—"How did you feel when the judge said you lost?"

They could use a split-screen when the verdict was announced, so you could see the loser burst into tears. Great stuff.

If you think I'm kidding or that I made that up, you're guilty of jumping to a wrong conclusion. That is a real show. Ralph Edwards—remember "This Is Your Life!"—is producing it. That means he is setting up his own court system. The trials, real and legal trials, will be on your local ABC station in several cities, including New York, Los Angeles, and Chicago.

The show is called "The People's Court." Under the laws of California—and other states—plaintiffs and defendants in civil suits have the right to hire a judge themselves and have the cases heard outside courthouses.

So why not in television studios? Edwards built a courtroom inside a studio, hired a retired Los Angeles judge named Joseph Wapner, and then went out and hired plaintiffs and defendants. He did that by checking calendars of local courts and offering trials to interesting defendants—and guaranteeing that he would pay all costs and judgments. The first trial involved a father and daughter who allegedly sold counterfeit Cartier wristwatches to a lady in a wheelchair.

"I am a real live judge; I won't hurt you," Wapner said when the lady in the wheelchair seemed nervous. "Can I say something?" she asked when he ruled against her. "No," Wapner said. Stephanie Edwards stepped into the picture and said, "We'll be back right after this. . . ." Cut to commercial.

"The People's Court" was the hit of the annual convention of the National Association of Television Program Executives in New York. Imitations, they say, are already in the works—we'll call it "The Case of the Courtroom Knockoff."

You've got to see it to believe it. And you will. Now if only television can figure out a way to create its own president, with a

White House out in Burbank. It probably wouldn't work, though, because no one would believe an actor as president.

In 1977, I had said that I was only sure of two overriding social effects of American television. Four years later, I was certain I knew of at least one more: When these people were through with us, we would not be able to tell fact from fiction, we would not know what was real and what was true.

Networks had become increasingly clever at creating new forms combining the real and the unreal and at using the techniques of entertainment to dramatize facts and the techniques of journalism to give credibility to fiction. "Magazine" shows looked like journalism but weren't; and "docudrama" looked like history but wasn't.

My fascination with flickering images—and flickering reality—led me to write a column about nothing but television for a television magazine, *Panorama*, which began publication in 1979 and continued only until June of 1981. It may have been an idea before its time. This is from the April 1981 issue:

Room 318 of the CBS building on West Fifty-second Street in New York is where you end up if you take a blue ticket from one of the young men who stand on street corners in midtown Manhattan calling out: "Free preview of a new TV show!" I did take one on a cold January afternoon and soon found myself in a comfortable chair with push buttons under each arm.

"We are going to see a magazine-type show," said a pleasant young man who told us—there were twenty-one of us gathered off the street—to press the right button, the green one, when we liked something we saw and to press the left button, the red one, when we thought something was "poor."

The show they screened for us was called "That's My Line"—a magazine show of sorts, an imitation of the "reality programming" of "Real People" and "That's Incredible!" Bob Barker was the host; my throat tightened and I pressed hard on the red button whenever he was onscreen, which was a lot. The gimmick—or the format— was that Barker ran the thing like a quiz show, going into the audience and doing his best to help people make fools of themselves between filmed segments about a blind carpenter, a lunatic dentist who tries to make kids laugh by dressing as a rabbit while he drills teeth, male dancers who strip to sell clothes to women in Topeka, Kansas, and a man who tells other men how to pick up women. Barker was helped by two women named Suzanne and Tiiu, who were described as "reporters."

The testing procedure I participated in, according to Jay Eliasberg, CBS's vice president of research, is used for most CBS series. The network simply pulls from one hundred to five hundred people, in small groups, off the streets of New York and Los Angeles and asks them to watch, push buttons, fill out a questionnaire, and chat for a few minutes with someone from the Program Analysis Unit. That unit, part of Eliasberg's department, then prepares a ten- to twenty-page report on the viewing sessions. Included is a long graph showing the minute-by-minute approval and disapproval rates—a chart displaying the red- and green-button percentage for each and every scene.

The results for "That's My Line" were somewhat distorted by the fact that I occasionally took my finger off the red button—just so that no one would think I had died in Chair 15. The show, as it happened, was about the worst I had ever seen. I thought it was significantly terrible because it was such a faithful synthesis of what makes most network programming so distasteful. It was almost a parody, a seamless web of "news" and "entertainment," presenting sex and exploitation—the humor of laughing at, not with, other people—as life, as a quiz show. Then, at the end, there was a brief disclaimer about "prepared dialogue," which I took to mean that the words in segments featuring "real" people were made up by writers somewhere.

I said some of that in the questionnaire, twelve pages of straight-forward questions like: Did you like Bob Barker? Did you like the reporter with the straight blonde hair? Would you watch this show if it played at the same time as "That's Incredible!"?

No. No. No, I would weep.

The man in 318 glanced over the questionnaires and began to ask us questions. "I liked the show very much," said the man in Chair 21, speaking very slowly, carefully. "Why?" asked the host. "I don't know," Number 21 said. "I don't speak much English."

The rest of us, however, did speak English. We understood what we had just seen. And—statistically—we liked it. Most of the people who were asked questions answered with a variation of the line from the middle-aged man in Chair 9: "It's all right."

Of Bob Barker, who really is unspeakable, someone else said: "He's OK. He does what he's supposed to do." These people off the street talked like professionals. No one got excited one way or the other. The show did what it was supposed to do—it filled the time. None of us expected more than that. We were part of our own seamless web—of acceptance, of mediocrity, of anaesthesia.

I hadn't been called on by our host—it makes you wonder where you went wrong—so I spoke up, asking about "prepared dialogue." He looked kind of blank about that, but my fellow panelists gave me this look of "So what else is new?" They, it became apparent, knew exactly what was going on, that "reality programming" is not real at all. It is programmed reality, a fraud. "I liked Tiiu," the man across from me said. "But you could figure out in five seconds that she wouldn't know what to say if they didn't hold cards up in front of her."

"The people at these sessions are usually quite articulate," Eliasberg told me. "They understand what they are seeing and they know what they want. What you want—or what I might want—is not important. . . . There is no question of knowing what people want. They want *this*. The argument that they want something better or that we don't know what we are doing is just bull!"

He was, I thought, at least partly right. The networks *do* know what they are doing. They have created a context for prime-time programming and have forced, or persuaded, viewers to accept that context. People, including the people who wander through Room 318 each day, are conditioned to accept familiar programming—things they are used to. "That's My Line" was a familiar product historically connected to every quiz show, to "The Gong Show," to "60 Minutes," and to every nightly news program.

Whatever else audience testing produces, it will favor programs that are like old programs. In fact, Eliasberg, who had said earlier that the process was generally predictive of ratings success, conceded that it had often failed to predict the success of programming that was in any way innovative. "All in the Family," he said, was disliked by preview audiences. Why? Because it wasn't familiar—it wasn't part of the seamless web.

"That's My Line" was part of it—and so were all of us in Room 318. My colleagues were unnervingly sophisticated about television practices; they sometimes sounded like network programmers. We talked about "reality" and "reporters" and "dialogue." We all knew that "reality" did not mean truth, "reporters" did not have to report, and real "dialogue" did not have to be the spontaneous words of real people.

"Reality programming," I thought, really did have a history, at least a television history, and perhaps that was why it did well in previews. "That's My Line," with its enhanced dialogue, was a modern version of the rigged quiz shows of twenty years ago. The difference now was that people were cynical enough—or conditioned enough—to accept the deception. Or perhaps it really isn't deception any more—it's just the enhanced reality of television, where one day very soon news will be entertainment, entertainment will be news, and it will all be real—as long as it's on television.

One of the pleasures of being a reporter, of course, is that, as everyone knows, the press runs the country.

That's not true. But I get a couple of dozen letters each week from people who sincerely believe it.

A more precise statement might be that one of the pains of being a reporter is explaining to friends and adversaries that the power of the press over events and government is more apparent than real. The press does have influence. At its most influential, it can set the agenda for a city, sometimes even for the country. Publicity—and the editorial and management decisions about which people, causes, and events get it—can greatly speed up or slow down movements and careers. But, as far as I have been able to tell over the years, public officials are far more likely to set the public agenda than newspapers and television, and great movements such as feminism and civil rights begin on the streets and in the hearts of America. It's only later that those movements begin to dominate news columns and news shows—by then, a real test of the power of the press would be to try to ignore them.

Trying to explain—or argue—that point became a recurring theme in my columns. I'm not sure I was convincing anyone, but I tried to show that the press is essentially a reactive institution, once in December of 1979 with this column about the coverage of the seizure of American hostages in Iran:

A few years ago, when plane hijackers began taking hostages, the high-minded thing to say was that television and newspapers should ignore what was going on. If there was no coverage, the argument went, these crazies would go away.

I happened to be in a network news department's meeting when a ban on coverage was discussed in those days. The men and women present seriously considered establishing a policy that taking of hostages would not be shown or reported under any circumstances. "OK," someone said, "what if the terrorists or kidnapper or whatever, said to one of us, 'Turn that camera on right now or I'm gonna blow this little lady's head off?' "

Every person in the room said they would turn the camera on. What would you do?

The fact we faced that day is that television is more than a news medium. It is a means of communication—the modern means of worldwide communication. Bank robbers holding a teller at the point of a gun don't send postcards to announce their demands. Iranians holding Americans hostage don't send letters by diplomatic courier or carrier pigeon. Television has been invented—and it is being used. Whether we like it or not.

The networks are doing the right thing in broadcasting the mobs, the demonstrations, and the propaganda. What else can they do? What would you do if the militants at the embassy in Teheran said, "Fine, we'll kill one hostage a day until you bring the cameras here and turn them on."

What would you do if the same images were being filmed and broadcast by television crews from France, from Germany, from Japan, from Canada?

The debate about the networks' role in the Iranian hostage crisis approaches the ridiculous. First, the networks have no choice, only an obligation to be candid about the circumstances or conditions of their reportage. Second, the White House statements and editorials denouncing television are based on the assumption that the American people are too stupid to know propaganda when they see it. Does anyone really believe that the Republic will fall because millions of Americans are hearing the crazed words of ranting men and veiled ladies?

I asked one editor, who had written an editorial condemning NBC

News for interviewing a hostage under conditions set by his Iranian captors, whether I, if I were still a reporter for the *New York Times*, should have gone into that embassy, under the same onerous conditions. "Sure," he said, "that would be different because you could exercise judgment about what to print."

Judgment? Why is my judgment better than anyone else's?

Finally, there's nothing new about conditions. Almost every story I have ever covered had conditions. "Off the record . . . This is for background, you can't use my name. . . . You can only ask about . . . You can ask . . . The questioning is over when the president's press secretary says it's over and the president will decide who gets to ask the questions. . . . Can I use your name, soldier, or would you prefer to be court-martialed for pointing out that the colonel is lying? . . . Would you spell your name for me, Mr. Throat? Is that D-E-E-P?"

The problem—the message—is the hostages and getting them out alive. The networks are just the messenger. If the people with guns in a television age want to talk on camera, networks and reporters are hostages, too. That's the way it is. . . .

One of the reasons that the power of the press is overrated, I think, is that the gathering and dissemination of news is still pretty much of a mystery to most people—which is just the way editors and reporters want it. Better than most, they understand the problems that come with aggressive scrutiny by outsiders.

In many cases, outsiders looking at the press might find less there than meets the eye. They might even find out about the McCandlish Phillips School of Journalism, which would explain how most of the reporters are treated most of the time.

Phillips and I were reporters together on the *New York Times* and he had this theory, widely shared, that journalism schools didn't know anything about journalism. In his school, the entire curriculum would consist of students being called to a front door each morning at eight o'clock, preferably in snow or rain. If it was not stormy, the professor would stand on the roof above the door all day pouring buckets of water on the class. At 5:00 P.M., the prof would run downstairs, pull open the door and say: "No comment."

The point: The people giving out the news have more control over it than they and we like to admit. That was also the point of this column titled, "Where the News Really Comes From":

The president is the source of 20 percent of the domestic news in the United States. That conclusion, which seems about right to me, comes from Herbert J. Gans, a Columbia University sociologist who studied national news operations for ten years in preparing a book called *Deciding What's News*.

The man in the White House, of course, does not spend all—or even much—of his time talking to reporters and editors. He has five hundred fifty men and women working for him, many of them periodically authorized to speak in his name. The main speaker— "the spokesman"—is his press secretary.

In fact, each weekday morning at eleven o'clock or a little later, the press secretary meets the press in a ritual known as the "Daily Briefing." The noisy gatherings are in the White House Press Room, a rectangle the size of a large living room built on top of the dry swimming pool where, legend has it, John Kennedy and Lyndon Johnson used to skinny-dip.

It's a circus—but children and television cameras are not invited. The incumbent secretary, Jody Powell, is the ringmaster, and thirty to one hundred reporters play the seals. They bark a lot. Powell barks back and, most days, throws them enough fish to keep them quiet for another twenty-four hours.

Everybody, actually, is pretty happy. The press secretary and his president keep the reporters from doing more serious work, and the reporters get their daily ration, a front-page story or a ninety-minute spot beginning, "The White House yesterday said . . . "

Just for the hell of it, I decided to record America getting its news during one week. This is, verbatim, what it sounds like with "P" standing for Powell and "R" for the reporter, any reporter:

R: "Extenuating circumstances aside, is there any way that you can say that the administration's record on the economy has been anything but a disaster?"

P: "Why should you complain about screwing up a piece last night? You've spent your whole life . . . "

R: "How many number one priorities has the United States got? You just said inflation is the number one problem, but I thought I heard the president say the other night that national defense is the number one problem?"

133

P: "Sarah, why don't you let me finish my answer for once, just once. . . ."

R: "Let's answer the question."

Those questions, answers, and insults, weren't sequential, they just give an idea of the tone—Washington testy. "If the *Boston Globe*," Powell said at one point, "is interested in doing a thorough investigative piece on these sorts of things, I think that would be a wonderful . . . "

He was cut off by the man from the *Globe*, saying, "If anyone at your committee would return calls to the *Boston Globe*, we would be."

So it goes. Every day. Powell answers (and these answers were consecutive): "I am not prepared to comment on that" . . . "I don't think it is my job to do that" . . . "I am just not prepared to comment on that issue today."

Things get nasty, but no one gets hurt. A lot of reporters who shouldn't will look like stars reporting inside stuff at the White House. The president lets out only the news he wants out—and keeps a lot of reporters from going out and covering the government.

It's an adult day-care center and at the end of one session Powell said: "We will have some announcements for you probably about as soon as you get back from your lunch lid."

One plastic star lit up outside his office. That's a "lid"—it meant no news would be released while the star was lit. When two stars light up, that means no news will be released until the next morning. The stars are a kind of Pavlovian signal. When two go on, the print reporters head for their typewriters and television types go out to the lawn in front of the White House to give America its news.

"P"—Jody Powell—did not necessarily agree with that analysis. But, then, he disagreed with more than a few of the things I wrote during the Carter administration and he would occasionally call to suggest that my parents were not married at the time I was born. As soon as he was out of the White House—it was not a voluntary exit, you'll recall—he announced that he would be joining our side and writing a book. I disagreed with his premise and said so in my March

26, 1981, column:

Jody Powell, who I always thought was the most impressive of President Carter's men, cut his deal last week. He will be paid, as they say, "in six figures" to write a book on the presidency and the press.

The former press secretary's proposal to his publisher, William Morrow and Company, has been floating around Manhattan. It's interesting, but it's a lot less intelligent than I know Powell is. This is how it begins:

"Much has been written about the relationship of the presidency to the Congress, the courts, the bureaucracy, and the political parties. Little has been said about the relationship of the presidency to what may be the most powerful institution in our society, the press."

Powell should know better. We're roughly the same age and we've lived through the same short stretch of American history. The biggest stories, the most important things that happened during our lifetimes, have been: feminism, which will change the way we live forever; civil rights and the resulting pressure for mandated egalitarianism; the dawning, for Americans, of the age of limits—of resources, of influence, of future.

All those stories crept up on the press. Television and newspapers, which were quite male and quite white, never really sensed the pressures building up among women and among black Americans. And the business of journalism is just now trying to become sophisticated enough to cover stories as complicated as economies and resources.

"That relationship," Powell says of press and presidency, "is more dynamic, more intimate, less stable, and I believe both more important and interesting than any of the others. I also believe that this relationship is basically flawed. It falls far short of providing the reasonably accurate information and impressions necessary for an informed electorate to govern itself. . . . That belief may change as I research and write this book, but I doubt that it will."

There are, as Powell says, many flaws in the relationship. But one of those flaws—a fatal political one for Powell and his patron, Jimmy Carter—is that too many public officials overrate the press and are more comfortable dealing with it than with the larger society and its problems. One of the reasons Carter failed as president was that he governed for the press rather than for the people.

The Carter presidency was, too often, a mobile media event. Fireside chats, town meetings, announcements timed for the "Today Show," making the president available to cameras about twenty hard-working hours a day became ends in themselves. More than most, Carter and Powell lost sight of the differences between governing, appearing to govern, and just plain appearing—on television or in print.

It is the presidency, not the press, that is the most powerful institution in the society. Ronald Reagan, not the people who talk and write about his ideas, is outlining the national debate. But any president has to master the press, a job that becomes more difficult as both the technology and the men and women of journalism become more sophisticated—changing what we know and when we know it.

A president has to know how to communicate through these people and technology, and he has to know what he wants to communicate. Jimmy Carter did not know what he wanted to say; that is why he and his people think the press is more powerful than it actually is.

What did Powell know? His candidate lost. True to the code of columnists, I had some gratuitous advice for the new president in a column called, "The Quiet Presidency":

After running around the country for a year in the great presidential marathon, Ronald Reagan decided to go to his ranch—by himself. No aides, no briefing book, no photographers. Just a wife.

The president-elect, apparently, did not feel the need to announce he was a on a "working vacation." That security, or laziness, or sanity, is a hopeful sign.

Without having been asked, I would like to offer the next leader of the Free World some advice: establish a Quiet Presidency. Stay off television unless you really have something to say. Don't brag about going to work at dawn's early light, or about falling asleep reading cables from Zanzibar and the collected speeches of Theodore Roosevelt. Don't propose a solution for every problem exposed by helpful assistants, ambitious congressmen, saintly preachers, and thoughtful editorial writers. Protect us from your children—if you can. And if the press complains that you are not talking or doing enough, tell them to shove it!

And keep your shirt on. Our last four presidents—each a bit manic in his own way—have had this compulsion to undress in public: Lyndon Johnson showing his scars; Richard Nixon changing clothes while discussing foreign policy in the Oval Office; Gerald Ford slipping out of his bathrobe and taking his morning plunge; and Jimmy Carter running up and down hills in his underwear until he collapsed. Who needs it?—except maybe *People* magazine.

My credentials for advising presidents are restricted to watching them. What I think I've seen in the past twelve years is men destroying themselves by being too many things, too often, to too many people.

On a superficial level, the three presidents I've covered have been obsessed with filling the insatiable celebrity demands of the press, particularly television. They never seem to be able to get it through their heads that trying to "use" television is riding the tiger. The medium itself is a people-eater. Viewers turn off overexposed comedians—and overexposed politicians. It should be an event when the president speaks to the nation. Most of the time, we can do just fine with printed statements.

On a more important level, the governing level, Nixon, Ford, and Carter consistently rushed in where angels feared to tread. As they used to say of Hubert Humphrey, he had more solutions than there were problems. Programs. Programs. Programs. Plans. Plans. Plans. Most of them forgotten or failed as each president became The Great Proposer.

The United States in the 1980s is not a good place or time to propose too much. Everyone else out there—Congress, special interests, the press—is just laying back, waiting to chip and claw away at the program of the day. Presidents are literally being nibbled to death by ducks.

So, let the ducks do the quacking. There is no good reason that the leader of the nation has to speak out on every issue. Talking about issues like abortion—unless you are an advocate of one side or another—is a no-win situation. There is no reason a president—even one, like Reagan, who has taken positions on such issues as he tried to build a constituency—has to strangle himself trying to make women or anyone else do or stop doing things they are going to do with or without executive permission.

Leaders are not people who take a leadership position on everything. Leaders are people with an agenda, with priorities—something Carter never had. Leaders are often people who hold back their words and their deeds until allies and opponents are worn out or cancelled out, until followers are ready to follow. If Franklin D. Roosevelt had practiced the leadership of his recent successors, he would have declared war on Germany and Japan in 1938—and no one would have come.

Reagan could do very well with a short agenda. Something like:

1. Peace in our time.
2. Prosperity in our children's time.

The rest of the national agenda—important though it may be—could safely be left to the busy, busy men and women who take working vacations.

Part 4
"Mr. President, Is It True . . ." Where'd He Go?

America elected a president in 1980. So, people like me saw even more of the country than we planned to—and less of the candidates than we had in past campaigns.

Campaigning, for candidates, is a seemingly endless round of meaningless encounters—touches, smiles, and waves. The modern political appearance is an introduction of bands, bunting, and posters followed by a man (usually) bounding onto a stage of some sort. He energetically defines an issue, a public problem, for the crowd, expressing great concern—then, smiling and waving, he gets the hell out of there before anyone realizes that he hasn't said what he intends to do about it or anything else. If that seems like a harsh judgment on what politicians do, think of what it says about political reporters—we follow them around and actually write down the words they say, no matter how meaningless.

Well, most of us used to write them down. Now the dominant

reporters on the campaign trail are the ones who photograph the candidates' rapidly moving lips. The coverage of campaigns has changed drastically since I hit the road for the *New York Times* in 1968. Then, despite books about television and the selling of presidents, the campaign was essentially print-oriented. The leaders of the boys on campaign buses were the most senior and most respected newspaper and magazine reporters—people like James Reston of the *New York Times* and, later, David Broder of the *Washington Post*.

There were daily press conferences on the road. They were most often trivial, but there was a regular opportunity for follow-up questioning by persistent and informed correspondents. A Broder or a Tom Wicker or someone less well-known, would lead the interrogation of candidates about ideas like nuclear disarmament or thousand-dollar-a-head poverty grants.

Now the traveling press, like a classroom of seventh-graders facing an uncertain substitute teacher, is dominated by whoever happens to be the loudest and most aggressive of the television correspondents. The model is Sam Donaldson of ABC News, moving noisily and menacingly through airports and auditoriums with a platoon of cantankerous equipment bearers. Among other things the number of electronic folk has multiplied because of technology and economics. Local television stations can now cover campaigns live for the nightly news programs because of the new miracle of satellite transmission, and television, profitable television, can afford the escalating transportation expenses involved in coverage while smaller newspapers and magazines are being driven out of the campaigning business.

So, there are fewer and fewer formal and informal question-and-answer sessions. They have been replaced by shouted—and filmed—cries of "Mr. President, you've been charged with . . ." answered by a smile, a wave, and a slamming car door. That was about all there was in 1980: rallies, "town meetings" with awed citizens, and chats with network and local anchormen without the knowledge or the requisite irreverence to push a president or a possible president.

The candidates, basically, only talked to cameras, crowds, and their own wives in 1980. By Election Day, November 4, President Carter had not agreed to an interview with *Time* magazine for more than a year. *Newsweek*, the country's other multi-million circulation weekly, had been shut out for two-and-a-half years.

My own campaign coverage, I was astounded to realize, totaled close to two hundred thousand words. Some of them were quite wrong. As I had since 1966, the year I first covered Ronald Reagan, I promised myself that I would never, never underrate him or his appeal to voters—and then I went ahead and did it again.

But there were things I said or that others said and I reported that still seem worth thinking about. "Leadership" is a subject that qualifies. It was one of the dominating issues of the campaign and I wrote this about it in *Esquire* in December 1979:

"The president ought to be a strong leader. . . . The president is the only person who can speak with a clear voice to the American people and set a standard of ethics and morality, excellence, greatness. He can call on the American people to make a sacrifice and explain the purpose of the sacrifice, propose and carry out bold programs."

The time was July of 1976. The speaker, of course, was Jimmy Carter, although it could have been anybody and the time could be now. Leadership is the issue of 1980 even if no one is quite sure what the word or the concept means. When I asked Howard Baker, the Republican leader of the U.S. Senate, to define leadership, he said: "Convincing the country to do the things that have to be done."

Baker's definition seems sensible. It's a variation on one of Harry Truman's better lines: "You know what makes leadership? It is the ability to get men to do what they don't want to do and like it."

Only one major American politician doesn't use that definition: Jerry Brown. Brown believes that you can't make anyone do anything he doesn't want to do—at least in a democracy. "To be a leader you have to be at one with the people you lead," he told me the first time we met. "You have to feel it." He reached back to Lao-tzu, the founder of Taoism, offering a Chinese maxim that translates, roughly, as "You can't go across the grain."

I think now—I didn't then—that Brown is right. Not that he, as governor of California, proved to be a great leader. His own faults and his careless cynicism eroded whatever benefits he might have gained from being that rarest of fauna, an American politician who thinks. Another one of his theories, the "canoe theory"—in politics, you paddle a little on the left, then a little on the right, to keep moving in a straight line—destroyed his credibility. Brown could not lead, finally, because no one was sure whether he meant what he said at any given moment.

But Brown's thought—you can't make the American people do anything they don't want to do—is a useful starting point for a discussion of leadership as a political issue. Most of us now know, or believe, that no one, certainly not one of the presidential candidates in the field, is at this point in time capable of uniting and mobilizing the American people around a single goal or set of goals. Someone could do it, perhaps, if the country were invaded by, say, Mexico—but then it would be the event, the invasion, that created the leader, not his or her own attributes or skills.

Why? Because the United States is more democratic and more open than it was in the good old days of "leadership." It is a better, if more confusing, place to live in now but a harder place to govern, populated by a people almost impossible to lead. Take the question of nuclear power. This was written by *Time*'s perceptive essayist, Lance Morrow:

> A pervasive, undiscriminating effort to be fair to everyone means ultimately that it is difficult to be fair to anyone; or at any rate, that all of the controversies of the society seem to be perpetually on appeal. It becomes impossible to build a nuclear plant . . . or to stop it. The entire nation is tied up in court.

The explosive growth of the legal rights of individual Americans since World War II is probably the most dramatic example of the expansion of American democracy. Try to build nuclear plants or highways or dams in a country where it's almost impossible for a boss to fire a litigation-minded employee. And if that employee is old or black or female . . . forget it.

But Franklin Roosevelt, or Theodore, could have built a nuclear power system. There was precious little recourse for individual groups who wanted to stop the Tennessee Valley Authority or the Panama Canal. And where would the dissenters get the information to stop it? Leaders once had the power to control information sufficiently to get people to do what they didn't want to do. That control—or that kind of leadership—no longer exists, is no longer possible, in America. Many people *do* think they know enough about nuclear energy to know that they don't want it.

The courts and information are destroying, or at least diminishing, classical American political power. We live in a society where congressmen, smarter and better informed than they used to be, think they know more than the president. And the rest of us, smarter and better informed, too, think we know a hell of a lot more than congressmen. We have congressmen and presidents who are afraid to make a move, and they can prove to themselves that they are right to be afraid by looking at some of the new information—the polls—and seeing that the public has already made up its unwashed mind. Why fight or try to lead them? Gallup and Harris and the rest have replaced, in the little minds of most politicians, what Jerry Brown and Lao-tzu might have called "feel."

There is also the effect of a superfluity of demeaning subinformation: items, circulated throughout the Western world, such as Gerald Ford's clonking his head every now and then and Jimmy Carter's collapsing on a public road in his short running pants. By contrast, in the good old days there was a gentleman's agreement that the public would never see photographs or mention of the fact that Franklin Roosevelt was a cripple, a man in a wheelchair. Now we see anything we want and know even more: that Teddy Kennedy has the maturity of a teenager when it comes to women, that Brown lives on sesame seeds or something, that Betty Ford . . . blah, blah, blah. The emperor has to rule with no clothes.

The rest of us have to lower our expectations, beginning by talking a little less about leadership. The thing we have been talking about, something that involves grandeur and mystery, unquestioned command and unthinking followers, really doesn't—probably can't—exist in the open democracy that has developed by common consent in the United States in the late twentieth century. A lady in Philadelphia, they say, asked Benjamin Franklin what had we here—a monarchy? a republic? a democracy? "A republic, if you can keep it," Franklin answered. That answer really isn't true any longer. We are much closer to a real democracy writhing within the framework and traditions of a republic. Americans are not willing to delegate that much to leaders anymore.

It is a little foolish and self-destructive to pretend, and expect, that the next president will be, in the old sense, The Leader.

Beyond the few who will follow him (or, someday, her) blindly, a modern president can depend on very little in the long run—and, as Jimmy Carter discovered, the long run seems to be shorter than four years. We, the people, with the help of dazzling communications techniques, television among them, have demystified the office to the point that anyone who wants to use it has to understand that the new leadership is more, and less, than standing up there and saying: "My fellow Americans, I'm going to tell you how it is and what we're going to do."

143

The next president is going to have to concentrate on a few basic leadership techniques—things like being consistent and relatively credible—and the voters who select him are going to have to look for some of those same elements and factors that give one man a chance to be a more effective leader than the next. Charisma. Vision. Consistency. Patience. A certain personal reserve. A touch of Machiavellian skills and more than a touch of common sense.

Jimmy Carter, sadly, failed as a leader because he had almost none of that basic equipment. He did not have charisma, which I'm defining here as nothing more than the almost chemical ability to get people's attention, to communicate compellingly in a society suffocated with messages. Worse, Carter thought he did have it and got so carried away trying to use it with fireside chats, town meetings, and the rest that when he really had something to say, no one noticed. He was, in television talk, "overexposed."

Unfortunately, it also turned out that most of the time he had very little to say. He could not offer a vision—even the kind of limited one that might be acceptable to a great majority these days—of what he wanted America to become and why Americans should want it that way. He was inconsistent, regularly attacking his own credibility at home and abroad—sending the navy steaming toward Iran during the revolution there and then, without public explanation, calling the ships back.

Always, it seemed, Carter was impatient and lacked understanding of the processes of governing that Machiavelli wrote about and that Franklin Roosevelt practiced. The critical failing of Carter as president was this: He would collect all the available information and opinion on a public problem, then say, "Ah, this is how it should be worked out, this is where it will end up after all the maneuvering and rhetoric." Then he would take, and announce, that stand, never anticipating that even if he had found the solution it could not be accepted by the nation until after all the speeches and moves had been made.

Under our system, the process called "consensus building" is the solution. Sometimes a leader leads by withholding his support and the information he has, choosing to wait until he can maximize his influence to guide the process toward the end point he has already chosen.

Finally, Carter had no personal reserve. That I would call a breakdown of common sense. People may like but not admire someone who habitually breaks down in public—lets it all hang—in tears and in marathons. But presidents should not be "open"; rather, they should be approachable, offering the mere appearance of openness.

Carter, and Gerald Ford before him, may be the models of future presidents—or a reflection of what an open democracy can do to its leaders. I hope not. I hope that cleverer leaders will learn to cope better with the new pressures and that the rest of us will, as Howard Baker pleaded in our conversation on leadership, "give them a little more room."

Nevertheless, we can live with all that, with the Fords and the Carters. This is a crisis of change, not collapse. You can go too far with talk of a lack of leadership, of national unity. The alternative is often worse: people chanting, "We want one leader! Nothing for us! Everything for . . .

"Germany!"

That was what the crowds chanted in Nuremburg in 1936.

Politics is fun; government is work. That's why candidates and reporters alike tend to prefer the chaos of campaigning to the business of governing. For both sides, traditionally, it was *Cosa Nostra*— "our thing"—a game in which only players knew the rules. Then, in 1976, bless them, the spectators seemed to catch on and began turning our thing into an unpredictable three-way tennis match.

Candidates and political reporters used to amuse themselves batting back and forth issues, analysis, and predictions. Now voters are beginning to play off the serves and lobs of the political press. So, when I reported on one of 1980s' first contests, the Democratic caucuses in Maine, I realized that the crowds, the voters we used to take for granted—they were numbers in the great computer of public opinion—were having a little fun with us. Turnabout is fair play . . . power to the people . . . and it gets tougher and tougher to make a living—at least if you make it by telling Americans what they are going to do. This is what I wrote after Maine, on February 14, 1980:

As Maine goes so goes the nation. And Maine was uncooperative.

Somehow, the forty thousand or so Maine Democrats who came out to vote in the state's Democratic caucuses did not do what they were supposed to do. They were told—by the press, with a little help from the White House—that they were going to ignore Jerry Brown and knock out Edward Kennedy. Instead, they spread their votes around, cheering up Kennedy and noticing that Brown existed.

I suspect those cantankerous folk up there were setting the pattern for what the 1980 primaries will be like. They will be like the 1976 Democratic primaries in Maryland, Michigan, and Oregon, and the '76 Republican primary in North Carolina. Unpredictable.

Those four primaries—and a couple of others—produced morning-after stories that began something like: "In a stunning upset . . ."

"Stunning upset" and "unexpected" and "surprising" are three of the phrases political reporters use to cover the fact that everything they'd been telling you about an election is wrong. Who's "surprised"? Not the voters. They only come out on one day and, on that day, their moment, they know what they're going to do. Reporters are the ones surprised—they've been talking to the wrong people, reading the wrong poll numbers, and making wrong guesses. Four years ago, most of the primary results were "unexpected," including the first ones in New Hampshire—the dead-head between Ronald Reagan and Gerald Ford on the Republican side and the "surprising" win of Jimmy Carter on the Democratic side. But the real "upsets" and near-upsets were Reagan's defeat of Ford in North Carolina, Brown's defeat of Carter in Maryland, the virtual tie between Morris Udall and Carter in Michigan, and Frank Church's easy win over Carter in Oregon.

There was a pattern to those results in 1976 and the vote-counting in Maine. Voters were rebelling against predictability and predictions; they were voting to slow the process down. When commentators and candidates agreed that Ford had the Republican nomination locked up and was going to knock out Reagan in North Carolina, people there came out and voted for Reagan. When Carter was conceded the Democratic nomination, voters came out in droves to vote for anybody but him.

What people were saying then, at least in the interviews I did in those states, was: "Wait a minute! We haven't elected anyone yet. Let's take a look at this thing."

I think the same kind of voting will happen again this time. Nobody likes being told what to do, and nobody likes being told what they're going to do. A few "favorites" are going to lose just because they are favorites—or they are going to do less well than expected. That's what happened to Carter in Maine—and it will happen again.

People, bless them, fool around a lot in primary elections. I certainly never talked to a voter who didn't understand that no one takes office after a primary. For voters, it's time to "send them a message." That's one of the reasons that the slogan was so effective for George Wallace—and why he was always so effective in primaries. A lot of people who would move to Canada if Wallace actually became president voted for him in primaries for personal and complicated reasons. But, they knew he was not going to be running the country.

The lesson, I think, is that it's really impossible to know what will happen in many primaries—or why it happens. This week, a lot of people in Maine may just have wanted to knock Jimmy Carter off his high horse. Next week, who knows?

That pattern did continue through 1980. Anytime a candidate pulled ahead, his high horse was kicked in the shins by voters—it happened to Jimmy Carter in New York and to Ronald Reagan in Pennsylvania. Political analysts were "surprised" by "stunning upsets."

The highest horse in American politics, of course, is the presidency itself. National campaigns are now fought out within the restricting financial guidelines of a multitude of reform laws and regulations. But, as I discovered without ever leaving my living room, you can't stop a president from spending money on ambitions. Our money and his ambitions. You also can't keep him away from your wife. This column appeared on April 10, 1980:

This is the story of Jimmy Carter's courtship of my wife. He's constantly sending her notes, cards, and gifts—and I want it stopped.

It began in November 1978. My wife—Cathy O'Neill—was president of a furniture manufacturing company in Santa Monica, California. She was elected, by local businessmen and women, as a delegate to the White House Conference on Small Business.

The purpose of the conference, according to the White House, was to assure "the continued vitality of America's small-business community." She was all for that—who isn't?—but she couldn't help but wonder what was really on the president's mind when he sent as his principal representative to the first conference sessions . . . his public relations director, Jerry Rafshoon.

Rafshoon, of course, didn't have much to say about the vitality of small business, but he did tell the assembled entrepreneurs how vital Carter was to America. Some delegates took that, not happily, to mean that the conference might be designed to assure the continued tenure of Carter—and Rafshoon—in the White House.

That began the flow of goodies to our house—cards and letters from the president and his wife, impressive packets on Carter's record on women's issues from Sarah Weddington, the White House's director of women's affairs, more packets on business from John Deveraux, the director of the conference. All on engraved White House stationery, all postage-paid by the taxpayers, all looking suspiciously like campaign material.

The best came last week: the lovely certificate, suitable for framing, signed by Jimmy Carter under a lithograph of the White House and next to an engraved, gold-plated seal of the president of the United States.

The certificate—eleven-by-fourteen inches with my wife's name written in by a talented calligrapher—proclaims: "In appreciation to Cathy O'Neill for outstanding contributions to the White House Conference on Small Business. January 13–17, 1980."

The thing must have cost ten dollars to make. Too bad, because my wife couldn't make the January 13–17 conference. They wasted their money—which, come to think of it, is our money.

Of course, the money wasn't wasted to Rafshoon and the rest of the people running the president's re-election campaign. Contact like that is the president's campaign. There were 2,100 delegates to the National Small Business Conference and another 23,000 regional delegates. If they all got anything like the attention my wife did, then a very significant portion of the conference's $4.7 million budget went for cards, letters, and certificates that had nothing to do with the vitality of their businesses.

Certainly the furniture business did not need the twenty-two-page package extolling Jimmy Carter's record on women's rights, which were sent out to the women on the conference mailing list but paid for by White House funds separate from that $4.7 million.

No one could ever add up the many millions that the White House spends on "public" business that is actually politics as usual—the sophisticated direct mail to people involved in dozens of conferences and commissions, the first lady's staff and travel, the trips by Cabinet members and other federal officials to dispense government money where the president needs votes. My guess is that the president can spend about five times as much as the $18 billion limit public financing laws place on his primary opponents.

The lovely souvenirs coming to our house are just one story. There are millions more. There are no such things as spending limits when you are the president and control the spending.

Cathy and I saw Jerry Rafshoon at a friend's house shortly after that column. "I can assure you," he said to her with half a smile, "that you won't be getting any more certificates from the White House."

The Pennsylvania primary, where voters were preparing to surprise us, was on April 23, 1980. There is almost nothing for politicians and reporters to do while voting is going on. During the primary season, the candidates usually move on to the next state. Reporters, with the bars closed by law during voting hours, sleep or read, sometimes even call home about leaky roofs and other problems patriotically left behind. In Philadelphia that day, I walked through downtown alone and reminded myself of why we were all there:

You swallow hard and, for a moment, you think you are going to cry when you step into Independence Hall, into the rooms where they signed the Declaration of Independence and wrote the Constitution. Right here, men like us created the United States of America.

The guide from the National Park Service says something, and you realize that you're not the only one. At midnight on January 1, 1976, in bitter cold and sleet, thousands of people stood silently for more than four hours to watch the Liberty Bell being moved from the hall to a new site a couple of hundred yards away.

Later, outside in the real world of 1980, there were things, too, that made you want to cry. Cry, the Pennsylvania primary.

—The voting was so negative. Democrats, most of them, did not vote for anyone or anything, they just voted against Jimmy Carter or Edward Kennedy. Republicans, a lot of them, for some reason decided to vote against Ronald Reagan. There could be no other reason to vote for George Bush because the man is not saying anything. The Bush campaign has less substance than any I have ever seen.

—The president of the United States, the inheritor of the corner chair where George Washington sat in Independence Hall, ran a rotten, vicious, dirty campaign here. Rosalynn Carter and Vice President Walter Mondale visited to be polite, but the real Carter campaign was hours of television and radio commercials with two-pronged messages: "You can't believe Kennedy," "You can't trust him," because he's not a "good family man" like Carter. The president, in fact, has a two-pronged strategy—Rose Garden and Scarlet Letter.

—Democratic voters, in their wisdom, easily renominated two Philadelphia congressmen—Michael Myers and Raymond Lederer—who have been accused of accepting bribes from FBI agents playing Arabs. Myers, who is also on probation for disorderly conduct for slugging a waitress, said he thought the publicity about the bribes might have won him "a few votes."

—The professional candidates—politicians who make no pretense about the fact that their business is running for office, not representing citizens—casually ran for two offices at the same time. State Senator Michael O'Pake—read the name aloud—ran ads saying, "Keep Mike O'Pake Working for You—Pull Lever 8F and 15F." He pledged his devotion to Berks County running for the senate—he won—and to the whole state running for attorney general—he came close. God forbid that they might have to get real jobs.

So it went. Democracy in action. But there were moments that made it all seem worthwhile.

In Scranton, a high school student proved to be more than a match for the platitudes of the vice president of the United States, stunning Mondale with this question: "In 1976, Jimmy Carter promised to curb inflation, never to deceive the American people, and to reach out to those people. However, inflation has never been higher, many Americans were deceived by the recent vote at the United Nations, and the president has remained in Washington for 170 days now, and we have no results, because our people are still in Iran. Why should the people of this nation give him another chance?"

In Philadelphia, on election night, Kennedy thanked a long list of elected officials and union leaders who made his small victory possible. One black American after another came on to the stage. That couldn't have happened at Independence Hall, and it made you think that maybe we are not doing quite as badly as it sometimes seems. The Liberty Bell, after all, had nothing to do with the Revolution—it was adopted as a symbol in the 1850s by Abolitionists because of the biblical inscription molded into it: "Proclaim Liberty throughout all the Land unto all the Inhabitants thereof."

See, we're not such cynics. But what do you do when you're sitting in the press section at Madison Square Garden, at the Democratic National Convention, chatting with friends, and you're interrupted by a shouting man. This guy starts ranting nonsense at the top of his lungs, disturbing everyone. Could it be? Yes, it was Phyllis George's husband and the date was August 14, 1980:

John Y. Brown, the governor of Kentucky, better known as Phyllis George's husband, was giving one of the most astoundingly silly speeches in recent political history as the Democratic National Convention began its third night. The man, whose speaking style owes something to confederate bugles, was arguing that Americans are better than other people because we are only 6 percent of the world's population but we have 30 percent of the world's wealth. Besides that, he blared, profits are higher here than in Russia.

Behind the podium, convention staffers and reporters listened intently—to the sound of a television set showing a re-run of "Star Trek."

The United States, it sometimes seems, is divided into two classes: politicians and real people. Politicians yell a lot, run for office for a living, and think that someday if they marry Miss America, they might be president. Real people watch "Star Trek" and do their best to ignore politicians. Judging by voting statistics and television ratings, there are a lot of real people in the country—perhaps two-thirds of the nation couldn't care less about this convention.

In fact, there were a lot of real people inside Madison Square

151

Garden. Bob Bernstein had one of the best seats in the house, just to the left of the podium. He is a cameraman for ABC News. "I wouldn't watch this if it wasn't my job," he said. "I'm not big on politics." Behind him, Lew Gluckin, a trumpet player in Peter Duchin's convention orchestra, said: "I'm not concerned with all this. I certainly wouldn't be watching at home. I'm not even watching now." Paula Thompson, serving Coke in the closest refreshment stand, said: "Watch? I don't even vote." Dan Weiner, a political science student at Princeton, was watching from a guest seat. "Look at them push and shove on the floor," he said. "For what?"

For jobs. For power. For money. For prestige. Pushing, shoving, and politics is the business of most of the people on the floor. There are careers being made in and around the convention—legislators trying to become governors, congressmen trying to become senators, governors and senators trying to become president. That's part of the action at Democratic conventions, particularly a Democratic convention where most of the delegates seem to think that their nominee is a loser and that they'd better watch out for their own future.

Sometimes it shows. Paul Tipps, the Democratic state chairman of Ohio, wanted the state's Kennedy leader, Tim Hagan, to switch votes from Kennedy to Carter during Wednesday night's roll call. Tipps dispatched Anthony Celebrezze, Jr., Ohio's secretary of state, to talk to Hagan with these words: "You tell Hagan that if he doesn't move those votes, he's finished"—no small threat to a candidate for county commissioner—"and I don't just mean in his commissioner campaign. I mean he's finished in everything."

Hagan angrily called his Kennedy delegates together and said: "In case you've been hearing rumors about careers being finished, don't worry about it. Vote your conscience."

Hagan decided to risk it. Most don't. They are in business, on the make, and in New York, you could hardly avoid the career thrusts of professionals named Brown. On one floor of the Sheraton Center Hotel, the governor of California was trying to build up a mailing list for his next national run. On another floor, William J., the attorney general of Ohio, was pushing his campaign for governor with Oysters Rockefeller. On a yacht in the Hudson River, John Y.—with Phyllis, of course—was telling anyone who would listen about his "national media interviews."

William J. Brown, who hosted a couple of receptions with pretty good food, had the most competition. A lot of people want the

Democratic nomination for governor of Ohio in 1982. Peace Corps Director Richard Celeste, a former lieutenant governor and unsuccessful gubernatorial candidate in 1978, repeated his 1976 convention schedule of parties hosted by his father, Frank Celeste, a wealthy Cleveland builder. Former Cincinnati Mayor Jerry Springer couldn't entertain delegates and reporters, so he walked around handing out gum and saying: "I don't have the money to throw a party here. But when you're chewing this, remember me."

Jerry Brown used the Sheraton Center on Thursday morning. After unsuccessful runs for president in 1976 and 1980, the Californian has decided that organization and mailing lists are the key to success. So, to get a free breakfast, you had to fill out a card putting you on the list to receive a newsletter covering only one subject, the thoughts of Governor Brown.

John Y. Brown seemed ubiquitous, spreading what he calls "The good news about America"—and about Phyllis and their new son. In addition to the cruise on a friend's yacht, Brown hosted a reception for delegates at the Empire State Building—delegates carefully picked from the largest and most effective group at the convention, the National Education Association. The best news, according to Brown aides who said their man had been "catapulted into national prominence," was interviews with the *New York Times* editorial board, the "Tomorrow" show, *Newsweek*, *Forbes*, the *Economist*, and *Parents* magazine.

The body of Browns goes marching on. The cameramen, the trumpet players, and the waitresses do their best to ignore the parade of professional ambition that representative democracy has become. On the whole, two-thirds of the Republic prefers old movies. That, Mr. Brown, is the bad news about America.

As the 1980 general election campaign began, I wrote a "wrap-up" on the conventions. It was one of several long columns that I wrote for Sunday newspapers during the political year.

I remember the column and the day. I was writing in the emptying convention bureau of the *Detroit Free Press*, which was my home paper that summer, on the mezzanine of the Statler-Hilton Hotel in New York. By "emptying," I mean that workmen were taking desks

153

and chairs away as I typed and they snatched my typewriter as I pulled out the last sheet of the column. Behind me, in the bureau of the *Chicago Tribune*, reporters were giving a small party for the *Tribune*'s Washington bureau chief, Aldo Beckman. People were drinking heavily, very heavily for late morning. We all knew Beckman was dying of cancer.

The newspaper business is like that. There's a "show must go on" feeling to it. You write in noisy crowded rooms, focused on the clack of your machine or, now, the flicker of a video display terminal. Around you, they're taking away the furniture and a friend is dying. Looking back, I'm not surprised that I began the wrap-up with a woman who was crying:

Rose Marie Schmidt, who is sixty-seven years old and has worked in the Democratic party for forty-three years, sat in the middle of the California delegation to her party's convention Thursday night and cried as the delegates around her booed their own nominee. "It hurts so," she said. "It's wrong, showing the whole world we have no respect for the president."

That was how it ended—in tears. There were few Americans who did not have some reason to cry over the process that began on August 2, 1978, when Rep. Philip Crane announced his candidacy for the Republican presidential nomination, and ended just over two years later with Jimmy Carter and Edward Kennedy avoiding each other's eyes on the podium at Madison Square Garden. The new American process for selecting a president is a national embarrassment.

Two years, millions and millions of dollars, and incalculable human energy were spent for . . . for what? To renominate a failed president, to nominate an actor who has routinely performed as an extremist, and to allow the press to select its own candidate, a losing politician who couldn't win a single primary election.

Campaigns are meant to test candidates. The 1980 nominating campaign didn't test much beyond patience. Two of the most vulnerable candidates in American political history—Jimmy Carter and Ronald Reagan—were able to glide through the process without answering, usually without even addressing, the serious questions their careers had raised. Carter, for his part, simply didn't allow any questions and may not have known what people, his own people, thought about him until the booing in Madison Square Garden.

The third candidate, John Anderson, failed within the political system, losing eleven straight Republican primary elections. But he survived as a candidate because the political system, and the candidates it is producing, is so discredited that a single profession, journalism, could muster enough influence and energy to nominate its own candidate.

Jimmy Carter won renomination, if not the real commitment of his party, because he was clever enough, and cynical enough, to exploit the seizing of American hostages in Iran last November. From that point on, his campaign was an appeal to patriotism and a successful attempt to explain his own failure by convincing Americans that no president can accomplish much. The politics of incompetence, practiced by a a master.

Ronald Reagan, it could be argued, won his nomination in about two seconds. The two seconds it took him to say, one night last February in Nashua, New Hampshire: "Mr. Breen, I paid for this microphone." That is an over-simplification, of course. Reagan worked for many years to win the devotion of Republican conservatives. But even that faith had been shaken by his confused, lethargic campaigning—raising questions about his age, energy, and intelligence. Then network television began showing, again and again, the film clip of an angry man in a dramatic confrontation.

Television, the technology and the business, is at the core of what has gone wrong with the process of selecting presidents.

The technology of instantaneous pervasive national communication has transformed local events—like the debate that night in New Hampshire—into national events. But the nation, the citizens of the democracy, only see those events. They can't *do* anything about them—most Americans have no power in the process. Votes are power, but only people in New Hampshire had votes in that case. Americans in New York or California could only watch helplessly— they were quite literally alienated from the process of nominating presidential candidates.

The Republican and Democratic conventions, which ended Thursday with Rose Marie Schmidt's tears, were meaningless in terms of the selection of candidates. In effect, the Iowa caucuses and the New Hampshire primary—national television events—were the real first ballots of the conventions. And, as in the past, the leader on the first ballot was almost certainly going to be the nominee—among other things, early losers have difficulty raising money.

That touches the business of television. Networks and local stations, the proprietors of the "public" airwaves, charge for the public's business. The cost of television advertising is what has made American politics so expensive. Once a candidate is behind, he or she has trouble raising television money, and without television money it's damned near impossible to catch a front-running Jimmy Carter or Ronald Reagan.

So, many people who care are left with an extremely difficult choice in an election that may very well be critical to the future of American politics. The conventions in Detroit and New York revealed dramatically that there has been a role-reversal in American politics. The Republicans, now, are the party of ideas; they want to change America. The Democrats are intellectually bankrupt; they are the party of the status quo.

Whether one agrees with it or not, the Republicans' platform call in Detroit for "a bold program of tax rate reductions, spending restraints and regulatory reforms" is an idea or a series of ideas. The Democratic paeans to Roosevelt, Truman, and John Kennedy, and the endless, exaggerated attacks on Reagan were substitutes for thought, a way to fill time because the party had nothing to say in New York.

Carter, the Democrats' winner, topped off last week's barren rhetoric with a couple of examples of how low the Democrats have sunk.

"We've reversed the Republican decline in defense," the president said, totally contradicting his record, his 1976 acceptance speech, and his attacks on Reagan as some kind of warmonger. "The Republicans talk about military strength, but they were in office for eight of the last eleven years, and in the face of a growing Soviet threat they steadily cut real defense spending by more than a third."

Statistics lie. And so do presidents who say that Republicans are less defense-oriented than Democrats. The reason defense spending dropped under Republican presidents is because Republicans ended the war in Vietnam.

But Carter's challenger, Senator Kennedy, was only offering a more stylish version of the same ideas the Democrats have been running on for almost fifty years. They were the ideas of the New Deal—government-enforced base-level economic security. The New Deal has been completed, generally successfully, and images of children starving in the streets don't seem particularly relevant these days. The United States has dealt with many of those problems, and the Reagans of the world—even if they didn't want to spend money for those kids—understand that fact and America better these days than the Kennedys.

If Reagan goes on to win this election, there will probably be a new kind of Democratic party by 1984. There should be. The one in New York isn't going to do anyone much good. If Republicans are nostalgic about their America, Democrats are nostalgic about themselves.

Whatever Carter does—and his own history indicates he will do anything for votes and survival—the tides of America seem to be running toward Ronald Reagan. He is the beneficiary of the frustration that has built up in the American political system as rules were changed with too little thought for the consequences and as the technology of television inevitably changed the society—changing what we knew and when we knew it.

What do voters do when they feel they are losing control of the political process? And of their lives? They look for change. They throw the rascals out. We seem, on the national level, to be entering a politics of changing. Ronald Reagan, right now, represents change—a release from the frustrations of alienation. He looks like our next rascal.

Ideas, despite the nonsense, the cynicism, and the despair of campaigning, are still the driving forces of democratic politics. The election results tended to confirm that. The party with ideas, the Republicans, won over the voters. Unfortunately, other people and parties with ideas found it almost impossible to get them to those same voters. In some ways—ways that favor the existing parties and the press—the American campaign process is closed to "outsiders." I wrote despairingly about that on September 4, 1980:

A presidential candidate actually had an idea the other day. Two hundred people heard it. Two other candidates, Jimmy Carter and Ronald Reagan, spent the day saying just about the same things they have been saying for years. Millions heard them that night on network news.

The candidate with the idea was Ed Clark of the Libertarian party. He told a Town Hall audience in Los Angeles that he believed government had no inherent right to control education—and that in recent years government had contributed, greatly, to the collapse of public education in America.

What would he do? He would end compulsory school attendance and give a $1,200 tax credit to any person or organization willing to pay for a child's education—at a private school or wherever else they thought the kid could learn.

It might be worth a try. Public education is costing more and accomplishing less every day. A new system is an idea worth talking about. But ideas, in general, are the last things talked about in American politics. "The two-party system is a failure," Clark said with some accuracy. "The Republicans and Democrats are both completely tied into the spending constituencies."

Certainly the Carter-Reagan race is not going to spark real national debate about education or much else. The Democratic candidate has no ideas beyond getting re-elected and then continuing to try to figure out what to do day-by-day. The Republican candidate is no prize, either—although he is backed up by a platform with a couple of ideas, supply-side economics, and demand-side morality.

Many of the ideas in this campaign, like most campaigns, will be on the fringes—the fringe candidates and the fringe of the press and public consciousness. The Libertarians and the Citizens' party—and their presidential candidate, Barry Commoner—have ideas, good ones and bad ones, but they can't be heard.

Clark and Commoner are very serious candidates, in the sense that they have serious things to say. But they are not considered "serious" within the definition used by the news business, particularly by network television.

"Serious" in media jargon means that a candidate has a serious chance to win a particular election. So, political coverage focuses on strategy and tactics, and candidate coverage becomes personality coverage.

The present two-party system—mandated by election laws and institutionalized by taxpayer-financing of the Democratic and Republican candidates—and the time and talent limitations of network television effectively guarantee that a Clark or a Commoner will be, as the Russians say, "non-personed."

And, even more than in a fairly dismal intellectual past, those laws and rules and limitations guarantee that campaigns will almost never be about ideas. If these laws—particularly public financing—had been in effect in 1856, this election would be between the Democrats and the Whigs.

It is a vicious cycle. The word "vicious" is appropriate because, more and more, the closed cycle drives outsiders to the streets, to confrontation. The press, of course, covers demonstrations, riots, and terrorism.

Ed Clark is a fifty-year-old attorney for an oil company; his speeches are delivered in a soft monotone. He is not likely to pick up either banners or stones. Commoner won't do much of that, either.

But both men, different men with different ideas, might be better off throwing a few rocks. At least that way they'd be able to get their messages on television.

Campaign reforms had always made me a little nervous. Maybe it was because I grew up in a "bossed" city, Jersey City, but I have never been comfortable with plans and people trying to take the politics out of politics. Many of the post-Watergate reforms have proved, to me, to be counter-productive, driving volunteers out of politics and forcing candidates to channel every precious and regulated dollar into more and more media buys. Given the choice between one more television commercial and setting up a small office with a coffee urn for volunteers licking stamps and telephoning their neighbors, candidates asked the volunteers to please stay home. Was that what we were trying to do?

Reforms, like other law and regulation, tend to have unpredictable results. That and the fact that, in this case, predictable results seemed appalling, convinced me that it would be a bad idea to eliminate the Electoral College. There is some unfairness in electing a president by state rather than by national popular vote, but, for me, the possibility of electing a president without a plurality is more than balanced by the benefits of forcing presidents to see America first. I got the chance to explain my anti-reformism while traveling with Ronald Reagan on September 17, 1980:

A horse, a big gray one being ridden by a man dressed as a caballero, lifted its tail and did what horses do—on my foot. What the hell am I doing here, I thought, why should I be in Harlingen, Texas?

What I was doing in this hot little city near one tip of the United States was watching Ronald and Nancy Reagan riding in a carriage

159

past the Benitez Grande Theatre. "Hoy All Seat One Dollar," the marquee said. Their carriage, horse drawn and driven by another American caballero, rolled into the local plaza past the World War II monument honoring dead soldiers named Benavides and Baker, Delgado and Durham, Rodriguez and Roberts.

Reagan, waving and smiling to a crowd of several hundred, came to Harlingen because he wants to be president of this country. To do that, he has to win a respectable percentage of the Mexican-American votes of south Texas. And three-quarters of the forty thousand people in the city are Hispanic.

It's about the same in Corpus Christi, where Reagan went next. Jimmy Carter had been there the day before, the first president to campaign in Corpus Christi since William Howard Taft in 1909. So, both candidates know about Felix Longoria, a local infantryman killed on Luzon in 1945, whose Mexican-American family was denied a memorial service in a Corpus Christi chapel because they weren't "American" enough or white enough. You have to know the story of Felix Longoria if you want to win Mexican-American votes around here—the 1980 election could be won or lost in south Texas. That's because of the way the electoral college system works.

Texas has twenty-six electoral votes. The number of Mexican-American voters in the state is eight hundred thousand, up from four hundred fifty thousand in 1976. Four years ago, Carter, the Democratic candidate, won 87 percent of the state's Hispanic vote. If Reagan can get 20 percent or more of that vote this time, he will almost certainly win Texas and those twenty-six electoral votes.

This election could be decided by things like that. There is a real chance that Reagan could win by getting the electoral votes of large states—California and Texas, for example—even while running behind Carter in the national popular vote. The president may just roll up large pluralities in a few Southern states, but lose close contests in Northern and Western states.

Is that unfair? It is very fashionable to say that the electoral college serves no purpose. But it does serve the purpose of forcing candidates to come to south Texas—to see and feel the place, to hear the voices and stories of these Mexican-Americans. It might be less than fair—and less than sensible—for would-be presidents in the future to travel a land seeing nothing but cities like Dallas and Houston.

Without the electoral college, candidates would be sorely tempted to campaign only in "media centers," in the big cities with the big television stations and newspapers. Presidential politics then could become even more like prime-time television—a contest for raw audience numbers. If we decide to choose presidents by nothing more than popular vote, then there might be no horses and caballeros, no re-telling of the story of Felix Longoria, no reason to go to Harlingen—or to the Bronx, or South Dakota, or Nebraska, or any place else off the beaten track.

Another trip to Texas with Reagan gave me a chance to grumble about something else that was bothering me. The column was called, "The Politics of Celebrity":

The crowd in San Antonio had been waiting almost an hour for Ronald Reagan and they burst into applause and cheers when he arrived. After all, he walked in with Roger Staubach.

Staubach, the former quarterback for the Dallas Cowboys, made his first political trip with the Republican candidate for president during this campaign. It may not be his last. A lot of people in Texas think that Staubach, now a sports commentator for CBS, will be a candidate for the U.S. Senate in 1982.

Roger the Dodger sort of denies that. "The reason I'm here is that I am a voter," he told a crowd later in Corpus Christi. "I'm not a Republican; I'm not a Democrat. I'm a concerned citizen. I am a grass roots guy."

Really he's an Astro turf guy. Staubach is the most famous guy in Texas, an authentic hero after years of football bravery for the Cowboys and, before that, for the U.S. Naval Academy. And celebrity is the coin of the realm these days in politics. Ask Jack Kemp, who went from quarterbacking the Buffalo Bills to Congress—and Kemp wasn't as good as Staubach.

Or, ask Bill Bradley, who went from playing basketball for the New York Knicks to the Senate. Or, ask John Glenn and Harrison Schmitt, the astronauts in the Senate. Or, Jesse Helms, television commentator turned senator. Or, John Y. Brown, who found out you can become governor of Kentucky if you marry someone as celebrated as CBS's Phyllis George. Or, Reagan . . . we all know where he came from.

It would be going a bit too far to say that the country is going to be governed by actors, professional athletes, anchormen, and astronauts. There will always be room for famous sons, particularly sons with names like Rockefeller, duPont, Heinz, Stevenson, Brown, or Kennedy. This year, candidates around the country include the sons of Thomas Dodd, Albert Gore, Richard Daley, Barry Goldwater, and Hubert Humphrey, and the grandson of Ernest Gruening. The daughter of Alf Landon, Senator Nancy Kassebaum, is not up for re-election and the daughter of Ronald Reagan, Maureen Reagan, doesn't plan to run until 1982 for the U.S. Senate from California.

It's at least as old as John Adams' son, John Quincy. Name recognition is the name of the game. We just have different kinds of celebrities—and more of them—these days. And they don't always win every time. You can never set hard and fast rules—after all, Bess Myerson, who was Miss America before Phyllis George, lost her race for the Senate in New York. Tom Hayden couldn't make it to the Senate even with Jane Fonda at his side. But it did work for John Warner and Elizabeth Taylor.

Celebrity is not only relatives, it's relative. To win lower offices, you can trade on fame of a lower order. Barney Frank, a Massachusetts legislator who just won a congressional nomination without ever having his own television show, told me that the new group turning up in state legislatures is high school football coaches.

Anyway, it was a pleasure to watch Staubach in action, as it was for fifteen years on the field. He seemed shy at first, but he was soon into the swing of things, shaking two hands for every one Reagan grabbed that day in Texas. "At a rally in a city park," one newspaper reported, "Reagan introduced the distinguished platform guest to the crowd. (Governor William) Clements, (former governor John) Connally, and (Sen. John) Tower were greeted in silence; Staubach received tumultuous applause."

"We need stability in this country," Staubach said. "We need leadership." Well, he led the Cowboys to the Super Bowl, didn't he? No one asked him about anything else, usually they just wanted to see his Super Bowl ring. No one, that I saw, tried to kiss it, although a few looked tempted.

Ronald Reagan, my neighbor in Pacific Palisades, won the presidency of the United States on November 4, 1980. It was a landslide, newspapers and television reported. But it was a narrow landslide. The Republican defeated President Carter by more than 10 percent of the total vote. But that total was the problem—almost half of the eligible Americans did not bother to vote. So, after taking into account the votes for John Anderson and other minor candidates, Ronald Reagan became the fortieth president with the support of about 25 percent of Americans eighteen years old and older.

No one is sure why Americans don't vote. Some are just lazy, of course. Some are too dumb. Many are very happy with the way things are. Some of us blame the complications of registering—but the turnout in North Dakota where registration is unnecessary has dropped faster than the national average during the past twenty years. Some say giving eighteen-year-olds the vote did it, because young people are usually less interested than their elders. Some blame television, theorizing that watching the processes of democracy provides an emotional or psychological substitute for participation.

Those factors probably all have something to do with it. So does the fact that there really are few passionate differences in American politics. The nation—Democrats, Republicans, and the uncommitted—is essentially united on basic values and attitudes toward economics, welfare, and foreign policy. The spectrum of American political dialogue, compared with other democracies, is very narrow. America seems to work pretty well for most of its people.

But, historically at least, the low 1980 turnout may one day be considered as significant as similar turnouts in the past. There have been peaceful revolutions of a sort when American voter participation has dropped near the 50 percent level. The figures are sometimes estimates and sometimes arguable, but there was significant political change in the United States after low turnout years in the 1820s, 1920s, and 1940s. New voters came out in relatively huge numbers after those low points, and the new participants overwhelmingly voted for change—in the persons of Andrew Jackson, Franklin D. Roosevelt, and, to a more moderate degree, Dwight Eisenhower.

If that historical pattern held, there could be a sharp rise in turnout in 1984—presumably, either because President Reagan succeeded on a scale that brought enthusiastic Americans to and back to the polls to endorse him, or because he so disappointed or angered large numbers of people that they worked up the energy to come out and vote for yet another change.

That, however, is in the future. The present—November 4, 1980—was exciting enough for me. I saw a permanent and exciting revolution in the returns and reported that in a column called, "Women Really Are Different":

Reagan won—that's the lead. But a reporter on election night is like a kid in a candy store. This kid couldn't resist three other stories; one of them, about the half of America that is female, could turn out to be more important than the results:

1. The biggest one is that women did vote differently than men in 1980 and that could change American politics.

2. Voting schedules must be changed before 1984, because many Westerners are not going to vote after they have learned that a presidential election has been won or lost on the basis of Eastern returns and projections.

3. Finally, the press may be in trouble during the Ronald Reagan years. You should have heard them yelling "Lefty!" at reporters during Reagan's victory celebration in Los Angeles.

—Election night and morning-after coverage emphasized that more women apparently voted for Jimmy Carter than for Reagan. Therefore, it was generally reported that there was no such thing as a "woman's vote." Wrong.

NBC, to pick an example, reported that women had favored Reagan by 46 to 45 percent. That network's analysis, and everything else I have seen, used those figures to say that both men and women supported the winner. But wait a minute! If women only gave Reagan a one-point margin and he won the nation by ten percentage points, that means there was almost a twenty-point difference in voting by sex.

Breaking down CBS's exit poll figures, women divided equally between the two major candidates, but men favored Reagan by 53 to 38 percent. That is a hell of a difference: Candidates beware.

—Alan and Susan Freidman allowed their home in Los Angeles to be used as a polling place. Voters pushed in and out all day. But after Carter conceded while polls in the West were still open, not a single person showed up to vote at that particular location.

Carter was, at best, thoughtless to concede with more than an hour of voting time left in Western states. Some candidates—

Congressman James Corman of California, for one, who lost by 864 votes—may have been defeated because their constituents figured what's the use after seeing the president. Normally about 10 percent of the vote in Los Angeles County is cast in the last hour, from 7:00 P.M. to 8:00 P.M. Pacific Standard Time. This year, the percentage of vote cast during that hour was only 3 percent.

Losers like Corman blamed the president. But the real problem is exit polling—the questioning of voters as they leave the booth. It's accurate; that's how Carter knew he had lost. NBC projected the election at 8:15 P.M. Eastern Standard Time, that's 5:15 P.M. on the West Coast where polls are open until 8:00 P.M. Pacific Standard Time. And, because I was working in an NBC studio that night, I know the network could have declared a Reagan landslide hours earlier than it actually did.

The technology—polling and computers—is there and the networks have the freedom of speech to use it. Someday they will—and there had better be a uniform national voting closing time before that day.

—"How do you liberals like this?" they shouted at Linda Douglass as she covered the Reagan celebration for CBS's Los Angeles affiliate. They were not friendly to the reporters they could recognize—"Hey, Lefty!" was the greeting—and television people took the abuse because people know what they look like.

The only surprising thing about this is that it took so long to happen. Conservative Republicans, who used to do things like that all the time, held back during the Republican National Convention and the long campaign. Now, they are free at last.

But the press isn't. One of Reagan's advantages may be that he is more invulnerable to press criticism and attacks than other politicians because his hard-core constituency is generally anti-press already. It could become a nasty four years.

The difference in male and female voting patterns—a first in American history—seemed of enormous and lasting significance to me. I was sure that it would affect the way President Ronald Reagan governed—and I believe it did. I was sure I would be writing about the differences in women's political views again and again from that

165

day on—and I did, particularly about female perceptions of war and militarism. The political year 1980 may have seemed dull, but it also may have changed history—or, rather, American women may have begun changing American history.

Part 5

Cruel and Unusual Government

I used to cover government. For a couple of years, I was the city hall bureau chief of the *New York Times*. I thought about and wrote about and supervised six other reporters who wrote about taxes, budgets, legislation and legislative priorities, police administration and sanitation strategies, urban renewal and urban design, public employees, public employees' labor relations, and public employees' pensions.

Crucial subjects, especially in a city like New York, which was facing the same crunching problems of all older American cities as its taxpayers, corporate and individual, dispersed and the poor and dependent congregated and multiplied. One of the things I remember about those years in city hall was that, except for my editors and the men and women actively involved in municipal government, hardly anyone ever mentioned the stories I wrote day after day, stories that usually ran on page one. No one, as far as I could tell, read them.

But when I wrote about politics—about, for instance, the ambitions of the mayor I followed around, John Lindsay—other reporters and friends would pester me with questions: "What's he going to do? . . . What's going on?"

It is an old problem—if "problem" is the right word. Where, after all, is it written that citizens have to spend their mornings and part of their evenings reading the Congressional Record and the Federal Register? It is impossible for one American to even begin to keep up with constantly expanding government—which is, of course, the way people in government often want it and gives the organism itself more reason to keep growing. And a columnist, even the best informed of Washington columnists, is in essentially the same quandary. How do you keep up?

Well, you have "access." Translated, that means people in government answer your phone calls. They talk to you because they think the publicity will help their careers or a program they believe in, or will hurt someone else's career or program, or just because they know you socially. That's part of the wonder of Washington for a reporter; the town, for all practical purposes, is American journalism's candy store. It is small, in both area and pertinent population. Almost the entire politics-government-journalism complex lives in "Northwest"—the quadrant of the city, including Georgetown, which houses the minority white population—and a couple of suburban areas in Maryland and Virginia. A columnist can do his work while he does his errands. Once, on the twenty-block walk from my house in Georgetown to a State Department office near the White House, I bumped into and talked politics with fifteen friends, acquaintances, and sources. I could have taken off the rest of the week.

Of course, there are problems with all that. The system is circular, so you tend to get the same information that everyone else is getting—that's why so many Washingtonians have the same opinions. And, in Washington, just like everyplace else, the conversation is much more likely to be about politics than government—it's even more likely to be about the Washington Redskins—and you often end up writing the worst of all possible columns, a Washington dope story. It is only by getting out of town that you are forced to face the fact that no one gives a damn about most of that, about the politics of the day with a Capitol spin.

Now, when I'm back in town, which I am frequently, it takes me a day or so to drop back into the local language: "There's a mark-up session today. . . . We're trying to find a budget line. . . . Who's the point man on S.182? . . ." It's wonderful. It's also questionable how much of it really has anything to do with the way people live in Phillipsburg, New Jersey, or Tarzana, California.

What does? War. Work. Money. Crime.

It is not always easy to write about the important things, about what government is really about. When I left Washington, I cut myself off, at least on a day-to-day-walking-down-Pennsylvania-Avenue basis, from the talk of the town. But I thought I could still write about work and money from Detroit and San Angelo and Fresno. And I thought I might be able to write—and think a lot more clearly—about war from luncheonettes rather than from corner tables at Washington restaurants like Mel Krupin's and Lion d'Or where it is discussed as a strategic and academic option. Between May of 1980 and March of 1981, I found myself thinking that the history of the United States might be changing right in front of us—that, short of the most flagrant provocation, the United States government was going to have trouble mounting even the most limited military action. Part of the reason for that was the new political independence of women that seemed so important to me in the 1980 national election results. Then there was the communications revolution. Something was going on, I thought, and one of the first of a series of pieces that I wrote about it was published in *Esquire* in May of 1980:

It was my first coffee of the day. I was in Los Angeles, sitting at a Formica counter in a coffee shop on Sunset Boulevard—not the fancy part of Sunset—grouchily looking at the paper. "Oh, mister, you're wonderful!" the young waitress said. "You just made my day."

I did? But she wasn't looking at me. She was looking at the *Los Angeles Herald-Examiner* in my hands, at the front-page headline: CARTER LOSES DRAFT VOTE.

A few days earlier, at Theodore Roosevelt High School in East Los Angeles—where there is no fancy part—I was walking through the halls with a friend, and she stopped to say, "Good morning, Mr. Gutierrez" to a young man. He glanced up unhappily. "He's one of our physical education teachers," my friend said. "He's upset about the students' reaction to the draft. Yesterday he told me, 'All the Gutierrezes went to Roosevelt. All the Gutierrezes went to war, and

169

the Gutierrezes will continue to go to war. *We* do our duty.' "

Roosevelt High men—the school's Rough Riders play football under Teddy's old motto "Don't flinch, don't foul, hit the line hard"—have always done their duty. In World War II, in Korea, in Vietnam, tough Mexican Americans fought and brought home their uniforms and medals to show the children who are today's students. The ones who came back proudly displayed their Purple Hearts and Silver Stars, many of these placed near framed pictures of Franklin D. Roosevelt and John F. Kennedy.

But half the kids I talked with at Roosevelt High that day said they weren't going anyplace for a Roosevelt or for a Kennedy or for Uncle Sam. "No way, Jose!" was a stock answer.

If that's the way they felt in East Los Angeles, what were they saying on the West Side of Los Angeles, on the East Side of Manhattan? As far as I could tell, parents on fancier streets were telling their children, "Take care of yourself." Only one person I talked to in those neighborhoods said he would encourage his sons and daughters to serve—and he just thought the draft evader's price of permanent exile was too high to pay.

The draft, I'm afraid, may be the issue of our time. It will tear the country apart—as it has before. This time, however, the upheaval will be worse. I was not impressed by the Gallup poll that indicated that 83 percent of the American people supported President Carter's call for registration of all eligible young men. First of all, he wasn't calling for induction, just registration. Secondly, 83 percent is not a consensus—far, far fewer than 17 percent in a democracy can cripple the most determined national leadership.

Consider the following statistics from the Vietnam period. According to federal figures, 26,800,000 men were eligible for military service during the war. Of those, 8,720,000 enlisted in the armed forces and 2,215,000 were drafted and served. A total of 15,980,000 never served—they were deferred, exempted, or disqualified for a variety of reasons. Only 570,000 apparently evaded the draft to the point of being classified as "draft offenders." Of those, 209,517 were actually charged with breaking the law and 11,750 either were convicted or became fugitives.

The point is that only about 2 percent, at most, of the eligible draft pool were willing to defy the government at risk to their own futures. The actual figure, which is impossible to calculate, was probably far lower. However, as you recall, the nation was pretty torn up.

I am convinced that dissent and disruption would be far more serious today, no matter how popular the military cause and policy. What has changed?

Everything has changed: Vietnam raised questions about the sense, effectiveness, and common decency of military action in far-off lands. More important, perhaps, the war and its aftermath demonstrated that America doesn't give a damn about its veterans. The men who fought in Vietnam—1,600,000 of them—were either killed, wounded, or screwed. That lesson is not going to be lost on the potential soldiers of the 1980s.

The American character has changed—or, at least, Americans are now willing to admit openly their own selfishness. The young people I talked with, like their parents, are focused on themselves, their own lives, their careers, and their hopes for the future. The phrase "national interest" did not come up in those conversations.

Since Vietnam, American political leadership has become weaker and more hypocritical. No matter how determined they are privately to strengthen foreign policy by backing it with a credible military presence, presidents and members of Congress don't have the guts to push unpopular programs at home. This year, as presidential candidates urge the rebuilding of American military strength and demand fortitude in facing foreign adversaries, they also claim that draft registration and painful economic policies, such as a grain embargo, are not necessary. It is a form of low comedy.

More important, the United States has become more democratic. Therefore, any new draft will be *fairer* than conscriptions of the past. And the more equitable the draft proposals are, the less chance they have of succeeding in a divided country. Serious plans to treat the sons and daughters of Harvard and Yale the same as the sons and daughters of Roosevelt High School are probably doomed to noisy failure—newspaper owners and rich people have never been unanimous in the belief that their kids' blood is as expendable as the blood of those kids from East Los Angeles.

But then, the United States has never had a fair draft. Democracy in foxholes and military cemeteries was not considered to be in the national interest. American conscription policy in the twentieth century was shaped by the national tragedies of England and France in the early days of World War I—when both nations, in patriotic frenzy, lost much of their future leadership in Flanders' fields. The United States was determined that it would not expend its educated, trained elite in the same way, as President Woodrow Wilson articulated in 1917:

> The nation needs all men, but it needs each man not in
> the field that will most pleasure him but in the endeavor
> that will best serve the common good. . . . People who
> work in deferred occupations will be serving the country
> and conducting the fight for peace and freedom as effec-
> tively as the men in the trenches.

But not as dangerously. The idea has always been to protect the
best and the brightest. Even during the Civil War, when the Union
conscripted only fifty thousand men, certain men were legally allowed to buy their way out of military service for as little as three
hundred dollars. After World War II, General Lewis Hershey, the
director of Selective Service from 1947 until 1969, often and openly
proclaimed that the draft was designed to exert " 'pressurized'
guidance to encourage young people to enter and remain in study,
in critical occupations, and other activities in the national health,
safety, and interest."

So Leslie Fiedler, talking at the height of the war in Vietnam about
his university colleagues, their children, and their students, could
say that he

> had never known a single family that had lost a son in
> Vietnam, or indeed, one with a son wounded, missing in
> action, or held prisoner of war. And this despite the fact
> that American casualties in Vietnam are already almost
> equal to those of World War I. Nor am I alone in my
> strange plight; in talking to friends about a subject they
> seem eager not to discuss, I discover they can, they must,
> all say the same. . . .

A survey taken in the early 1970s of one hundred Vietnam draftees from northern Wisconsin showed that not one of them came
from a family with income of more than five thousand dollars a year.
In a survey of a different group of Americans—the Harvard class of
1970—only fifty-six of twelve hundred men served in the military,
and just two of them went to Vietnam.

It was ever thus—the Confederate Army exempted plantation
overseers, government officials, lawyers, and newspapermen—but
it will not be that way in the future. A lot of Americans, including
some Americans at Roosevelt High School, have figured out the
class discrimination behind the draft. They're not going unless my
kids go—and maybe they won't go even then. The United States is
not the place it used to be. That may be for the better, but it may also

mean we're not about to build large armies.

The CARTER LOSES . . . headline that gave so much pleasure to the waitress in Los Angeles was a result of a relatively unimportant subcommittee vote. The irony was that she got so much happiness, at least for the moment, from Washington, which is, outside of a couple of marine bases, the most militaristic place in America. "Internationalist" is the word congressmen and other federal officials would prefer to "militaristic," but it is nevertheless true that a kind of war fever has been infecting the Capitol for two or three years. Those who've caught the fever—whether or not they admit it in public—have their reasons: They know that the United States does not have all the military strength and resolve it needs to pursue its traditional foreign policy goals, most of them economic, and they know that the volunteer army is a disaster and is probably going to get worse.

Whatever the fighting capabilities of the untested volunteer army formed in 1973, the experiment—at least when viewed in traditional perspective—has been a failure. It is very expensive. It is, even more so than a conscripted force, a lower-class mercenary army. The core of the problem is that most Americans, quite sensibly, don't want to be in the army. The original plans for the volunteer army called for a standing force of 2.3 million. The original goal is never going to be reached, because the products of the baby boom have already come of age. There is a smaller pool to draw an army from because there are fewer young people.

Those facts have been haunting official Washington for quite a while—but official Washington and other people who know have been way out of step with most of the country. One area in which this discrepancy shows up is the periodic surveys sponsored by the Chicago Council on Foreign Relations. The council sponsors dual polls on foreign affairs—one a standard national survey of the opinions of fifteen hundred "average" Americans, the other a questioning of four hundred or so "opinion leaders," that is, White House officials, members of Congress, important academics, corporate leaders, editors. The last complete survey was done in late 1978 and early 1979. It showed striking differences between "elite" and "average" thinking. When asked what the United States should do if the Russians invaded Western Europe, 97 percent of the opinion leaders said we should "send troops," but only 59 percent of the general public gave that response.

Since then, Washington and other centers of internationalist in-

fluence have been trying, consciously or unconsciously, conspirato-
rially or by unspoken consensus, to get the rest of the country in
line. The hyped-up excitement in the summer of 1979 over two
thousand to three thousand Russian troops in Cuba was part of that
informal campaign. Troubles in Iran and Afghanistan and potential
threats to the oil fields of the Persian Gulf countries served the same
purpose more effectively.

The public opinion stage is being set to reinstitute conscription—
to go back to the draft. Then, I think, the real problems will begin.
Many Americans will say yes; many will say no. We will disagree on
what is in the national interest—and in the end we will find that we
live in a different country, a nation that isn't sure, that can't agree on
whether there is such a thing as the national interest.

I had not, at that time, thought that a new assertiveness by women,
an independence of attitude, might be part of the cause of a change
in public opinion surveys on militarism or internationalism. But,
after looking at the 1980 election results and differences in male and
female voting patterns, I thought I was beginning to understand
part of what was happening. Carol Bellamy, the president of the
New York City Council, read, in the *New York Daily News*, what I had
written after the election and sent me a copy of a speech she had just
made. Another column resulted, this one on December 4, 1980:

The time has come, said the president of the New York City
Council, to "renounce our obedience to the fathers and recognize
that the world they have described is not the whole world."

Carol Bellamy was quoting poet Adrienne Rich to a state conference of Business and Professional Women's clubs in Louisville,
Kentucky. She was analyzing this year's election returns—in which
American women voted quite differently than American men—and
preaching some revolutions of the 1980s.

It was pretty good analysis. She argued that the big story of 1980
wasn't the victory of a conservative hero, Ronald Reagan; it was that
there was a twenty-percentage-point difference in the winner's
support among men and among women. Reagan has come and will
go; women are here, and American politics is never going to be the

same.

"A tremendous change has occurred in American politics almost without notice: Women now hold the balance of voting power," concluded Sandra Baxter and Marjorie Lansing in *Women in Politics*, published last month by the University of Michigan Press. "Whatever happens to the Equal Rights Amendment or feminist movement, plain statistics clearly show that the political opinions of women will count for more than those of men in the 1980s and decades beyond."

What Baxter and Lansing document in their book is that by the middle 1970s, after a history of relative uninterest, women began participating in politics—talking and voting—at the same levels as men. And, since there are more women—they live longer—their political ideas will inevitably become more important than men's.

If women's ideas are different. They were this year—polls indicate that women voters split evenly between Reagan and Jimmy Carter while men favored the Republican by almost twenty points. There was a reason: Reagan was seen as being more militaristic than Carter, and the one thing survey data has shown about male-female attitudes is that women are far less likely to favor military action than their brothers. In 1969 Gallup polls, for instance, 64 percent of women identified themselves as "doves," compared with 48 percent of men.

Whatever the rhetoric of Reagan or any other national leader, public attitudes like that will inevitably change American foreign policy. What does a president do if, say, Russia invades Poland, and he knows that a majority of the majority opposes any and all military action? The times are not changing; they have changed.

For better or worse. The men who opposed female suffrage because they thought women were different were right all along. It just took more than fifty years for the differences to become apparent and operative.

And it is not only on foreign policy. "Fundamental," Bellamy said in Louisville, "must be a recognition at all levels of government and society that the two-adult family with one primary (male) wage earner is no longer the main economic and social unit of America. . . . The classical romanticized middle-class family of breadwinner and homemaker is no more. . . . it is high time that childcare is seen as a public responsibility in this country—as fundamental and necessary as the provision of public schooling or police, fire, and sanitation services."

Whether you agree with that or not—I think public childcare would be worse than public education in Bellamy's city—it is going to be part of the public debate in a society where women have more and more voting power.

Women are still maturing politically. Many still haven't learned the value of voting for their own. Attractive, articulate, and assertive women still have trouble being elected to high office—the qualities that make a man charismatic seem to be viewed as somehow threatening in a woman. Voters like women officeholders to look like mothers, librarians, or construction workers. But that will change, too, because 1980 is going to be remembered as the year all women were created politically equal.

Within two months after becoming president, Ronald Reagan had moved on two of the issues that people care about—money and war. He had proposed a series of programs to reduce the expenditures—or the rate of increase of expenditures—of a wide range of government programs from social welfare to foreign aid. At the same time, he advocated sharply increased military spending and his cabinet members and assistants were making belligerent noises about a civil war in El Salvador. It was, the Reagan men hinted, a tidy little "easy win" situation involving left-wing guerrillas and Russian weapons. A few marines and . . .

Then, in late March, national opinion surveys showed that the new president, who had seemed to be riding a wave of popularity, was, in polling fact, less popular than his predecessor had been at a comparable time. The White House had a quick explanation. I had another and did this column on March 29, 1981:

The official White House line, as articulated by the president's pollster, Richard Wirthlin, is that Ronald Reagan's popularity ratings have dropped because his economic program is so tough that it is making everybody a little angry.

Those nice folks from California may not be lying about that, but they are trying to kid us a bit.

There really was some shock around Washington last weekend when the second Gallup poll of the new administration was released. After all those nice stories about Ron and Nancy and all that talk about national optimism . . . the president came out sixteen points lower than Jimmy Carter had during the same week four years ago.

The question, asked year after year, is: "Do you approve of the way _____ is handling his job as president?" When that blank was filled with Jimmy Carter's name in March 1977, 75 percent of those answering said "Yes."

This year, with Reagan's name in the space, only 59 percent said "Yes."

But economic boldness was not the principal reason for Reagan's decline, whatever the White House would have us believe. The reason, shown by other polls and by some of Gallup's figures, is not spending cuts. The reason is El Salvador.

In the Gallup poll, the tip-off comes when you compare the president's approval rating among men with his rating among women. Male respondents backed Reagan by 64 percent to 22 percent—a 42 percent positive margin—with 14 percent undecided. Women supported him 56 percent to 25 percent—a 31 percent margin—with 19 percent undecided.

That's an 11 percent overall difference. It's already getting close to the difference on Election Day last year, when men voted for Reagan over Carter by more than twenty percentage points while women divided their vote equally between the two candidates. The reason then, polls and interviews indicated, was that Reagan was perceived as being more militaristic. He was, many women thought, more likely to get us into war.

"He has had some slippage because of the economy, particularly among blacks," said Patrick Caddell, who was President Carter's pollster, and has been independently surveying Reagan's popularity. "But the major reason for his popularity drop is that the tough talk on El Salvador just confirmed a lot of fears that women had about Reagan. He was weak already with women and his patterns of support are tending to go back to where they were before the election. One of the reasons these numbers might be more significant than they seem to be is that women have always tended to be a bit more supportive of incumbent presidents than men."

Those numbers already seem very significant to me—both for the future of Ronald Reagan and the country. They reaffirm, at least for me, the biggest story of the 1980 election: Women are declaring political independence. They are thinking and acting differently than men. Polls have always shown women to be less militaristic than men—and in 1980 they began to vote differently. In a big way. This was only one little poll. There will be another next week or next month. But already Ronald Reagan should have figured out that if every man in the country is behind him, that only guarantees him an approval rating of 50 percent.

I am not a pacifist. I was also too young for Korea and a safely married father of two during Vietnam. But, in a democracy, it does not matter what I alone am—or, often, what the president is, or wants—it requires the consent of the overwhelming majority of the governed to fight a war. Women, I was becoming convinced, were finally claiming, independently, their half or more of the majority. Also, the technology of communications would make a mockery of the kind of propaganda the United States government used, for instance, before and during World War II to keep the nation at a fighting pitch. Now, often via satellite, potential draftees, and their mothers, get their information about battles and blood at the same time as the Joint Chiefs of Staff. I'm not sure Americans will fight a war again. That statement is probably far too grand, but I do believe it points in the right historical direction.

So what do we do? What I am, I hope, is an optimistic realist. When Russian troops first massed on the border of Poland at the end of 1980, I wrote a column called, "Is There a Substitute for War?":

What do we do if the Russians invade Poland? The best guess in Washington, even if tough-talking Ronald Reagan is president, is another question: What can we do?

We could go to war—but we won't and everybody, including the Russians, knows that. We could sputter and wring our hands—and the Russians could continue on their not-so-merry way, invading a country a year. Or, we could try to find a middle way before the old men in the Kremlin decide to lurch someplace that will force us or somebody into the beginnings of a world war.

The United States may not exactly be a "pitiful giant," but it is a giant and it is to be pitied, at least in the traditional terms of imperialist history. We have gigantic power, interest, and appetites, but we are in the not necessarily unhealthy process of eschewing the use of the usual means of preserving affluent bulk: military force. The leader of the free world, for all practical purposes, is not ready, willing, or able to fight. We may never be again. Our military capacity, again for all practical purposes, may be "limited" to destroying the world—or, at least, huge chunks of it at a blast.

But the problem, if that's what it is, is far more fundamental than how many men (and women) we have in uniform, how good their guns are, and how rapid our rapid deployment forces really are. The fact is that most of the people of the democracy do not want to fight and the propaganda machinery traditionally used to whip up a people to dying for a cause can't work in an open, information-gorged society. Americans have too much true, untrue, confusing, and contradictory information to be mobilized; we know too much to charge out there to win one for the Gipper.

It is impossible for me to conceive of any leader or leaders of this country being capable of controlling the flow of information well enough or long enough to persuade large numbers of Americans to risk death or the death of their children. This is not 1940. I don't think a Roosevelt, Franklin or Teddy, could stir the mass against the conflicting voices on the nightly news. Whatever else it is, television is a force for peace, or pacifism; the new technology provides too much knowledge, including the knowledge of what it looks like and sounds like to be shot in the stomach.

The Russians know or sense that. Obviously they would prefer not to go in and start slaughtering Poles, but they seem to think that, if they have to, they can get away with it. They probably can, and they might think they could one day in Iran, or Saudi Arabia, or West Germany.

So, what do we do? In the short run, I assume, we would, despite Reagan's pandering campaign promises to farmers, end all grain shipments to the Soviet Union and clamp on a few other embargos. It may not be nice to use food as a weapon, but it's nicer than using weapons as weapons. But, in fact, we have about run out the string of our own trade weapons. We used them up when the Russians went into Afghanistan.

Still, trade has to be the key to a de facto pacifist foreign policy attempting to deal with an aggressive and unscrupulous adversary. The United States and its allies do need a moral equivalent of war, or rather, a practical substitute for war.

For trade war to be effective as a deterrent to the uncontrolled acting out of Soviet ambitions and concerns, legitimate and illegitimate, it would have to be waged by more than just the United States. France. West Germany. Japan. Canada. Argentina. Many more. Effective economic action takes real allies these days. And if we are really great leaders, the United States will have to give up a great deal—that dirty word "sacrifice"—to construct a new trade order that satisfies more than one self-interest, our own. There could be more rather than fewer foreign cars on our roads, but maybe there would be fewer tanks massed on borders.

The wrecks of the United Nations and the League of Nations are testimony to the fact that it is almost impossible to deter military force without military force. But the increasing interdependence of national economies—including those of the Soviet Union and its allies—provide another opportunity to reach for the oldest dream. And the inevitable reluctance of a real democracy—I think the United States is more democratic now than its founders and our fathers could ever have imagined—to go to war makes Americans the people who have to try again.

In the beginning of that year, 1980, I thought, in several cities, that you could sense the beginnings of a domestic war. Majority attitudes seemed to be hardening about crime as the violence that had always plagued poor America, random violence, began to happen, again and again, in "better" places.

There had been a tax revolt in the 1970s. I thought there would be a crime revolt in the 1980s. Los Angeles was the first place I saw it—a city that scared very easily in vulnerable, isolated homes of glass walls and French doors—but I was soon reporting the same kind of panic from other cities.

It would be, I thought, a frightening time. Not only were the aimless new criminals frightening but the reaction was as well because the crime issue, like many American issues, was essentially racial. The kind of crime that was being reported and discussed as the nation turned from the 1970s to the 1980s most often had an affluent white victim and a poor black or Hispanic assailant. If it did come to that kind of war, it was obvious to me who would win—the majority rules.

One of the first things I noticed was a growing reaction—just some surprised and surprising conversation—by people on the west sides of both Los Angeles and New York, by the activist liberals of the 1960s. This case, which I wrote about on November 22, 1979, was the kind of thing they were talking about:

Barry Floyd Braeseke appeared on "60 Minutes" last year and told Mike Wallace how he had killed his mother, father, and grandfather in their home in Dublin, California, on August 24, 1976. He had, he said, been using the drug PCP—"angel dust"—and: "I was in my room and had a rifle with me. And I came downstairs and walked into the family room. And the family was watching the TV set with their backs to me. Then I started firing the rifle. . . ."

Braeseke was convicted of murder in April of 1977. That conviction was overturned last week by the California Supreme Court.

The court ruled 4-to-3 that there was not "proof beyond reasonable doubt" that Braeseke had made a "knowing and intelligent" waiver of his right to silence before making two separate confessions of the murders.

There was never a question about whether Braeseke had been informed of his rights to counsel and to remain silent—he had been. This, according to court records, is what happened:

Braeseke voluntarily went to the police after the shootings and was informed that he was a suspect only after officers spotted blood on his clothing. He was then informed of his rights and said he did not want to talk about the crime until he had seen an attorney. Later, however, while he was being booked, he told Police Sergeant Bernard Cervi that he wanted to speak "off the record" because he was afraid children might find the rifle and he was afraid of jail.

He was again told that he could remain silent. Cervi said he would appreciate any information Braeseke had, but warned him he would still be put in jail. Braeseke then told police where the rifle was hidden and confessed the killings in detail. Several hours later, Braeseke was questioned again by Alameda County Deputy Prosecutor Michael Cardoza. The prosecutor, according to the transcript of tapes of the interrogation, read the defendant his rights to counsel and to remain silent four times, and asked thirty separate times whether he had understood them. One of the questions Cardoza asked was: "Did you have these rights in mind when you asked to talk to the sheriff, Cervi?" Braeseke said "Yes" thirty times and said he wanted to talk. At the trial, the judges ruled the first confession inadmissible, but accepted as evidence the Cardoza interrogation. Braeseke was convicted.

The Supreme Court overruled the trial judge, saying that the second confession was a product of the first. The police, the high court ruled, should have informed Braeseke that they would not accept off-the-record statements.

"Sergeant Cervi," the majority ruled, "then contributed to the defendant's lack of understanding by agreeing to the (off-the-record) request rather than informing the defendant that there could be no such thing as an off-the-record discussion."

The minority of three dissented, saying: "The conduct of the police was irreproachable . . . recognition that some (criminals) desire to tell the truth—and should be permitted to do so—escapes the majority of our court. . . . His desire to describe his conduct to those charged with its solution is clear and should not be frustrated by the court."

Cardoza, the deputy prosecutor who handled the first trial, now says: "I'm just sick. Getting a second conviction will be very tough. All of the evidence obtained after the confession may be tainted. I don't even know if we can use the tape of the '60 Minutes' segment."

That confession, after all, was only witnessed by 30 million Americans. Forty years ago, in a case that may have been precisely the opposite of this one, United States Supreme Court Justice Felix Frankfurter wrote a decision throwing out the confession and conviction of a man who had been interrogated for five straight nights by relays of policemen. "There comes the point," Frankfurter wrote, "where this court should not be ignorant as judges of what we know as men."

Within a year the terror had become quite specific in West Los Angeles. This was my column of November 20, 1980:

A twenty-three-year-old newspaper writer and her date, a Stanford economics professor, stepped outside Chez Helene, a restaurant in Venice, at 10:15 last Wednesday night. Two young hold-up men stepped out of the shadows and demanded money. The professor handed over his wallet, containing $200. Then one of the men shot the young woman to death and the gun misfired when he aimed at the teacher.

It happens every day, and night—here and everyplace else. It was the forty-ninth murder this year in half-chic and half-slum Venice; last year at this time there had been nineteen. Few people would have noticed this one except that the victim was named Ribicoff, Sarai Ribicoff, a niece of the U.S. senator from Connecticut.

There is a murder epidemic in the United States. Los Angeles county may well have as many as 2,500 this year, compared with 1,557 in 1979. New York, where there are an average of five a day, may have more than 2,000, compared with 1,733 last year.

So, the Los Angeles city council will hold hearings next month. And it will find out what everybody already knows: The borders between affluence and poverty in the United States are prowled by hungry, armed, and amoral young men who kill the way the rest of us jaywalk. Nihilist guerrillas.

"The mental image that keeps coming back to me is coyotes raiding a flock of sheep;" said Lieutenant Glenn Ackerman, a Los Angeles homicide detective. "As long as the coyotes grab a lamb here, an ewe there, individually, and drag them off to consume them, the flock is not that much discomforted."

The police really can't do that much about what's happening. There will never be enough cops to prevent random violence, and it is almost impossible for detectives to find killers who never knew the victim and leave no witnesses.

Perhaps politics is as good a place as any to begin looking for help. Politics, liberal and conservative, has had a lot to do with the current slaughter of the law-abiding flock.

Liberals have had a heavy hand in, for all practical purposes, eliminating the death penalty and life imprisonment as punishment in our enlightened society. I have yet to talk, privately, with a policeman or a defense attorney who did not say that a lot of the killing was simple elimination of witnesses to other crimes. If the punishment is roughly the same for all crimes, why not dispose of the prosecution's chief weapon, witnesses?

And speaking of weapons: It's guns that kill people. It is damn difficult to kill a healthy human being with your hands, or a club, or a knife. With a gun, it's nothing. It is insane for the United States not to restrict the manufacture, sale, and ownership of handguns. No one wants to take guns away from hunters—and the conservative politicians who go along with that line of crap are the nation's real

183

gun nuts.

But the problem of random, guiltless violence, of the increasing murder without reason, goes deeper than Senate votes and council hearings—and it goes much further back than 1979. The problem is "haves" and "have nots," the comfortable and the poor, living within walking, driving, and shooting distance of each other in a free society. The $500,000 condominiums on the Venice Beach are bordered by black slums.

Race is tangled in the roots of this problem, as it is with many American problems. Black Americans, particularly young black males, are the most desperate Americans. Those young men commit significant percentages of violent crime—usually against other blacks, more and more against whoever happens to walk out of a restaurant door.

One hundred and fifty years ago, in New Orleans, a French consul, a man named Guillemain, commented on the repression of black Americans, saying: "If, without giving the Negro rights, (the United States) had at least taken in those of the colored men whose birth and education most nearly approximated its own, the latter would have infallibly attached to its cause . . . only brute force would have remained for the Negroes . . . however, the white aristocracy gives the slaves, on the contrary, the only weapon needed to become free: intelligence and leadership."

Guillemain, succinctly and cynically, stated the essence of European colonial policy: Pick off the native leaders; make them sergeants in your own army. And we have gradually adopted that policy over a century and a half. The talented poor—black, white, and brown—are sought out, educated, and promoted into and within the majority aristocracy. Their poor brothers are left, as Guillemain would have left them, with nothing but brute force.

That brute force is emerging—like coyotes, killing sheep one by one.

Within a couple of months—and after several more senseless killings—crime had replaced real estate as the usual conversational opening in Southern California. It was the only subject many politicians were talking about, and I wrote this on January 22, 1981:

Los Angeles City Controller Ira Reiner, one of the best known public officials in Southern California, announced last week that he had decided to run for city attorney. "We are facing a clear and very present danger," Reiner said. "Our first responsibility is to protect the public."

Those were pretty strong words from the candidate for an office that is restricted to acting as counsel to city agencies and prosecuting misdemeanors. But they were no shriller than the first paragraph of the lead story in the next day's *Los Angeles Times* about "the city's wave of violent crime."

Los Angeles is a frightened city. It reminds me of New York in the middle 1960s or Washington in the late 1960s. Angelenos are so scared because they are still so innocent. They thought it wasn't going to happen to them; they thought they could live without keys and alarms and dogs, that they could walk down the street without checking the lights and doorways first.

Now they know. They know that their stereos and their purses are going to be ripped off—and, every once in a while, someone's head is going to be blown off. The random violence that hit Eastern cities fifteen years ago is now everywhere; no one is completely secure from the roving bands of outlaws in Adidas shoes.

Even in the East, with self-defenses refined over a decade—weapons, devices, and animals purchased in recognition that the police can't protect you—the fear is still growing. "Major Increases in Burglaries Troubles New York Suburbs," reported one headline in Monday's *New York Times*. Another, from an affluent New Jersey suburb, said: "In Ridgewood, Theft Is Table Topic."

The only difference back East is that people take some of this for granted. They expect to be violated, they hope to survive. That fatalism has not yet reached the West, or, at least, the middle-class West.

The West wants to fight back. And I think it will. Politicians are going to give people what they want—and the people want blood. They also want tougher laws, mandatory sentences, overcrowded prisons—who really cared or ever cared about prison reform?—and more guns. Gun control, for this time, is dead—middle-class people, honest people, scared people are the ones who want the guns now.

More and more politicians will be sounding like Ira Reiner. Or, to be more precise, like George Deukmejian, who may very well be the next governor of California. Deukmejian, a Republican who is now the state's attorney general, has moved his career along by becoming California's leading capital-punishment advocate. Last week, as he has for years, Deukmejian was making speeches that tracked the rise in California's homicide rates since the effective elimination of the death penalty in the early 1960s. When the state was executing killers its murder rate varied between 3.0 and 3.9 for each 100,000 residents each year. Since the last execution, that number has steadily risen to 15.0 per 100,000.

(On a national basis, there has also been a rise in homicides, but the numbers have not been as dramatic. In 1963, there were 4.5 murders for 100,000 people in the United States. Now there are 10.0 per 100,000.)

Deukmejian may be our dark prophet. Whether capital punishment is revenge or deterrence or both, it is almost certainly inevitable. The panic in Los Angeles reminded me of a conversation I had in early 1968 with John Mitchell, who was then a Wall Street lawyer who happened to be a friend of Richard Nixon. We were talking about black riots that were then sweeping American cities and he said they could be stopped quite easily.

How?

"By killing a few of them," Mitchell said. "As soon as they know we are shooting back, that we mean it, they'll think twice about burning property."

It has gone much further than burning property now. There are desperate and amoral men and women, killers, among us. And soon there will be killers on both sides.

Political outrage and opportunism over crime seemed to be vibrating between coasts. I could feel the angry rhythms in February traveling from New York to Los Angeles and then up the Pacific coast to San Jose and the small towns north of San Francisco Bay. The target of politicians and the public seemed to be judges. I wrote on February 12, 1981:

New York Mayor Ed Koch, a politician with a good ear for public outrage, began attacking judges again last week. This time he was blaming the judiciary for the apparent lack of success of New York's six-month-old "toughest in the nation" gun law.

The law essentially eliminates plea-bargaining for defendants with previous felony convictions who are convicted of carrying a loaded gun. In theory, those people must go to jail for at least a year. They're not, Koch says. The mayor's office studied the first 4,106 arrests made under the law. There were 2,222 resulting indictments and, so far, the courts have disposed of only 239 of those cases, imposing sentences in 104. Only seventy-seven defendants received the one-year term. The mayor, who admitted that it might be a little too soon to evaluate the full impact of the law, still went ahead and accused judges of "abusing" the latitude they have in sentencing defendants who claim mitigating circumstances.

Koch, who is running for re-election this year, has picked the right target. A national poll done late last month by the *Los Angeles Times* prompted that newspaper to report: "Public discontent about crime is focused chiefly in the judiciary, and there appears to be general across-the-nation outrage aimed at lenient judges. An overwhelming majority of people hold their court systems in contempt and believe the courts are not tough enough on criminals."

The *Times* survey—a nationwide sample of 2,063 people questioned between January 18 and 22—reflected the fear and the hardening attitudes toward crime that I, and I'm sure other traveling Americans, see and feel in places large and small all over the United States. Of that sample, 77 percent said the courts do not deal harshly enough with criminals, and 68 percent said they favored the death penalty.

That poll showed high favorable ratings for police departments and a general willingness to pay higher taxes to fight crime. People, at least the ones I've talked with, are scared and angry—much more so than I can ever remember. One indication was the answer to the *Times'* question about the purposes of punishment. Only one in five respondents mentioned "rehabilitation," while "isolating criminals" was mentioned by 52 percent, "deterrence" by 38 percent, and "vengeance" by 30 percent.

The courts and the prisons—that's what people seem to be thinking about. A retired Los Angeles police officer, now working in a small town in northern California, a place experiencing its first crime, said: "The bottom line is that there are just too many criminals, and we have no place to put them and not enough courts to handle them all."

As if to underline that point, the *San Jose Mercury News* recently reported on a day in the courtroom life of California Superior Court Judge Peter Stone. The judge called the roll of 294 felony cases, including 9 killings, 31 robberies, 84 burglaries, 2 kidnappings, an indecent exposure, and a salmon poaching.

Judge Stone spent an average of twenty seconds per case. "It's like watching a conveyor belt go by," he said. "A lot of the items you see week after week, with a lot of new stuff. Meanwhile, at the end of the conveyor belt, only a few trickle off."

The belt doesn't work any more; American criminal justice has broken down. The first things the country seems to want—and the hell with the cost—are more prisons and more judges willing to send criminals there.

Then, one week after that, I was in Washington. The conversations were the same and this is what I wrote under the title, "The Crime Revolt":

Crime became part of Margaret Benson's life a little more than a year ago when someone broke into her home and took the silver. Despite all the talk about the dangers of the Capital, she and her family had lived in Northwest Washington, the city's most expensive section for six years and had never had any trouble. Many of their neighbors didn't even bother to lock their doors.

Then, last summer, she was forced, at gunpoint, to lie down in the street near her home while two men took her money and jewelry and pistol-whipped her husband. In November, she sent her twelve-year-old daughter home early from a family picnic and the girl just missed a confrontation with a burglar.

Mrs. Benson (that is not her real name) then began telephoning every home in the six-block area around her own. Of 110 homes, 12 had been burglarized during the year. Some of the victims hadn't even bothered to call the police. She knew why—the cops hadn't come when she and her husband called after being assaulted in the street.

The Cathedral Neighborhood Watch evolved out of those calls. "Block captains" and "block alternates"—people who are home during the day—have been appointed in the neighborhood. Residents in their own cars—two to a car—patrol the streets, in scheduled shifts, for six hours each night. "I never thought the patrols would work," Mrs. Benson said. "When we called for volunteers, seventy pairs showed up."

The citizen patrollers, armed with nothing more than notebooks and flashlights, cover forty square blocks. If they see anything out of the ordinary—strangers or strange cars on the street—they call the Washington Police Department. After some early misgivings and suspicions, the cops and the citizens decided they were all in this together.

There has been only one attempted burglary in the area during the past three months—no one is sure why, but both residents and police are happy at the moment.

That news spread by word-of-mouth and now, neighborhood watches are being organized all over Washington. Not everyone is happy about that. I happened to be visiting friends in Northwest when they were approached to contribute five dollars to begin the organization of a "Neighborhood Alert" on their block.

"I don't want to do that," the wife said. "What it really means is that we'll be out there calling the police to hassle young black men."

"Who do you think is breaking into these houses?" her husband said. "Middle-aged white women?"

Race is at the touchy core of Washington crime. The neighborhood watchers, so far, are mostly white. The criminals being arrested are almost all black.

But the members of the District of Columbia City Council are also black and many of them have begun to introduce tough anti-crime legislation—mandatory sentencing bills, for instance—partly because of pressure from the new groups.

And those groups have begun going a lot further than just looking for people in sneakers running out of houses with television sets. The leaders are sophisticated people—wise in Washington ways of government and bureaucracy—who have begun monitoring court and parole proceedings to see whether the criminals they fear are actually going to jail.

"One thing we wanted to find out was why crime was up and why we were targets," one of the Cathedral founders said. "We found out a couple of things. One, crime pays. The risks are low because very few people are being punished. Two, the rising prices of gold and silver and the ease of fencing stolen precious metals made it pay even better than it used to. . . . All those ads from jewelry stores that say "We Buy Old Gold" are invitations to crime."

"The fact that there was gold and silver in our houses may have been what made criminals bolder," Mrs. Benson said. "I don't know. What I do know is that there was more fear because people were afraid of confrontation with the criminals. They were breaking in while people were home and getting away with it.

"We had to do something," she said. "And we found out that the police couldn't stop it. Maybe we—or we and the police together—can't either. But we have to try."

People will try. They are in Washington now and they will do the same thing across the country. Crime has increased, is increasing, and we will see more and more citizen action and pressure. Tax revolt and Proposition 13 in 1978; crime revolt and neighborhood watches in 1981.

It was an explosive situation, I thought—and it would probably last at least through the end of the 1980s. There was, too, a sad irony to the pressures that were building in Washington, in San Jose, in all the cities from which I had reported. Politicians were joining the public in screaming, but politicians had been part of the problem, not part of the solution. As yet another case on the rights of prisoners, of convicted criminals, came before the Supreme Court in March of 1981. I wrote about that in a column called, "Cruel and Unusual Government":

The Supreme Court heard the arguments on "double-celling" in Washington last Monday and, one of these days, will be deciding whether the placing of two convicted criminals in the same cell in Lucasville, Ohio, is a violation of the Constitution of the United States.

And, during the week, a federal judge on Long Island ruled that the Nassau County Jail was overcrowded and ordered the county and the state of New York to reduce the jail population of 930 by half within sixty days. He didn't care how they did it—just do it!

Part 5: Cruel and Unusual Government

And, same week, the Department of Justice petitioned a federal judge in Houston to order the Texas Department of Corrections to end the practice of putting two inmates together by 1983. The feds also want to limit the jurisdiction of state wardens to a maximum of 500 inmates and to immediately eliminate "triple-celling."

Same week, again, the New York State Commission of Correction announced that it was prepared to go—where else?—to federal court to force New York City to reduce jail overcrowding. The city has 9,243 prisoners in facilities designed for 8,300.

All of this governmental action is based on—and presumably will be decided by interpretations of—the Eighth Amendment to the Constitution: "Excessive bail shall not be required, nor excessive fines imposed, nor cruel and unusual punishments inflicted."

I am tempted to follow my gut instincts and say that it's getting to the point where the courts might rule that it's cruel to force criminals to make their own beds. But, of course, there is a history of cruelty to convicts and a need to protect their rights, which are really all our rights. Fifty years after the Eighth Amendment was written, American convicts were routinely kept in chains in Cincinnati and forced to sleep with hogs in New Orleans.

So, we have to do this. But why the courts? Because our elected officials—our executives and legislators—are so pathetic in Ohio and New York and Texas and a lot of other places. Governors and mayors, legislators and councils have refused to deal with prison issues. There seems to be no great constituency for spending more money on jails even if it might mean less crime, and the federal courts have taken over.

What should be a political question—what kind of punishment do we want for crime?—has become a legal question to be decided on the narrow basis of a few words written in the eighteenth century to prevent the use of torture.

With these foolish results:

—Judicial decisions tend to favor criminals, who are, after all, the people the Eighth Amendment was written to protect.

—Criminals, dangerous ones, are being set free or never sent to overcrowded prisons at all to satisfy judicial orders and guidelines. Letting crooks go is a lot cheaper and easier—for a governor—than building more cells.

—The current overcrowding and the judicial reaction to it could force many states to build prisons that will be unnecessary before they are completed. One thing we know about crime is that it tends

191

to be proportional to the number of young males in a society, and we may be experiencing the peak of the crimes committed by all the young men of the "baby boom" of the 1950s. Things may be about to get better—and we could, ten years from now, have new "baby boom" jails that will stand just as empty as those "baby boom" elementary schools built in the 1960s and early 1970s.

No one, least of all me, is certain what the effects of this particular piece of government by judges will be. But it is cruel and unusual government: judges doing a job, very badly, because politicians are afraid to do theirs.

It was one thing for me to say things like that. It was quite another for the Supreme Court of the United States to begin dealing with the problems I found cruel and unusual. That is what finally happened early in 1981 in the Ohio case and in one involving the court and the government of Pennsylvania, and I tried to point out the importance of a few judicial words in my column of April 26, 1981:

"If Congress intends to impose a condition on the grant of federal monies, it must do so unambiguously." Those words, written by Supreme Court Justice William Rehnquist and released by the court last Monday, have no ring or poetry about them, but they could be the most important ones Americans will hear this year.

Congress must "speak with a clear voice," read the majority opinion of the court's 6-3 decision overturning a ruling of the Third Circuit Court of Appeals in Case No. 79-1404, *Pennhurst State School v. Halderman*. What those legal words and numbers record is the fact that the Supreme Court ruled that states cannot be forced to spend enormous amounts of money because of vague judicial and bureaucratic interpretations of even vaguer federal laws.

In this case, the Third Circuit in Pennsylvania had ordered that state to correct "abominable" conditions at a state hospital and school for the retarded, under the effective management and control of the federal courts. A district court judge in 1977 ruled that the state was in violation of the Developmentally Disabled Assistance and Bill of Rights Act of 1975—and that the court, the judge himself, had the power to take over the facility and force the state to empty it and open new facilities.

The district judge assumed that power by ruling that Pennsylvania was in violation of the "Bill of Rights" for the retarded, in which Congress said a retarded person was entitled to "appropriate treatment." Pennhurst State School, the lower court ruled, was "not appropriate."

Wrong, the Supreme Court ruled—perhaps beginning the reversal of the trend toward federal court takeovers of hospitals, prisons, school systems, and other state and local governmental units found in violation of federal laws or regulations.

It is always possible, of course, to overinterpret Supreme Court rulings. Decisions, in the end, mean whatever the highest court says they mean in later cases. This one could be interpreted to be focused only on the problems and rights of the retarded—and the lower courts were upheld on many of the restrictions they placed on the state of Pennsylvania.

But the majority's language seems clear enough to me to guess that the Supreme Court is going to roll back some recent history. For years, lower federal courts have been taking over state and local government—usually for good reason. The courts have been moving in where politicians, legislators, and governors have feared to tread. Elected leaders have dodged expensive and controversial questions involving prisoners, patients, the handicapped, and undereducated minority students. Judges have taken over the prisons in Alabama, the schools in Boston, and—until last Monday—institutions for the retarded in Pennsylvania.

What the Supreme Court seems to be saying—and what needed to be said—is: Congress is elected to write laws, not vague guidelines to be interpreted by judges and federal agencies so that congressmen can then disclaim responsibility (blame) for the consequences (including taxation) of their actions. The Supreme Court may be opting for putting the politics back in politics, and letting essentially political questions, like unpopular spending for small constituencies, to be debated in the political arena instead of being decided by judicial fiat.

I will not like all the decisions or non-decisions that those politicians will make if they really start using the power granted to them by the Constitution of the United States. Neither will you. There are hard questions: Build new prisons or mistreat prisoners? You decide. Or, elect representatives who decide for you—in your name. That is what democracy and republican government are about. The alternative we have been slipping toward is almost a dictatorship of judges. If that is what the Supreme Court ruled against last Monday, then it has used its power clearly and wisely.

Politicians who avoid all decisions are doing what they're supposed to do—for themselves. The public's business is their profession. They are different from you and me and that difference is always worth thinking about. This column was written on May 3, 1979:

Jimmy Carter has just become the third recent president to advocate that the nation's chief executive should be limited to a single six-year term. He said, as Lyndon Johnson and Richard Nixon did before him, that whatever he does now the press and public inevitably suspect him of playing politics, of making his own re-election his first priority in the White House.

I happen to think the press and the public have it about right. Running for office is what professional politicians do for a living—and Carter began in 1960, running for the Sumter County, Georgia, school board. I also believe that the process, perpetual campaigning, makes (or breaks) the man (or woman) and that Carter didn't go nearly far enough.

We are a people led by professional candidates. A few years ago at a Pulaski Day parade in New York City, an acquaintance bumped into Nelson Rockefeller, then the governor of New York, and said: "Governor, we seem to meet only at parades." Rockefeller winked and said, "Son, parades are my business!"

Campaigning, too, is the business of Sen. Thomas Eagleton of Missouri, one of the men in American politics who succeeded by holding each of his public offices for as short a time as possible and doing as little as possible. Politics is one of the few businesses where accomplishment is measured by how little one does, where success is determined by how often one changes jobs.

In the sixteen years up to 1972, Tom Eagleton, who was very successful indeed, had gone from county circuit attorney to state attorney general to lieutenant governor to United States senator to Democratic nominee for vice president.

When it became known that his climbing was periodically interrupted by emotional problems, Eagleton talked about his first secret hospitalization, which came after he had been elected attorney general of Missouri in 1960: "There is a letdown mood after an election. I guess it's like the closing night of a show. You go from frenetic activity to nothing. . . . there aren't any more speeches to give, there aren't any more airplanes to catch. So you sit around and this mood of depression comes on."

That's a very human reaction, but "nothing" in Eagleton's business was being the chief law enforcement officer of a state of five million people. Campaigning, now that's something—adrenalin and plasma to most politicians.

It's heady stuff for any man. Robert Redford, who gets his share of adulation as an actor, once told me that he had never experienced anything like the overwhelming sense of power he felt when he pretended to be a senatorial candidate in an unannounced lunchtime motorcade for the business district of San Francisco. During the filming of "The Candidate," he said, "the people on the street didn't know who I was. We just came in with loudspeakers and signs as if it were a real campaign. They were just giving themselves completely to the man waving on the back of a convertible."

And it does not have to be a man.

In a study of fifty women state legislators for the Center for the American Woman in Politics, Jeane J. Kirkpatrick of Georgetown University found that forty of them enjoyed campaigning to the point that the phrase, "I love it!" became boringly redundant. "Smiles, speeches, favors, exclamations, congratulations, ingratiation, deference," is the way Dr. Kirkpatrick described the work. "Campaigning gives them a chance to seek and receive attention—all in a worthy cause."

It all seems demeaning, to an outsider, but candidates enjoy their work. Unfortunately, they don't like government that much and their work, campaigning, makes them different from other men and women. They say they've been "talking with the people"—usually saying nothing but "Hi! Howareya?"—but actually they develop a guarded contempt for constituents. People, when you see too many of them for the briefest and most artificial moments, when too many of them want and need something from you, become so many objects to be quickly and professionally stroked and manipulated.

Multiply those experiences thousands and thousands of times from school boards to the presidency, and you are on to something about the way American politics and government really work. Representative government too often becomes officials representing themselves and their class, the small cadre of professional candidates. We should protect the rascals from themselves by throwing them out—regularly.

Let a citizen serve eight years in elective office, then be forced to follow that with four years in private life before he or she can run for anything again. Let him work in the real world, away from the joy of campaigning. If Thomas Jefferson could periodically go home to Monticello to check the fields and do painful things like thinking, then so can the rest of them.

Jeane Kirkpatrick, a scholar when I first met her, became the United States ambassador to the United Nations when Ronald Reagan took over as president. Judging by past experience, she and other new appointees were probably not going to suffer for their service to the Republic.

Public office may once have been a service, even a personal sacrifice—and the holders of the titles still complain about low pay—but so far as I've been able to tell, over the years it's an investment. "They Call It Public Service" was the name of the article I wrote in April of 1980:

The premiere issue of a magazine called the *Corporate Director* is not for everyone. In fact, it is designed for the few who are members of boards of directors and are willing to pay the $890 subscription for six issues.

One feature in the magazine caught my eye: "Directors' Register—A listing of recent board elections." There were some familiar names on that list—Juanita Kreps, W. Michael Blumenthal, John O'Leary.

It was another small example of how to win friends and profits from government service. Mrs. Kreps, who resigned as secretary of commerce, was recently elected to the boards of Eastern Kodak, JC Penney, and Citibank, the New York bank holding company, bringing her board memberships up to six and her annual income from directorships to more than one hundred thousand dollars. Former Treasury Secretary Blumenthal was elected by Pillsbury and the Burroughs Corporation. O'Leary, who was deputy secretary of energy, was elected by the General Public Utilities Corporation, the holding company that owns, among other things, the most famous nuclear plant in America, Three Mile Island. Mrs. Kreps was elected to the six boards—including American Telephone and Telegraph, United Airlines, and RJ Reynolds Tobacco—between November of last year and this January. Blumenthal, who earns more than four hundred thirty thousand dollars a year as a vice chairman of Burroughs, has also been tapped by Chemical New York, another bank holding company, and the Equitable Life Assurance Society.

These are very capable people. Kreps and Blumenthal served on a couple of the same boards before their brief tenure in Washington. But they are still examples of one of the real fringe benefits of government service: When you leave the Capital you are a hot property because every major corporation in the country is now interlocked with the federal government. Lobbying and friends in Washington are as essential to a big company as profits—and those things, lobbying on tax and regulation legislation and profits, are interlocked, too.

And, you don't have to be a corporate mogul before you go to Washington to cash in after you leave. Donald Rumsfeld was a relatively obscure congressman from Illinois when he was tapped for Richard Nixon's White House staff, and went on to work for Gerald Ford and become secretary of defense. Today he is president of GD Searle, a pharmaceutical company, at a salary of more than four hundred thousand dollars a year and serves on the board of the Bendix Corporation, Sears Roebuck, and the People's Energy Corporation.

The annual compensation for these board memberships—which, face it, don't require a lot of work—ranges from ten thousand to fifteen thousand dollars each. The directors are also paid an additional three hundred to seven hundred fifty dollars for each meeting they attend—usually from ten to thirty a year.

It is a very old story, repeated on lower levels throughout the government. Justice department lawyers join the companies they are suing. Defense department bureaucrats and generals join the weapons companies they buy from. Press secretaries become television commentators. Speechwriters become newspaper columnists. All this happens usually because of the contacts these people make on the private side—and the contacts they still have on the public side—and usually at salaries that are a multiple of what they were

197

earning before they went to Washington.

Nice work if you can get it. And you can get it if you work for the government. They call it public service.

Public "servants" became the enemy, the rhetorical enemy, at least, of many Americans in the 1970s. The most prominent and certainly one of the loudest rhetoricians was a California character named Howard Jarvis. A household name now, but he wasn't when I first stumbled across him and wrote that I wasn't crazy about him, but he sure had helped provide living proof that "government" now included more than politicians and civil servants. Big government was an establishment made up of millions of people depending on some sort of public subsidy. What was most interesting about Jarvis were his opponents—he united and revealed big government and its friends. He, of course, won this fight—later he was to lose a couple—which I first wrote about in *Esquire* in May of 1978:

"It's either us or them," growled Howard Jarvis, swinging the clumsy right hook of a dumpy seventy-five-year-old man into the hot air of the San Fernando Valley. "We have to change this California government from of the bureaucrats, by the bureaucrats, and for the bureaucrats, to government of the people. . . . We're going to say to government, 'You're not my master! I'm the boss!'

"A politician comes down the street, you take off your hat and bow six times to the east. You're looking at a potentate. . . . They get elected, they become part of another world. They have had so much money to spend—do you know it costs us five hundred fifty thousand dollars for every legislator up in Sacramento, for the office and staff and everything. It costs us one and a half million for every senator and congressman. . . . Let me tell you about politicians. They have two eyes just like you and me. One is always on re-election and it never blinks. The other one is fluttering at you. . . . They say I put the politicians' feet to the fire. Well, that's OK—but I want to put the fire up a little higher than that."

He is a nut. An ugly, angry one, the kind you see on the fringes of political rallies, mumbling paranoia and handing out badly lettered mimeographed tracts raging that Washington, the Rockefellers, and

198

the Commies are part of a worldwide conspiracy to get him. He's right about at least one thing: *They* are out to get him. Among the people and organizations saying that Jarvis must be destroyed are: Governor Jerry Brown and almost every other major and minor politician in the state, the *Los Angeles Times* and virtually every other major newspaper in the state, the California Taxpayers' Association, the California Tax Reform Association, the California Labor Federation, the AFL-CIO, the state board of education, the California Teachers Association, the California Supervisors Association, the California State Employees' Association, the League of California Cities—and the Bank of America, League of Women Voters, Common Cause, the Sierra Club, and the United Way.

Howard Jarvis is the executive director (paid) of the Apartment Association of Los Angeles—the city's landlords—and the director (unpaid) of something called the United Organization of Taxpayers. What he did to unite almost the entire California establishment against him was to collect 1,264,000 signatures on petitions placing Proposition 13 on the ballot for the state's June 6 primary election. In the simplest terms, Prop 13 is a state constitutional amendment that would require California to reduce immediately all property taxes to one percent of the 1975 assessed value of land, homes, and commercial properties—in other words, cut all property taxes by 57 percent.

"An atomic bomb," said Conrad C. Jamison of the Security Pacific National Bank. "A temporary mirage that in a few months will blow up in everybody's face," said Governor Brown. "If I were a Communist and wanted to destroy this country, I would support the Jarvis Amendment," said Governor Brown's father, former governor Pat Brown. "It would do nothing short of destroying education in California," said state schools superintendent Wilson Riles. STATE EMPLOYEES' JOBS AND RAISES IN JEOPARDY, headlined the newsletter of the California State Employees' Association. "Whenever I tell an audience that Jarvis will bring local government to a halt, all I see is smiling faces," said Paul Priolo, Republican leader of the state assembly—and Priolo decided to become one of the very, very few public officials to support the amendment.

Actually, some of those are understatements. The Jarvis Amendment is not just a bombing, it is a revolution—or, more precisely, a realignment or redefinition of American political forces. Crazy Howard Jarvis, a Republican who has been defeated every time he has run for office, has isolated the Government-Constituency Complex. "Them" is everyone in government or so linked to governmental spending that their defense of the status quo is self-preservation. "Them" may be the political majority, the sum of the governors, public employees and pensioners, the givers and receivers of welfare, big business and do-gooding special interests. "Us" is everybody else, the leftovers—or leftouts.

How else can you explain what's happening in California? This guy jumps up and says let's *really* cut taxes and just about every organized constituency in the state screams that he's a danger to the republic.

What Jarvis is trying to say is that republican government has already broken down—that the delicate system of checks and balances went out of whack when the Government-Constituency Complex reached a critical mass. There came a time when elected representatives interested in being re-elected representatives, when government employees and institutions dependent on government spending or preferential tax treatment, discovered a community of interest—they were all served by rising federal, state, and local budgets. We may have reached the point where that complex of interlocking interests politically controls the society; if they do, there is no effective check on public spending. The example: The reason most often cited by California political experts forecasting the defeat of the Jarvis Amendment is that one out of seven people working in the state is directly employed by government, and with their families, they may control enough votes to eliminate any efforts to drain the tax pool from which their salaries and pensions are drawn.

But if republican form—elected representatives—has failed, democracy is alive and quite well in California. Since the days of Hiram Johnson, any Californian has had the right to write state law or, at least, to place an initiative on the ballot and ask fellow Californians if they will approve something that the legislature has not seen fit to enact. Howard Jarvis is the kind of gadfly—"pain in the ass" is the euphemism usually used in Sacramento—who does things like that. Maybe he has nothing more profound in mind than doing a good deed for his bosses, the landlords, but the unwritten meaning of the Jarvis Amendment is this: Do the citizens of a democracy have the right to draw a line, to say this is how much government is worth to us, and no more!

All that is phrased a bit differently than how Jarvis himself would say it. He is a decidedly unattractive character, an arrogant egotist who prefers to bully honest questioners like the ones who approached him the first time I saw him in the San Fernando Valley, at a crowded luncheon of the Woodland Hills Chamber of Commerce. If Howard Jarvis is the voice of the people, then the people sound like a mad bullfrog. Anyone who disagrees with his voice is quickly and personally attacked as a "phony" or a "liar" and risks comparison with "Goebbels in Germany."

There is also an undercurrent of racism in the Jarvis pitch— "screech" might be the word—as there is in most things American. At least that's what I heard when he began throwing around lines like, "The schools in Los Angeles are in the business of manufacturing illiterates, future and permanent welfare recipients. . . . Why should property owners in the San Fernando Valley pay for the redevelopment of downtown Los Angeles?"

Race certainly was one of the factors that led to the California property-tax increases that made Jarvis such a serious threat to the status quo. State-ordered desegregation of Los Angeles city schools—the city's minority group population is expected to be a majority by 1985—led to serious house hunting by white parents in parts of Los Angeles County outside the city itself. Real-estate values on blocks in places like Santa Monica tripled and quadrupled in three years—in California, when one house on a street is sold, all houses are reassessed to reflect the recent sale. It is hard to avoid friends who want to talk about nothing but the fact that their property taxes have gone from, say, one thousand four hundred to five thousand nine hundred dollars since 1975—and many, particularly older residents, have had to sell out because they simply didn't have the income to meet those taxes.

Now, with the voters being threatened from all sides with dire consequences if Prop 13 passes, most knowledgeable Californians are predicting that the amendment will be defeated, that nothing can stand up to the political juggernaut of the government-union-business-newspaper complex and the threat of chaos if Jarvis wins. On the other hand, it's difficult to find many people who have definitely decided to vote against the thing. The amendment is the principal topic of conversation in the state, and about a hundred interviews I did in the San Fernando Valley, Santa Monica, and Sacramento produced two equally divided groups of responses. Roughly:

"You're goddamned right I'm for it. Those bastards are stealing us blind."

Or: "I don't know. I know Jarvis is crazy, but this may be the only way we'll ever have to shake the politicians up. They just won't stop:

They're killing us and then throwing our money away. I'll tell you, I'd really like to vote for it."

Ed Salzman, the editor of the *California Journal*, was one of the few who said he had to vote against the amendment. "In my gut, I want government shaken up, and I know it needs it," he said. "But this scheme is crazy. It's hitting where government can least afford it."

He talked for a while about California government, something he knows well. Once, he paused and interjected: "You know, if this thing were directed at the federal government, I'd vote for it in a minute—in a minute!"

So would I. Howard Jarvis is a nut, but in my heart I know he's right.

That from California. It made a real difference where I wrote from. After a dinner in Manhattan—and a few unpleasant subway rides—I wrote this on January 28, 1981:

A group of repatriated New Yorkers, six people who had just moved back to the city after being away for five years or so, had dinner together the other night. Obviously, the subject turned to what had changed most in those years. More dirt, more crime, unbelievable rents, the thrilling comeback of neighborhoods on the west side of Manhattan—people argued back and forth.

Then someone said: "The transportation system has broken down."

That was it. Five years ago, in 1976, you could stand on a corner or go into a hole in the ground and a bus or a train would come by and take you where you wanted to go. It might not have been the most elegant, and you had to be careful about the people around you, but you got there. It was pretty sure.

It's not sure anymore. This week, the *New York Daily News* confirmed the impressions of those returned natives, in a sad and alarming series that began:

"The world's most famous and for years the best-run subway system has come down to this:

"On a Tuesday earlier this month, one third of the New York City Transit Authority's 6,409-car subway fleet was out of service, mostly because of a lack of parts. . . . Subway riders board trains today knowing that a trip that took ten minutes in 1910 may take four times as long today."

Statistically, this is what has happened to the subways in just four years, from 1977 to 1980: The number of cars out of service on an average day has increased from 600 to 2,141; the number of canceled trips each day has increased from 86 to 300; the number of fires per year has increased from 2,243 to 4,908; the number of miles between breakdowns has decreased from 13,900 to 6,000.

In the next four years, there will be derailments, collisions, and death. Inspection of equipment, tracks, and roadbeds, and preventive maintenance are, for all practical purposes, a thing of the past.

There is no money and the rest is inevitable. "We have a subway that is about to die," said Carol Bellamy, the president of the New York City Council.

So it is. A great and necessary national resource—the economic lifeline of the greatest population concentration in the country—is collapsing in as dramatic an example of governmental lunacy as the world will ever see.

The city of New York, beginning in the 1960s, began abdicating its management role and began slowly turning the transportation system over to public employee unions—to the point that public tax money, and there was, in real dollars, less and less of it as Eastern urban population declined, was going to salaries, overtime and pensions, rather than to equipment and maintenance.

The state of New York ignored the problem for as long as possible and the federal government moved in on the assumption that the problem was equal geographical allocation of mass transit money. While the greatest mass transit system in the history of mankind is collapsing—a system that carries 6.5 million people to work and home each day—the United States Department of Transportation is planning "people movers" in parts of Los Angeles where there are almost no people.

Federal mass transit policy seems based on "fairness." It is sets of formulas that attempt to allocate money by population. That sounds good, but it means that the less mass transit a city has, the more of its costs will be paid by Washington. In New York and Boston, which have multiple transportation options, 9 percent of mass transit costs are paid by the federal government. In Los Angeles, where buses come by the day, 26 percent of those costs are paid by Washington; in Phoenix, the figure is 40 percent.

The whole thing makes no sense. It's as if federal dams and water projects were distributed by population, with Minnesota getting twice as much irrigation as Arizona. Let's build an eighteen-mile subway under Wilshire Boulevard—which is on the federal books—and let the Broadway line grind to a fiery halt.

Los Angeles, of course, should have mass transit—not subways, but surface trains down the center of its freeways. But tilting federal mass transit policy toward the West would be a national tragedy. If New York's subways decline, so does its economy and then more of its people will leave—for the West. There will be empty houses and factories in the East and no houses or factories in the West. Both coasts will be the worse for transportation policies as fair as they are stupid.

Beyond New York, other Eastern and Midwestern cities were . . . well, they were just growing old. Then, a presidential commission chaired, appropriately, by a college president who had recently retired from New York to the Southern California paradise of La Jolla, William McGill of Columbia University, recommended that we let the old places die. That may be overstating the controversial conclusion of the Commission for a National Agenda for the 1980s, but not overstating it by much.

It was not that the commission had any power to actually do anything, but it did validate what I thought was a profoundly dangerous—and selfish—strain of American thinking. I tried to use Tocqueville, once more, to set up the argument I made in a column on February 25, 1981:

In the summer of 1831, two young French aristocrats came to Saginaw in the Michigan Territory, even after they had been warned by an innkeeper outside Detroit: "Do you realize what you are undertaking? Do you know that Saginaw is the last inhabited place till the Pacific Ocean; that from here to Saginaw hardly anything but wilderness and pathless solitude are to be found?"

They went anyway and one of them, Alexis deTocqueville who was later to be celebrated as the author of *Democracy in America*, wrote an essay about the journey into "le desert"—"the wilderness." It was swampland and virgin forest of pine then, but Toc-queville knew the great and greedy Americans would take every tree and move on to someplace else, some place momentarily wealthy.

"It's this nomad people which the rivers and lakes do not stop," he wrote, "before which the forests fall and prairies are covered with shade, and which, after having reached the Pacific Ocean, will reverse its steps to trouble and destroy the societies which it will have formed behind it."

We have reached the Pacific. Now, Saginaw, which once had a population of almost one hundred thousand, is just one of the societies formed behind the frontier. It is being destroyed now—its population was down to seventy-seven thousand, five hundred in the 1980 census.

That census tells the story of the new—or continuing—movement west. The population of St. Louis, which was a fur trading post in 1831, has declined from eight hundred eighty thousand to four hundred forty-eight thousand in the past thirty years. Buffalo dropped from five hundred eight thousand to three hundred fifty thousand. New York City lost almost one million people. Philadelphia . . . Detroit . . . so it goes.

People, it seems, would rather live in little boxes in the desert where Los Angeles meets San Bernardino or on top of what the Lord meant to be a swamp in Florida than stay in brick houses in Baltimore or Pittsburgh. Federal and local programs to create and save industries and jobs in the old cities during the 1960s and 1970s may have kept a few people around for a few winters, but only a few. Human nature still counts for more than public policy.

So, the new conventional wisdom will be: Let's forget about Saginaw and the rest—what can we do? That "idea" has been given impressive respectability by one of President Carter's creations, the Commission for a National Agenda for the 1980s. The commission has recommended a total change in federal urban policy—from trying to do something for the losers to joining the winners.

"When the federal government steps in to try to alter these dynamics," the commission reports after reviewing population shifts from east to west, from cold to warm, "it generates a flood of demands that may sap the initiative of urban governments via the expectation of continuous support."

"Cities are not permanent," the commission said. Perhaps, but, in general, they should be. The United States is no longer a country of expanding will and energy. We can destroy St. Louis or Saginaw, but we probably can't replace or rebuild them.

There is, it seems to me, a tremendous danger in the coincidence of the 1980 census and the coming to power of men who are both conservatives and Westerners. The new president, Ronald Reagan, a Westerner, and his friends have always tended to believe that there is something evil about "teeming cities"—the phrase is from the letters of an anti-urban politician named Thomas Jefferson, a Westerner in his day. The numbers and the reports are telling our new leaders exactly what they want to hear: that they should help themselves, help San Diego, rather than help the unwashed, the left-behinds of Pittsburgh or Milwaukee.

But the fact is that the left-behinds are still the real America. There are so many more of them back East; only 20 percent of the nation is in the West. It would be a mistake to throw good money after bad into the old cities—massive new job creation is probably impossible in many places. But we need to preserve those places, particularly their irreplaceable physical plants—buildings, roads, water lines, public and private facilities of all kinds—because it would be a tragedy to live in a country that decided its proper function is to subsidize the prospering minority rather than the struggling majority.

Cities and their environs may not be permanent, as the Commission for the 1980s argued, but they seemed natural to me. Driving up the Hudson River, north of New York City, through Tarrytown, I turned to my wife and said: "Look at this! Look at this! Look at the housing—this must be a wonderful place to live. There's nothing like it back in California. It's . . . there really is such a thing as developed ecology."

Yes, there is. I tried to write about that in a column on March 1, 1981:

A weekend drive up the Hudson River Valley from Manhattan into Westchester, Putnam, and Dutchess counties provides a wondrous education in the evolution of the older regions of the United States. Miles and miles of housing for millions and millions of

206

people, networks of roads and reservoirs, factories, schools, stores, hospitals, and fire stations all swirl out from downtown nuclei in dazzlingly intricate, interdependent patterns.

This must be something like the most basic unit of life—a cell, or whatever they call the latest thing they've discovered. My God, did men and women really do all this? How long did it take? Could it all be done again—the building of the roads, the lovely towns, and the marvelous homes, fifty, one hundred, two hundred years old? The railroad tracks? The pipelines for water and steam and electricity? The tunnels and the bridges?

The word that comes to mind is "ecology." There is such a thing as "developed" ecology. A man-made ecology is what you see in Manhattan and around that island, or in Philadelphia and beyond, in Chicago and Detroit and Des Moines.

That American ecology is why it is important to consider whether New York Governor Hugh Carey is right when he says President Reagan's proposed budget is "regionally biased" against the old states. New York City Mayor Edward Koch may well be less hyperbolic than usual when he attacks the president's plans to eliminate mass transit subsidies as "the dumbest thing I've heard of in years."

In less colorful language, Robert Mandeville, the director of the Illinois Bureau of the Budget, says: "We do not have a clear understanding yet of the new federal policies, but the indications are that states with mature economies will be hurt even more than they have been in the past."

Something is happening. There is a "cowboy tilt" or a "freeway tilt" to the Reagan administration. The new folks in Washington, many of them Westerners, seem to have taken literally the recommendations of President's Carter's Commission for a National Agenda for the 1980s.

The commission, which issued some preliminary reports last month, basically advised future presidents to go with the flow—to let people and jobs drift toward California and Texas and other newer, warmer places. The full report is now available and it says things like:

"Contrary to conventional wisdom, cities are not permanent. . . . Many cities of the old industrial heartland—for example in the states of New York, Pennsylvania, Ohio, Michigan, and Illinois—are losing their status as thriving industrial capitals, a position they have held through the first half of the century.

"These cities are not dying. Rather they are transforming—and in the future they will likely perform a narrower range of vital and specialized tasks for the larger urban society. . . . Thus, as the major long-term goal of federal urban policy, the commission urges government to place greater emphasis on retraining and relocation assistance efforts designed to link people with economic opportunity, wherever that opportunity might be."

While it is hard to disagree with some of that reasoning, the report does sometimes seem to be saying that not only are New York and Detroit dying, but we should put them out of their misery and move the people, quickly, to Albuquerque and San Bernardino. That idea often seems to be shared by the people now in the White House, men from warm places called Pacific Palisades and La Mesa.

Our new leaders from the West and the bold commission report are undoubtedly right and visionary in many of their perceptions and proposals. But if you travel the country, you wonder whether it's all as simple as it seems to them. If you encourage people to move from, say, Tarrytown, New York, to La Verne, California, how do you support them in their new desert home? Support, after all, is more than a job. Where does the water come from? The roads? All the complicated components of a metropolitan area?

The question may be whether we are rich enough and strong enough to rebuild Tarrytown and Queens and Cleveland in those warm deserts. Maybe we are. But we should be very careful about the destruction and decay of what we have already built. Surely, there is as delicate an ecology in the works of Man as in the wonders of Nature.

Part 6

Different Faces

I was on United Airlines Flight 5 from JFK to LAX, when a small man wearing glasses came up to my seat and introduced himself. His name was Abraham Lass. He said he was a retired high school principal from Brooklyn and that he had once taught a close friend of mine. We began to talk.

There has always been a legend in the newspaper business that a competent reporter can knock on any door and come away with a good story. And that's true. Everyone has a story. Some may be better than others but you never know what's going to happen when you listen.

Not that I always want to do that—just listen. One of the ways that I, and I'm sure other people, justified the drain of bicoastal living and all those long flights was to say that we got a lot of work done on the planes. No telephones, no one to bother you . . . all that. Would that it were true. After a while, most of us have trouble concentrat-

ing on airplanes and we give in to sleep, or conversation, or movies
that more and more seem to break or stop in the middle of the last
reel.

And if you're a columnist, and you're lucky, you get another day's
column. I was lucky—to meet Abe Lass and hundreds of other
Americans on planes, in hotels, offices, bars, gas stations, sometimes just down the street.

I got off Flight 5 and wrote a column called, "The Princess and the
Principal" for October 28, 1979:

The newspapers in Los Angeles last weekend were filled with
stories about the parties for Princess Margaret, which was kind of
silly when you consider that Abe Lass was also visiting. Abe Lass,
after all, has done more for America than Margaret ever did for
England.

Abraham H. Lass was the principal of Abraham Lincoln High
School in Brooklyn, on Ocean Parkway in Coney Island, from 1955
to 1971. I sat next to him flying from New York to Los Angeles. He is
retired now, after teaching for forty years, and was flying out to be
the guest-of-honor at a reunion of Lincoln graduates in Beverly
Hills.

This was no ordinary party. Not many high schools have reunions
three thousand miles away at the rambling home of Bernie Cornfeld.
He couldn't make it because he was in Switzerland, where he had
just been acquitted of fraud charges stemming from the bankruptcy
of his old company, Investors Overseas Service. Cornfeld is hardly
the best-known of the school's graduates, which include Arthur
Miller, Joseph Heller, Herschel Bernardi, Mel Brooks, Neil Sedaka
and Neil Diamond, Lou Gosset, Rep. Elizabeth Holtzman, doctors
and lawyers beyond counting, and two Nobel Prize winners.

"The times have changed," said Lass, who managed to write
thirty-six books after he began teaching English in 1931. "Abraham
Lincoln is not what it used to be, few schools are. Students are
different and family structures are different, but the changes that
have been made have actually made things worse rather than better.
I know it's not popular to say today, but schools should be essentially repressive. You have to stand up and confront the obvious
threats to order because you are always on the edge of anarchy when
you deal with immature and undeveloped people. I wouldn't want
to be a principal today because without authority you can't run what
should be an authoritarian structure."

Lass used bilingual education as an example of turning the schools over to students and well-meaning pressure groups. "It's a lousy idea dictated by the politics of the day," he said. "No one is learning how to live in the real United States. We had to learn English and learn it well, and, it happens, that I could only speak and understand Yiddish when I began school. The same was true for a lot of students I taught."

Old-fashioned. But apparently it worked for Lincoln students. There were eight hundred of them at Cornfeld's mansion to hear Lass introduced by Bernardi. Some had flown in from as far away as London. Their old principal said, "I bring you greetings from Brooklyn and from the past."

"There was a lot of hugging and kissing," Lass said later. "For me it was a spiritual experience. But it must have meant something to them, too. Most were from California—that's where a lot of Brooklyn is now—but they came from all over the country. I couldn't believe it."

I could—because I knew about Abe Lass before he sat down next to me on that plane. A friend of mine, who was a hood thrown out of Abraham Lincoln, had told me about Lass many times. "I was on the streets and that's where I'd still be," said Ken Auletta. "Mr. Lass sought me out at home and got me back into school and then into college. He saved my life."

Auletta, a writer for the *New Yorker* and a columnist for the *New York Daily News*, couldn't make it to California because he was finishing up the manuscript of his second book on urban problems. "We were hostile kids," Auletta said, "and he was a tough guy, compassionate but tough. God, I owe him."

We all owe him. The stories in the Los Angeles papers were about Princess Margaret dedicating a Rolls-Royce service garage and then being entertained by the city's elites. This is dedicated to Abe Lass.

Edward Koch, who is condemned to preside over the brutal and spectacular decline of Abe Lass's Coney Island, invited me over to dinner at Gracie Mansion in New York a couple of weeks later. He gets to live in the mansion because he's the mayor of the city. And he doesn't consider the job a sentence at all. For him, it's a joy. Why

211

not? He's paid to do what New Yorkers do best: gripe. Ed Koch has succeeded politically not by governing brilliantly or by being a demagogue; he doesn't just tell people what they want to hear, he says what they are saying. Or, he articulates what they are only thinking and he says it in their accents. For years, they've loved it.

The thoughts in this interview, which not only showed some vintage Koch, were later repeated and repeated in speeches and Congressional hearings and news columns and articles as Koch began to expand on our long conversations. Then, other mayors and public officials began picking up the same themes. But at the time, he was a Democratic mayor who seemed to be speaking the unspeakable. The column was published on November 11, 1979:

You can't go anywhere these days without hearing someone griping about how government is ruining the country. Take dinner the other night in New York with Ed Koch.

"It's insane," he said. "They're ruining us."

Koch, of course, is hardly your average citizen. He's not only the mayor of New York City but, before that, was a congressman for almost a decade—a very liberal congressman. But, *kvetching* that night, he sounded like a cab driver thinking about voting Republican.

"Washington just sits there and tells us to do this, do that, do it this way, do it that way," Koch said as we sat around with some of the highest officials of his city. "They're looking over our shoulder all the time, threatening to take us to court all the time. Keep the hospitals open even if they don't have any patients or we'll cut off your aid. Help the handicapped, help the children. Put white teachers in black schools. No, we changed our mind, put black teachers in black schools. Teach in Spanish. Now we have English and Spanish treated equally in the schools. It's crazy. It never ends."

"But Ed," interrupted his counsel, Alan Schwartz, "you voted for all those things in Congress."

"I know that," Koch continued. "I was dumb. We all were. I voted for so much crap. Who knew? We got carried away with what the sociologists were telling us. . . . we have permitted a small number of people, generally gifted, elitist, to dominate the society. This was their view. It was never the majority view."

"Well, what happens when you go back to Washington? You know a lot of people in Congress," I said. "You must be telling them the same thing."

"I am," he said. "They say they know I'm right. But it doesn't make any difference. They keep voting for more and more—and they say they have to. They're afraid of pressure from every group that wants something from them."

No one, in short, wants his office or campaign picketed by Hispanics, or children, or people in wheelchairs . . . or whomever.

"Congress has just become more responsive, too responsive," said Ronay Menschel, a mayoral assistant who once ran Koch's congressional office. "The winds of change would have once come and gone, but now they're institutionalized in regulations. . . . The regulations have a life of their own. Facility access for the handicapped is an example. The Department of Transportation is blindfolded to reality. In New York, they ignore the fact that our bus system shadows the subway system. We say we'll make the buses accessible to the handicapped, but they say it has to be both buses and subways, even if no one in a wheelchair will ever use the subways and the money doesn't exist to rebuild them." "We could shut them down," Koch joked sourly, "then we wouldn't be in violation of the regulation."

"New values have found a home in those regulations," said David Brown, a former deputy mayor who is now teaching at Yale. "Environmental regulations are an example. It's process run amok. Times change, but the old plans—the agenda of the 1960s—have this life of their own through federal courts and bureaucracy.

"We're heading for a crisis," Brown continued. "We can't get this thing back in the bottle. We won't be able to come up with all the money to do all the things that have been mandated. Government may not be able to carry the burden; it'll be run into the ground. You'll have public officials who are not upholding the law."

"The people out there have nothing to do with what's happening," Koch said, pointing in the general direction of Queens and Brooklyn from his elegant, temporary home in Manhattan, Gracie Mansion. "How do they feel? I know how I feel. I want to exercise the authority I'm supposed to have under the City Charter. I can't. Most of the time I feel I can't do anything. I'm telling you, it's insane."

William Green is a peer of Ed Koch's. He became the mayor of Philadelphia after this interview. It speaks for itself even if he can't. The title was, "The Very Model of a Modern Politician":

Publishers of paperback books favor a certain kind of cover for political novels. There's usually a scattering of small paintings: the Capitol or the White House, a bunch of people waving campaign posters, a panting couple beginning to take off each other's clothes, and, the centerpiece, a strikingly handsome, dark-haired candidate who looks like a face-lifted Kennedy.

Bill Green looks exactly like that painted candidate. He is forty years old, tall, dark, and very handsome. He was elected to Congress when he was a twenty-five-year-old law student because his full name is William J. Green III, and his father, William J. Green, Jr., was Philadelphia's political boss and used to have the same seat. Now the son wants to be mayor of Philadelphia. In fact, he is the Democratic nominee for mayor, having won a tough primary election last month. Why does he want to be mayor of the country's fourth-largest city? Because it's there; as far as I can tell, Bill Green's business is running for office. This is a verbatim account of the heart of a conversation we had the other day:

What groups or interests do you have to appeal to and to represent to be mayor of Philadelphia?

"I represent everybody. I want a constituency that includes everybody."

How do you put a constituency like that together?

"By visiting everyone."

There was a pause, and I waited.

"By meeting with them."

I waited again.

"By telling them what I want to do."

What do you want to do?

"Bring the city together."

Pause.

"End the corruption."

Pause.

"End waste. Government wastes a lot of money."

I waited again for something more specific, but that seemed to be the end of the Green program. He is the very model of a modern politician. Polls by Peter Hart of Washington. Media by David Garth of New York. Positions and programs—none if he can help it.

There were more questions, of course. Are the decisions on what to do about poor people in Philadelphia made in Philadelphia, or are they made in Washington?

"They are made in many places."

Where should those decisions be made?

"In many places."

Green, to say the least, is cautious. Perhaps he should be. He got only 51.7 percent of the Democratic primary vote against a lightly regarded black opponent. White Philadelphians voted for Green, who is white; blacks voted against him.

Maybe his color—as projected by hundreds of thousands of dollars worth of television commercials—was all voters really knew about him. Maybe they couldn't figure out what he planned to do as mayor. I couldn't.

That's the way it is with many of the young politicians who want to take over America. They prefer to campaign as media shells. Other people write their speeches and position papers. They are never forced to confront their own thinking. Their job is to be out front, looking good, promising to visit people. They want to bring people together—at the polls to vote for them. If they manage to win that way, they run for the next highest office as soon as possible.

Rosalynn Carter, I thought, was to first ladies what Bill Green was to mayoral candidates. That is not gallant, I know. It was also not a universal opinion. When I caught up with her in Los Angeles, Mrs. Carter was being projected as the president's most important advisor, sort of the power behind the Oval Office.

Maybe that was all true, but I never saw it in covering Carter for four years. As far as I could tell, she had the same kind of influence over her husband as many spouses do and it did show itself sometimes in personnel decisions. "Jimmy, I'm not sure I'd trust him. Isn't there someone else who could . . . ?"—that sort of thing.

I was mildly outraged by the first lady's little diplomatic jaunts and "substantive" meetings with leaders—she was never elected and as far as I was concerned was just another citizen—and I was probably just plain mean to her. I am told she thought that. But I did think it was what I called it in this column, "Parody Politics with the First Lady":

The deputy president of the United States came to Los Angeles the other day. She giggled a lot and said, several times, that she was having a lot of fun and these were sure exciting times. She added that polls are showing for the first time that Americans are pessimistic about their personal futures.

Rosalynn Carter is on tour. She stopped here after hitting Fresno and Dallas and Pine Bluff, Arkansas, lots of places. She is a gutsy, charming, tireless lady who has absolutely nothing to say.

If she is the president's principal advisor, as the White House seems to be signaling, then she must be telling her husband substantially more than she told the two hundred faithful Democrats who heard her, politely, at the Beverly-Wilshire Hotel.

They heard Mrs. Carter say:

"I'm having such fun. . . . I just talked to Jimmy. I call him every day. . . . He's lonely. . . . Amy is fine; she's at tennis camp. . . . He promised he would reorganize the government—and he did. . . . These are such exciting times. . . . Our country is good; our country is strong. . . . It really is an exciting time. The polls show for the first time that a majority of Americans are pessimistic about their own futures. . . Jimmy is, without a doubt, the best possible person to lead us through this time. . . . It was such a fun week."

She giggled after many of those lines. The crowd, as far as I could tell, was stunned. This must have been a significant event—there were a dozen television cameras. This must be a significant person—*Time* magazine and everybody else is saying that she's number two at the White House.

Somehow the signals got mixed. Somehow, the signals always seem to get mixed from this White House. Is Rosalynn the Iron Magnolia? Or, is she this gracious, slightly giddy lady standing up for her husband? Whatever she really is, she's no Eleanor Roosevelt. If Mrs. Carter believes in anything but Jimmy, you can't tell it by hearing her in public.

The trip was parody politics. A candidate tour without a candidate, trying to raise $250,000 from people who are mostly just being polite to a first lady. One man stood in the doorway as Mrs. Carter began speaking and said: "I can't force myself to step into that room and listen to that crap." He was a congressman for fourteen years.

The first lady's trip is a small thing. Contradictory, like almost everything out of the Carter White House. The lady being presented as the deputy leader of the free world acts like an aging debutante. All this in the name of her husband who has denounced *People* magazine as a symbol of the new American decadence and then sends his wife out to play *People* magazine politics.

Unfortunately, the signals are just as scrambled on the big things. Carter says the SALT agreement is his top priority as president. But when his administration spokesmen traveled to Capitol Hill to sell the treaty in open hearings—sent there by him to try to focus American attention on a complex issue—he decides to go to Camp David and hold his traveling domestic summit meeting with Who's Who in America. Result: No one pays any attention to the pro-SALT testimony.

Then, of course, he diverted attention from the domestic summit and the crises of energy and immorality by, in his wife's words, "reorganizing the government."

"It was not rash," Mrs. Carter said. "It's really great for the country. It's going to be good. There will be hard times, inflation, unemployment will be going up, the energy crisis will get worse . . . we'll need a good cabinet. I'm so excited about what's going on in this country."

The former congressman, walking out on Mrs. Carter, wasn't. "It's like watching a Greek tragedy that you've already read," he said. "We all know how this is going to end and no one can change it—certainly not Rosalynn Carter."

Brent Musburger was not important to me. He just happened to be the anchor person I picked to make a point about something that bothered me after traveling the country and watching night after appalling night of local television news.

Later, I admired Musburger's guts when he came up to me at a mutual friend's wedding and asked why the hell I was picking on him. It doesn't, after all, take all that much courage to sit behind a typewriter. You can say what you think and then try to stay out of sight for awhile. I learned how to do that a long time ago, back in Phillipsburg—in a small town the slum landlord you discover behind fancy corporate names can turn out to be your children's pediatrician.

Anyway, Musburger, guts and all, went back to sportscasting several months after this column appeared on August 2, 1979:

Brent Musburger, the smiling young man who used to announce pro-football scores with Phyllis George, is now the Walter Cronkite of Los Angeles. He is the new principal anchor man on KNXT-TV, the local CBS station, telling the nation's second-largest television audience about SALT and cabinet shake-ups and the state budget.

He trained for the job by being a baseball umpire and going to basketball games. It was decided he could handle affairs of state, according to CBS management, because "he's a real upbeat person."

That seems to be true; he sure smiles a lot.

That also tells you almost everything you need to know about where television news is going after the generation of Cronkites and Chancellors passes on. Their successors are being trained now as jock sniffers, charm school instructors, and weather girls—those are the backgrounds of three of the anchors giving you the news right now in New York and Los Angeles.

They are picked, as Musburger was, by audience research. I tried to get my hands on the KNXT research that resulted in Musburger's elevation, but CBS's security is better than the Pentagon's. I was told that he was picked because he had the highest "Q"-rating of any of the station's personnel—"Q" is the ratio of viewers who like your personality to those who don't like it.

The same system is sometimes used to pick the actors and actresses on comedy shows.

Earlier, KNXT and other stations had experimented with another research system that judged anchor and reporter competence by the amount of sweat each one raised on the palms of the hands of test audiences. The sweat production is supposed to be proportional to the sex appeal of the person seen on the screen. Musburger must leave them dripping.

Better things may be coming. A company called Psychophysiological Research Management is using a system that measures the brain waves of test audiences to determine their response to anchor persons. Beta waves, they say, may be even more reliable than sweat weight.

The ideal systems for television ratings and on-air auditions might not even involve test audiences in the future. The testers would scan your house and head from trucks or wristwatches.

This is a report on the possible future by Media Science Newsletter:

> The future of television and radio audience ratings may lie in personal exposure meters, worn as wristwatches; which record . . . second-by-second exposure to specific TV channels and radio stations. These instruments would measure the wavelength of broadcast stations being tuned to by receivers within twenty feet of the respondent. Would yield meter-hard data on an individual person base. Would require very little respondent effort, making high cooperation rates achievable.
>
> Tanner Electronics, Van Nuys, California, indicated the technical feasibility of these meters . . . after its earlier unsuccessful attempt to market a new rating system based on truck-mounted electronic scanners.

I just thought you'd like to know what those trucks cruising your neighborhood might be doing. I have to go now. My hands are dry and Brent Musburger is coming on.

Walter Cronkite and his retirement as the anchor man and managing editor of CBS News gave me a chance to emphasize the same point almost two years later:

> Watch the network news tonight—on CBS or NBC or ABC—and compare it with your local television news. Harry Hotcomb and Jessica Junkfood with the Eyewitness Action News Team On-the-Scene Tonight!

That is why Walter Cronkite is a great man and deserves every one of the soppy things being said about him as he retires this week. What Walter Cronkite helped to do—"helped" is an understatement—was to establish a history, a heritage, traditions for national electronic journalism.

About twenty-five years ago, Cronkite—and David Brinkley and John Chancellor and others whose names are not household words—took over, almost by accident, the most powerful journalistic medium the world has seen so far. It was a medium that happened to be run by show business and advertising people. News was a sideline, forced on the electronic media by government regulation.

Most of the new electric newsmen, but not all, came from print backgrounds, from newspapers or wire services. Cronkite, for instance, had been a reporter for United Press.

Now, reporters, specifically print reporters, tend to be a pretty shabby bunch. You might not want your son or daughter to marry one. But we do believe in certain things, like accuracy, fairness, a certain skepticism of established authority, maybe a gut instinct for injustice. We consider ourselves outsiders—even, I suspect, when we make a million dollars a year and own yachts—and we have our own language: First Amendment, anonymous sources, check the records, "But . . ."

Whatever you think of the press, those traditions and notions, I think, have served the United States pretty well over a couple hundred years. And Cronkite may have been the single most important individual in making those ideas and words part of national television news.

On the local level, in most cities, sadly, the advertising and show business folk have taken over. Cronkite, judging by a conversation we had last spring, is as worried about that as the rest of us should be. If he were to give a farewell address, as President Dwight Eisenhower did twenty years ago to warn of the dangers of the "military-industrial complex," I think he might have included some of these excerpts from our conversation:

"The new people coming into television are not print-trained, and it worries me to a certain extent. Not that print training is an absolute must, because you can prove that by the exceptions—Edward R. Murrow, Mike Wallace, for instance. But, I think, as a general thing, there are a lot of young people coming into television for the glamour of television—they don't really have a gut instinct to be journalists. And I'd kind of like to weed them out. . . .

"Up to now, those who are rising to the top in network television news are the best newspeople, not those who are seeking only the glamour. They fall by the wayside. I don't have a terrible worry about the immediate future. But as it goes down the line a couple of generations or so, I'm not sure what you are going to end up with.

"But it would be disastrous, disastrous . . . if we start using the local formula of funny talk, pretty boy-pretty girl news, trivializa-

tion of the ultimate, of the news."
That's the way it is. Good night, Walter. Thank you.

Fred Silverman, the president of NBC, not Cronkite, was the dominant figure in American television during the 1970s. That was as good a reason as any to be glad when the seventies were over. As the anchor man symbolized some of the best values of the news business, the programming "genius" promoted the worst values of show business. He was a hustler—hustling from the programming department of CBS to programming chief of ABC to president of NBC. His heritage and his legacy were lasciviously silly shows like "The Love Boat" and disturbing mixes of reality, manipulation, and deception like "Real People."

I had written about him over the years. A cover story I wrote for *Esquire* in 1978 was titled, "The Most Dangerous Man in America." That was when he moved over to NBC, where he failed so badly that the network profits began dropping almost as quickly as the money came in—and money comes in very quickly in television. But, out of false pride or real hope, NBC kept him on until June of 1981, prompting me to comment on September 14, 1980:

Fred Silverman's contract as president of NBC was renewed last week, giving him another year and a half to play tricks on television-watching America. More power to him; he is the P.T. Barnum of our time.

He's bigger than Barnum. The old showman thought there was a sucker born every minute; Silverman operates as if there were millions born every half hour.

Fast Freddy's latest trick is mortgaging the future of prime-time television. That's part of the reason he was able to save his own job despite lousy ratings at NBC. He had to keep Johnny Carson at NBC and he wanted to deprive ABC of people like Ron Howard and Rona Barrett—so he guaranteed those folks, as he has others, that they would produce and own substantial chunks of future programming on NBC.

The contract is quicker than the eye. Silverman is making a mockery of network assurances to the public—and the Justice

221

Department—that there is a free market operating in television programming. The network line is that the "viewers" dictate what's on television each night through ratings. Not true. By Silverman-negotiated contracts, Carson, Howard, and Barrett apparently have that power—and so does Gary Coleman and O.J. Simpson.

The case of Coleman, the star of a show called "Different Strokes," is an example of just how much contempt NBC has for viewers. To persuade Coleman not to leave NBC and one of its few popular shows, the network apparently guaranteed to broadcast at least three films that will be produced by him. The first of the movies is based on the life of Eva Peron. Gary Coleman, who should make about four hundred thousand dollars profit on each film, is twelve years old.

The details of these contracts are closely guarded corporate secrets. NBC has never released the details of these contracts and I have pieced together as much as I could from other industry sources. As far as I can tell, Carson will produce, and NBC must broadcast, three films and three prime-time series. Howard, whose defection from ABC is expected to kill one of that network's most profitable shows—"Happy Days"—will produce three films and two series. Simpson, the football player turned actor, will produce and star in a number of films filling eighteen hours of prime time. Barrett, NBC said, "will have something to do" with a future prime-time series.

Obviously, if those stars-turned-producers are guaranteed air time, outsiders cannot compete for those time slots. Future prime time is already spoken for, contractually. So much for open competition in the marketplace of ideas.

The Simpson case—guaranteed stardom and production revenues from NBC—raises even more interesting questions to me. He is a very visible spokesman for Hertz Rent-a-Car, which has a big financial stake in his continued celebrity now that he can no longer dodge National Football League players. NBC is essentially guaranteeing that celebrity in prime time. Both Hertz and NBC are owned by the same company, RCA—the company that just renewed Silverman's contract.

So, Silverman, who has worked for all three networks and is proudly responsible for shows from "Charlie's Angels" to "Real People," will continue to be responsible for what millions of Americans do in their spare time. And he and the rest of the people who run television will continue to make speeches boasting that "the public" decides what it wants to see. The suckers will never know the difference.

Harold J. Haynes was another corporate executive with some little power over the way Americans—and other people—lived from day to day. This column, unfriendly, was a way of talking about the real relationship, as I saw it, between "American" oil companies and Americans. It was called, "The Quotations of Chairman Oil":

"News availability" with Harold J. Haynes. It was the public relations department of Standard Oil of California's way of saying that the company's chairman and chief executive officer was holding a press conference.

Forgetting the PR jargon, the invitation was irresistible. I wanted to see one of the men who had the power to make me wait an hour and a half in a gasoline line. I wasn't disappointed when I drove up to the Biltmore Hotel in Los Angeles—a long line of Cadillac limousines, fender flags fluttering in the breeze, blocked off the street as uniformed guards and elegantly dressed men milled purposefully around the hotel lobby. It was like a movie version of power!

It was a movie version. Walt Disney Productions was filming something called "Whispers of the Gloom." Ah, California! Haynes was upstairs in a small conference room. A very ordinary looking middle-aged man. He looked as if he had worked his way up the corporate ladder of America's sixth largest industrial company from somewhere deep in the engineering department. Which he had. He began as an engineer at a Gulf Coast refinery in 1947.

Tell us about your power, everyone asked. He said he had no power, and recited a lot of mathematical formulas related to gasoline allocations and refinery capacity. He said his company and its subsidiary, Chevron, had a 16 percent shortfall against world petroleum demand and it treated all customers equally. He also used the following words and expressions: "Gee whiz . . . gosh . . . by golly . . . darned . . . my Lord!"

"Gosh," I said to Chairman Haynes after the news availability, "how many countries are your customers?"

"Seventy," he said.

223

"And you're giving each of them 16 percent less gasoline than they want?"

"Yes, that is our obligation under the law."

"Under the law? You mean federal law, treaties, things like that?"

"No, our contracts."

That was what I had come to find out. Standard Oil is not a California company. It is not an American company. It is extranational; it is a government unto itself. Its contracts are the law of the globe.

These are other quotes from Chairman Haynes:

"What do you mean, power? That is just an intelligent decision you have to make.

"It really is a very, very simple mathematical computation. There's really no mystery to the whole thing.

"There is no way that we can cut back on our operations or our customers preferentially in one part of the world compared to another. . . . We have to allocate on a fair and equitable basis around the world."

This is an exchange between Robert Scheer of the *Los Angeles Times* and the chairman:

Scheer: "But why would you want to expand in Saudi Arabia at a time (1974) when they wouldn't sell us any oil and may not be willing to sell us any in the future?"

Haynes: "When you say 'us' don't forget that we're a multinational company and we have markets in Australia, we have markets all over the world. . . . the world was not embargoed. We have responsibilities all over the world."

If he keeps talking like that, the public relations department may not make Chairman Haynes available for news any more. What he was saying, the truth, by golly, is that Standard Oil feels no particular obligation to the United States. The U.S.A. is the place it's from, the place where it goes to the government for drilling incentives, tax breaks, and subsidies to sell oil around the world.

Having made all that clear, Haynes was asked, naturally, whether he thought the United States should consider nationalizing the oil companies. He looked at his watch and said, "I guess we're running out of time." Then he looked up again and said, "They're ridiculous. Do you want the oil industry run by the postmaster general?"

No, I don't. But I would like to see the U.S. government put the screws to Chairman Haynes and his peer group. We should recognize them for what they are—as Haynes says, they are not "us"—and consider things like taking over domestic oil land that the American companies say they won't pump out or explore because it would be unprofitable. Give them two years to decide whether they'd rather do it themselves, or, have those fields put out to bids to other drillers or a public corporation that would agree to extract the last drop. It might make the oil companies reconsider their reluctance to sell anything at prices they don't set themselves; it would certainly be cheaper, no matter what it cost us, than the OPEC price increases that are inevitably coming along.

Betty Friedan. I was back to people I liked. I was back to heroes.

I was also back to the place that had come to mean the most to my wife and me, Sag Harbor, far out on Long Island. "Sag," as it is sometimes called, is a National Historic District because it still looks something like the whaling village it was in the early nineteenth century—the reason for that preservation being, as is usually the case, the fact that the town was economically depressed for more than a hundred years. Nothing new was built, so nothing old was torn down. People like us could end up owning the Greek Revival house on Main Street that a ship's captain named George Tooker had built for himself in 1841.

Things get a bit unclear here. Captain Tooker, they say, was a navigator on Commodore Matthew Perry's voyage to Japan in 1853. Whaling men were among the few Americans who really knew the Pacific in those days. Sometimes, when the old house creaks awake in the morning, we feel touched by history. Perhaps more history than we know. Tooker, it seems, may have signed on for Perry's journey to earn a presidential pardon for smuggling. The alternative was hanging.

We loved his house. There was, we knew, someone else thinking about buying it when we did. That person, we later learned, was Betty Friedan, who decided on another, older house down the street. An extraordinary woman—since I've already offered the opinion that feminism has been about the most important development of my lifetime, she seems to be an even more important

225

American than Commodore Perry. This is what I wrote about her on August 19, 1979, the first time I ever got to use a "Sag Harbor" dateline:

Newsweek magazine, in a recent cover story on American heroes, mentioned one of my summer neighbors in this little Long Island village. "The latter-day women's movement has produced no leader of a classically heroic mold," the magazine said in a statement I would disagree with, "but Betty Friedan was greatly daring in her challenge to social institutions that had hardened over the centuries."

The greatly daring Ms. Friedan was the speaker last Sunday at a fund-raising lunch for the Sag Harbor library. I wanted to hear what she had to say sixteen years after she challenged a number of hard and hardened things by writing The Feminine Mystique.

When the little lunch was over, someone asked what I thought. "I didn't hear anything particularly new. It sounded like common sense." "Maybe that's the message," said the woman with me, who is my wife. "It was not common sense to a lot of people when she started saying some of it in 1963."

No, it wasn't. Betty Friedan is significant, a hero, because she changed the way people thought—and not just American people. Over the years, she has changed some of her own thinking and this is what she had to say last Sunday:

"Don't think that I or some other witch of Salem seduced women who would otherwise be having orgasms of happiness waxing kitchen floors. The whole thing would have happened anyway . . . the women's movement was profoundly American. The values of American democracy were translated concretely in the movement. Women from Peoria, which is where I'm from, were simply saying, 'I am a person who can move in society by myself.'

"Now there are a whole new set of questions, a whole new set of problems. Women think they have to be superwomen. They have to be better than men at the work place and still have to maintain a home. Because of that pressure and the fact that so many women are being forced into the work place by inflation, there are a lot of tired women and a lot of lonely women, women alone.

"The movement will have to much more involve men than we thought back then. We should not deny the things that used to deny women—the need for security, for intimacy. I worry about the women who are not having children. Childbearing or not should be a free choice. But it is not a light decision not to have children. And the new pressures of being a superwoman are harassing a lot of younger women into making that decision."

She said she was not sure she understood all that the women's movement has wrought, that she was just beginning interviewing for a new book. But, she said, the original value of the movement—that women were people, too—has been overwhelmingly accepted and now men and women had to figure out where to go next, together.

Women, she said, could not win what they needed now by themselves. What did they need? For one thing, she said, changes in traditional working hours, modifications in the pattern of five nine-to-five days, fifty weeks a year. Those modifications would make shared parenting possible and would allow women who want to have children to pursue the same career goals and chances as men—and also keep that necessary second paycheck coming to families with children.

Changes in work patterns would not, after all, be the worst thing that ever happened to men. In America, as Ms. Friedan pointed out, men are now living an average of something like ten years less than women. We are working ourselves to death—and we probably should be listening to this fiery, wise woman again.

Arthur Angel was a Harvard Law School graduate, an attorney for a federal agency in Washington. It was the classic path of upward mobility—until he walked away from it all. It was the kind of story I had always been attracted to and I called this column, "The Greening of a Bureaucrat":

Arthur Angel, FTC GS-15, had about had it with being a bureaucrat when he read about Karen Silkwood in an old copy of *Rolling Stone* while waiting for a tennis court in Arlington, Virginia, across the Potomac from Washington. The hell with it, he thought, and he was soon on his way to Oklahoma City, volunteering to help in the lawsuit of Silkwood's heirs against Kerr-McGee Corporation.

That was in June 1978, a year ago. It hadn't been all that bad for Angel at the Federal Trade Commission. He was frustrated, but he had worked his way up from staff attoney GS-11 ($13,000 a year) to staff attorney GS-15 ($38,000 a year), and had paid off most of the $13,000 in student loans that had got him through Harvard Law School.

Something had gone wrong at the FTC, he thought, or maybe he had just stayed too long, six years—usually lawyers built their resumes for two or three years and headed for private practice. But Angel had loved the agency and his work, the primary investigations and regulation recommendations concerning funeral costs and the financing of condominiums in Florida.

Ironically, those investigations had real direction and impact when Richard Nixon was president. The reason, everyone said, was that Nixon's son-in-law, Edward Cox, had persuaded the president to take seriously the FTC critiques of Ralph Nader, for whom Cox had once worked.

But when liberal Democrats took over the agency in 1977, the talk got bigger and the results smaller. "All these 'good guys' came in with great ideas," Angel says now. "They'd expand someone's staff from six people to twenty-five and suddenly there would be three more levels of review. Everything started slowing down and you'd lose direct access to the commissioners. Finally everyone was just passing around memos saying that it would be a wonderful idea to break up the automobile companies. Talking about things that were never going to happen."

It reminded him of his undergraduate days at Berkeley. "The demonstrations were really jive," he said. "Talk, talk, talk and nothing happened. They made people feel good but they didn't accomplish anything. I figured I could sing 'We Shall Overcome' at home, then really try to hunker down and do something, something that could be done. That's when I decided to forget a doctorate in psychology and be a lawyer."

But not, anymore, a government lawyer. Angel moved to Oklahoma City and took $400-a-month in expenses to work on the civil suit that Karen Silkwood's father had filed against Kerr-McGee, the $3-billion-a-year conglomerate with major nuclear interests. The news was that Ms. Silkwood had died in a mysterious auto accident while harassing the company; the law was that the company might be held responsible for her contamination by plutonium or for violating her civil rights with clumsy surveillance.

Angel was joining the Silkwood team pretty late in the game. The

National Organization for Women had financed most of the groundwork and a roaming gang of saints and/or fanatics headed by an attorney named David Sheehan had prepared a case emphasizing the civil rights violations. A flamboyant Wyoming liability lawyer named Gerald Spence had been hired to handle the actual trial—he spoke the language of Western juries.

The kid from Washington—Angel was thirty—thought contamination was the stronger case and he began putting that together on his own, with the help of a local attorney named James Ikard. It turned out that the federal judge assigned to the case threw out the civil rights counts and Art Angel ended up planning most of the battle against a legion of Kerr-McGee attorneys.

The Silkwood team won—a $10.5 million punitive verdict. Legally, the important precedent was the ruling that a company in an inherently dangerous industry has obligations beyond meeting government safety standards.

"I'm not sure the legal results are the most important," Angel said. "We pretty well showed that everyone lied to the people working with plutonium, that's why the jury gave that award. Scientists, the government, the company, and politicians all had reasons to lie, and they did. There was a fundamental corruption. Beyond that, we showed that a ragtag bunch of unemployed lawyers, hippies, and priests could actually accomplish something against Goliath."

Now it's all over except the appeals—Angel has decided to stay in Oklahoma City and practice law—and the fights between attorneys over the contingency fees. Angel's share would be $800,000. He says he wants most of the attorney's fees to go into establishing a foundation to finance similar cases against Goliath—"I want it spent for things that can actually be done, public outrage isn't enough anymore." He does, however, want some of the money. He still owes Harvard $4,000.

Laurence Kirwan was no hippie and he was certainly no saint. He was the political boss of Rochester, New York. How he got that power was a story I wanted to tell. He, as my father used to say, got off his ass and did something about it. I wrote this column on May 20, 1979:

Larry Kirwan is one American who does not feel powerless. The president of the United States calls him every once in awhile, bankers and mayors come to his office to try to work out local problems and he personally picked a lot of the people who run his city, county, and state.

Laurence Joseph Kirwan, Democratic chairman of Monroe County, New York, has clout. This is the story of how he got it.

In March of 1970, six months after he moved to Rochester, and five years after he came to New York State, Kirwan and three friends who had worked together in local civil rights organizations went to see their Democratic ward chairman. They said they had not been active in partisan politics but wanted to be. Could they get on the ward committee?

You're kidding, the chairman said, there are no vacancies. Kirwan, an insurance underwriter, knew that wasn't true because he had bought his house from a committee member who had moved out of town. "Get out of here," the chairman said.

The four friends did, going to the county court house and looking up the list of 2,000 Democrats registered in the ward. They knew 141 of them personally. They called them, lined up candidates for the forty-eight committee seats, and then began going door-to-door. The campaign cost less than twenty dollars and they won forty-three of the forty-eight seats.

Two years later, using the same mundane techniques, Kirwan was elected chairman of the county committee. One of the techniques, incidentally, was running women candidates for half the committee seats—that was considered revolutionary stuff in 1970.

The title was nice and so was the pay, $24,000 a year, but it wasn't as if the thirty-one-year-old "boss" had anyone to boss around. Monroe, with a population of seven hundred fifty thousand people, had been Republican as long as anyone could remember—and Kirwan was elected chairman on the same night in 1972 that his party nominated George McGovern for president. George Eastman used to run Rochester politics as conservatively as he ran his company, Kodak. When Kirwan took over, the Republicans held every county-wide office and controlled the county legislature and the Rochester city council. Not surprising, considering that over 70 percent of Monroe's voters were registered Republicans.

"We studied each constituency," said Kirwan, "and figured out what would sell." One assembly district, for instance, was about evenly divided between Italian working-class families and people associated with local colleges. Kirwan found a State University of New York dean with an Italian name. The dean is now a three-term assemblyman, one of three Democrats representing Monroe in the state's lower house. The Rochester Council is now eight-to-one Democratic, the party controls the county legislature and has elected a state senator, sheriff, district attorney, and six judges.

And Larry Kirwan is a happy man. Politics is a helluva lot more fun than selling insurance, even if he still earns more money from his own agency—which has no government business. He handpicks candidates who just might win and has used his position to become a civic leader bringing together Republican businessmen and Democratic politicians.

"It was extraordinarily easy," he says now. "There is no system that is more open and vulnerable to takeover than politics. The organizations are a myth. You touch them and they crumble. That's the dirty little secret."

So, Kirwan's a force in Rochester—a force for good or bad, depending on who's talking. He found it as simple as Sen. Gary Hart says it is in Colorado. Hart once told me he thought any public official in his state could be elected by as few as ten people, if they were willing to work hard enough.

Maybe all that just demonstrates how low politics has sunk in public interest and esteem. But that's the way it is these days. People who think it isn't may be spending too much time watching television and complaining about how they're being screwed by big shots like Larry Kirwan.

William O. Douglas died while I was in his home state of Washington. I thought he was a great man and, now, a little bit of a Westerner myself, a very little bit, I thought I knew more about why he was extraordinary. This is what I wrote on January 18, 1980:

I was driving from Walla Walla to Seattle last weekend and the little city of Yakima was the place to stop for coffee. I picked up the local paper, the *Herald-Republic*, and found myself reading that Roy Neilan had telephoned Al Egley the day before and said: "Al, Bill Douglas died this morning."

It's the kind of call men their age, in their eighties, have to make every once in awhile. Another friend was gone. Well, not just another friend. This one was William O. Douglas, the man who served the longest on the United States Supreme Court.

"Yakima's most famous man," the *Herald-Republic* called him. This same paper, on the day in 1939 when Franklin D. Roosevelt appointed Douglas to the court, had published an angry editorial under the headline, "Don't Blame Yakima."

There was no sign that Douglas had ever lived in this city of fifty thousand. The house on North Fifth Avenue where Douglas grew up on the wrong side of the railroad tracks that bisect the town was torn down about twenty years ago to make room for a school administration building. The three-story United States post office and court house at South Third and East Chestnut streets is officially named the William O. Douglas Court House, but there is no plaque or sign mentioning his name. Someone, though, did think to lower the American flag to half-mast on Sunday.

Hell, Yakima never knew what to make of Douglas, even when he was the debate coach at Yakima High School back in 1922 before going on to Columbia Law School and controversial fame as chairman of the Securities and Exchange Commission and thirty-six years on the Supreme Court.

Even though he kept his vacation home near here, at Gooseprairie, in the Cascade Mountains, and was often around town, shopping and talking to friends, he was an outcast. The three divorces and the young wives, the liberal decisions and dissents— they didn't like that here. And he didn't like the feudal society of the Yakima he remembered, the nice Presbyterians who ignored his widowed mother and let him go to work when he was six years old.

But Yakima, the isolation, the free, breath-taking beauty of the mountains, and the class system made him what he was. The town's strange, bitter son was a true Westerner and, modern history has shown, a great man.

Somehow he understood America. "The right to be left alone is the beginning of all freedom," he said. And: "This country is the product of revolution. Our very being emphasizes that when grievances pile high and there are no political remedies, the exercise of sovereign power reverts to the people. . . . The airing of ideas relieves pressures which otherwise might become destructive."

A conversation I had a few weeks ago with another Supreme Court justice clarified my own ideas about what Douglas meant to the country and why it was important that he was from a far place, a Western place like Yakima. We weren't talking about Douglas, but about the modern role of the courts and the justice said: "When the country began, a non-conformist could always go West. There was always space for people who were different. Now that frontier, the West, is gone, and the courts are providing that space. The courts have been called on to protect the right of individuals, to replace the frontier."

That's what William O. Douglas was about. That's what the Revolution was about. That's what the United States of America is about.

On Sunday, the *Herald-Republic* conceded that Yakima should be proud of its most famous son. Now, maybe somebody will finally get around to putting a plaque on the front of the William O. Douglas Post Office and Court House.

The space for people who are different—it is the most precious American resource and one of the hardest to keep. And some of us have to fight the battle to keep that space, which is called freedom.

They are the heroes of our time. That, at least, is what I thought when an editor asked me to write about heroes. It was Clay Felker, again. After losing the magazine he had created, *New York*, he came back to become the editor of the magazine where he had learned his trade, *Esquire*. In his first issue—March 1, 1978—he wanted a cover story on heroes. He said to go find them. I tracked down four men and *Esquire* called them, "The Last Angry Men":

"Whatever happened to that guy Hanrahan?" I asked a friend who worked on the *Washington Post*.

"I don't know," he said.

"Did he go back to the *Post*?"

"No."

Nobody I knew at the *Post* wanted to talk about John Hanrahan. He had been the newspaper's assistant Maryland editor on October

1, 1975 when pressmen vandalized their own equipment and went on strike.

I began asking out of vague curiosity; I had never met the man. Friends just changed the subject, usually shifting their gaze to something on my left shoulder. What was going on? All I knew was that he was one of the reporters who had said that they could not stand by if management brought in strikebreakers to replace the pressmen—but a lot of reporters, some of whom worked at the beginning of the strike and some of whom didn't, had said the same thing. What I didn't find out until later was that Hanrahan was the only one who meant it. John Hanrahan would not cross a picket line: "Everyone here on both sides has something to be ashamed of," one friend said. The strikebreakers came and he was the only reporter who gave up that kind of career because . . .

Because . . . why? Because of a principle? A thousand men and women can live with crossing a line—but one will not, no matter what the price. Maybe he was just a nut—before my friends at the *Post* turned away from the subject of Hanrahan, a couple mumbled something about his being "a little crazy." Maybe they all were, the angry ones: Curt Flood suing baseball; Ernest Fitzgerald blowing the whistle at the Pentagon; Frank Johnson taking on the whole state of Alabama for more than twenty years. There must be others, but the list is short—there are not many that brave in the land of the free.

The price, I thought, must be very high. It turned out to be higher than I had imagined. While I was looking for Flood, the little St. Louis outfielder who sued professional baseball over the reserve clause in 1969, a friend of his said: "Maybe you should leave him alone. Look, he took on something very big and it broke him." Being curious about John Hanrahan became a search for heroes—for men who stood up to the system. I wanted to find out why they did it, what happened to them, what they accomplished. What I found out seemed crushing at first: If you buck the system, you are almost inevitably going to be destroyed. The men I searched out lost jobs and friends, endured a frightening loneliness punctuated by death threats and bombings, three of their children ended up deeply disturbed and one a suicide. All of that came to seem almost predestined: To keep the rest of us in line, established power had to make brutal examples of those who dared to challenge the order of things. In the end, though, it wasn't sad. Because some of us would not bend, the rest of us had the small measure of freedom that came with the tiny chance that we might be the next to stand up.

John Hanrahan hardly looked like the one guy who would stand up. But he didn't look crazy, either. He was just a slight, bearded thirty-nine-year-old man who gave up a $30,000-a-year job near the top of his profession because he believed in something: unions. "No matter how imperfect they are," he said when we met, "unions are the only existing means workers have to get a fair shake from management. If I crossed that picket line, I would have tilted the balance slightly more in favor of management, and I couldn't do that."

It cost him. Hanrahan lives only a few blocks from me in Washington, but it's a different kind of neighborhood. His house cost him $17,500 four years ago in one of the most inflated real-estate markets in the country. Still, the mortgage, taxes, and utilities cost $750 a month. He made less than $15,000 in 1977—half his 1975 earnings—from some free-lance writing and study projects for a union and a citizens' group auditing the military budget. There's no money now for the renovation he and his wife, Debby, began when he was at the *Post*. The walls and ceilings are exposed and blankets cover doorways and windows to keep in the heat.

"The money part is tough, but you just cut back," A. Ernest Fitzgerald told me. When the air force eliminated his job as deputy for management systems in 1969, he was making $31,000 a year. He made about $20,000 a year for the next four years while he sued to get his job back, essentially arguing that his dismissal was retribution for testifying before Congress that cost overruns might reach $2 billion on Lockheed's C-5A transport aircraft. He simply believed in the first principle: telling the truth.

He proved that point in court and the air force was forced to give him back his office and a salary, but no work. They try to ignore him, but that's not always easy because Fitzgerald is a gregarious man who loves to play Alabama country boy. "Hi, Whitey," he called to a barely nodding man as we walked into one of the Pentagon's generals' messes. Who's that? "Hans Driessnack," Fitzgerald said. "He used to be my military assistant; he was also 'T-1,' one of the informants listed in the Office of Special Investigations reports when they were after me, trying to prove I had a conflict of interest or was a homosexual or something." Driessnack was a colonel then. He is a major general now and budget director of the air force. Like almost everyone else involved in destroying Fitzgerald's career—including Defense Secretary Harold Brown, who was then the secretary of the air force—Driessnack has since done very well for

235

himself.

"I didn't get it at first," Fitzgerald said. "I had made more than thirty thousand dollars a year as a consultant before coming to the air force in 1965. My old clients wouldn't talk to me in 1970. Somebody finally told me that I was blacklisted in the defense business. They told me I should open a gas station if I wanted to work."

Blacklisting is in the frequent nightmares of Curt Flood. Money is, too, even though he insists that he put some away in his $100,000-a-year days as one of the finest center fielders in the recent history of the business that calls itself the Great American Pastime. He's forty now and he has not really worked for the past two years, not since spending $100,000 in legal fees and returning home from five tortured years in Europe. What he wants to work in is baseball— "C'mon, I'm just a jock"—but he is convinced that he is the last man baseball will ever touch. He was—and is reminded of it every day— the black man who sued professional baseball over its legalized slavery, the reserve clause. When his suit was filed in 1969, the clause totally bound each player to one team—the athlete could take what they offered him or leave the game.

Flood did leave in 1970, refusing a trade from the St. Louis Cardinals to the Philadelphia Phillies. He stated a rather basic principle then, one with more than a few echoes in American history: "I am a man, not a consignment of goods to be bought and sold."

The United States Supreme Court ruled two years later that that was true, unless you were a baseball player. He lost, but the Flood case did help set in motion a series of events that won those rights for other men, people like Reggie Jackson, who was able to sell his talents to the New York Yankees for $600,000 a year. But by that time Curt Flood was home, alone, in Alameda, California.

"Please, please, don't come out here," he said when I reached him by telephone. "Don't bring it all up again. Do you know what I've been through? Do you know what it means to go against the grain in this country? Your neighbors hate you. Do you know what it's like to be called the little black son of a bitch who tried to destroy baseball, the American Pastime?"

We talked, and finally he agreed to meet me at a junior high school in Sacramento. A friend had asked him to speak at a Martin Luther King Day assembly. Most of the kids did not know who he was and asked the questions you'd expect: How many years did you play with the Cardinals? What was your lifetime batting average? How many homers did you hit? How many World Series did you play in?

What was the most money you made? Twelve. .293. Not many. Three—against Boston, New York, and Detroit. A hundred and ten thousand dollars a year. But a fourteen-year-old named Eddie Mejorado did know what Curt Flood had done. "What did the free agents give you? Do they write you to thank you, or call?"

"No," Flood said. "No one has called."

At that moment, he looked very alone and small. He is only five feet nine and his athletic stardom must have been classic over-achievement. And he must often feel that way. When he talked about the owners of baseball, Flood said, "I suddenly realized that it was just me against nineteen multimillionaires." For a long time he looked into the straight vodka he was drinking, then said, "The first trial in New York lasted six weeks. No one showed up. Not one ballplayer came. My roommate didn't come. I roomed with Bob Gibson for ten years. Maybe I wouldn't have showed up either. I would have been afraid, too."

That isolation is a more fearsome price than the money. The Amish know exactly what they are doing when they "shun" a brother; so do the Russians when they make a comrade a "nonperson." Fitzgerald remembered the moment he returned to his office after testifying about the Lockheed cover-up. There were the beginnings of a small pile of call messages on his secretary's desk—each one a cancelled invitation to a meeting, party, or dinner. It works both ways, though—Debby Hanrahan carries sunglasses everywhere and puts them on when she sees acquaintances from the old days. "It triggers too many memories to see an old friend," her husband said. "It just hurts too much."

The lasting image of Federal Judge Frank Johnson that comes to me is not one of a stern jurist ordering Montgomery, Alabama, to integrate or the police of Selma to allow a civil-rights march. It is one of Johnson, with armed U.S. marshals watching, playing golf at Maxwell Air Force Base, walking on the green, alone. Marshals have been guarding the fifty-nine-year-old judge for twenty-two years, since he gave Martin Luther King, Jr., his first victory, ruling that a black woman named Rosa Parks could sit anywhere she wanted to on a Montgomery bus. That and a hundred locally unpopular decisions like it did not cost Frank Johnson any money. But it twice may have cost him appointment to the United States Supreme Court because of the livid opposition of the Alabama congressional delegation, and it may have cost him much more. His only son, Johnny, who was harassed in classrooms and on the street all through school, once said: "You have no idea what it's been like being Frank Johnson's son. . . . There has always been something to keep us on edge." A year after he said that, Johnny Johnson committed suicide in his father's guarded home.

Johnson does not like to talk about himself, but his friends explain him by pointing to a three-word answer he once gave when asked about principle: "Follow the law." He is a Republican and had never been involved in civil rights or anything like it when he was appointed a federal district court judge by President Eisenhower in 1955. He dealt with the cases that inevitably filled his docket in troubled times—eliminating the Alabama poll tax, abolishing the red-neck power of justices of the peace, reapportioning the state legislature, integrating the state police. And they hated him for it.

The troubles—and heroism, if it is that—come gradually, incrementally. Ernest Fitzgerald says that the people who hate him have forgotten that he did not exactly roar into a hearing room in the New Senate Office Building demanding that the government clean up waste in defense spending. He was asked directly, by Senator William Proxmire, about the accuracy of congressional reports that the C-5A was running $2 billion over air force cost estimates. Others lied: Fitzgerald waffled bureaucratically for a few sentences and concluded: "Your figure could be approximately right."

Hanrahan sure as hell never intended to take on the *Washington Post* all by himself. He was just another guy, a member of the Newspaper Guild who avoided the union's boring, internally politicized meetings, when the tangled history of confrontation between management and Local 6 of the Newspaper and Graphic Communications Union came to violence in 1975. After busting up the pressroom, more or less depending on which side's damage estimates one choses to believe, and beating up a foreman, the pressmen threw their picket line around the *Post* building. Almost in tears, Hanrahan called his boss and said, "I can't cross a picket line."

There was no easy decision for reporters, many of whom had always been pretty articulate in arguing cases for the downtrodden against capitalist oppressors. The Washington-Baltimore local of the Guild voted to honor the picket line along with fifteen hundred members of craft unions, while the *Post* unit voted to cross the line. More than five hundred Guild members went in and about three hundred stayed out, including fifty reporters and editors. Like most reporters, the ones who stayed out probably had no great love for the Guild but were grateful for the wages and working conditions it

238

had won in an industry where company benevolence was increasingly tested by the number of young people who wanted reporting jobs and were willing to do them for less than the people who had them, particularly at a glamour paper like the *Post*. Joseph Mastrangelo, a fifty-four-year-old writer in the paper's style section, was haunted by scenes of soldiers tear-gassing strikers that he had seen as a child outside Boston. "I had to decide," Mastrangelo said, "between pulling my kids out of college and kicking myself the rest of my life." He did walk through the pickets, then ran—ran into a men's room and threw up.

Ten weeks after the strike began, the *Post* announced its intention to hire permanent nonunion pressmen at less than six dollars an hour and assign them to nine-man crews, compared to the nine-dollar-an-hour and twelve-man crews of the union. The *Post*, in its own statements, was regaining control of its own property from thugs; in the language of organized labor, it was busting a union. For John Hanrahan, it was only a matter of time before he had to decide whether to keep his job or his resolve.

Fitzgerald knew that much on November 25, 1968, twelve days after he testified before Congress' Joint Economic Committee. He received a "notification of personnel action" that day stating that the earlier notification that he held Civil Service tenure was "a computer error"—the first and only error of its kind in air force history, according to later court testimony. What he did not know yet was that memoranda were already being prepared for Secretary Harold Brown on how to get rid of him. Or that a memo in the secretary's office on the day of his truth telling was headed "Re: Fitzgerald spilling his guts" and included these recommendations: "Prepare bland responses . . . muzzling."

Fitzgerald, who was then forty-two years old, had struck deeper than he knew into the inner life of the fabled military-industrial complex. By exposing cost overruns, he was attacking the spectacularly high overhead charged by defense contractors. What that meant was angrily explained to him once by an air force general: "Look, Fitzgerald, I'm going to retire in a year or two and I'll become part of some contractor's overhead. If I cut overhead allowances, I'll be cutting my own throat."

He was going to be hit hard and the people doing it were going to laugh at newspaper puzzlement over why the Pentagon would make a martyr of him. "What they did was good, sound management practice," Fitzgerald told me nine years later in his impotent office. "They were offering an object lesson to everyone else. They've got to make an example of people who get out of line. They teach it in business schools—communicating by deeds. They can say whistle blowing is wonderful as long as they show what happens to people who try it."

Management called Curt Flood on October 8, 1969. The man on the phone was Jim Toomey, assistant to the general manager of the St. Louis Cardinals of the National League. "Curt, you've been traded to Philadelphia," he said. "You, McCarver, Hoerner, and Byron Browne. For Richie Allen, Cookie Rojas, and Jerry Johnson. Good luck, Curt." First he thought he would just retire—he was thirty-two and might have only two or three good years left—but on December 24, he decided to sue, sending a letter to baseball commissioner Bowie Kuhn that said: "I do not feel that I am a piece of property to be bought and sold irrespective of my wishes. . . ." Kuhn answered: "I certainly agree with you, that you, as a human being, are not a piece of property to be bought and sold. . . . However, I cannot see its application to the situation at hand."

He spent the summer of 1970, in his words, "bedding and boozing"—and watching his case and his career booted through the federal judiciary to the Supreme Court. It was destined to end up there because what Flood was challenging was baseball's unique exemption from U.S. antitrust laws, an exemption sanctioned in 1922 by the Supreme Court because baseball was, after all, America. In 1971, he made a sad thirteen-game comeback with the Washington Senators, but it was gone—he couldn't hit the high fast ball. Already starting each day with a beer and ending with vodka martinis, pained that people were watching him play badly, Flood disappeared; he fled to Majorca and bought part of a small bar and restaurant that he called the Rustic Inn. He was there on June 23, 1972—four days after it happened—when he read in the *International Herald Tribune* that he had lost in the Supreme Court; the score was 5–3. The bitterness sank in deeper; even the justices who voted against him attacked the reserve clause, but they said that Congress, not the Court, was responsible for remedying such an obvious injustice.

In Sacramento, after Flood talked to the students, the past seven years of his life were replayed. There were two television sportscasters waiting for him. Creighton Sanders of KXTV was first, repeating the old questions: "Aren't these big salaries ruining baseball?" "Aren't ballplayers really overpaid?" *Aren't you trying to destroy the*

American way of life, you black son of a bitch? Flood was polite, pointing out that baseball is making more money than ever and asking how much a Reggie Jackson or a Tom Seaver is worth when all those people are willing to pay to watch them. The second questioner was Bill Madlock, a twenty-seven-year-old black man who works for KCRA when he isn't hitting .302 and earning $200,000 a year with the San Francisco Giants. "Would you do it again?" "Are you blackballed from baseball?" "Would you like to get back in?" Yes. Yes. Yes.

Madlock, who is one of the beneficiaries of the reserve-clause modifications the Major League Baseball Players Association won in arbitration in the years after the Flood case, was almost in awe of Flood when we talked about him later: "You know, if it weren't for Curt Flood I wouldn't be living in that big house and getting a couple of thousand dollars for going to a banquet. . . . I grew up in Decatur, Illinois. I saw him play a lot. He was *good*. It's like a war. You send your best soldier out to scout and he doesn't come back. He's not there to celebrate the victory.

"He says he's doing fine. That's not true, is it?"

Something like that. Flood and I talked for a long day in the comfortable little town house he shares with an impressive woman and her two teen-age sons in Alameda, just across the Oakland line. Nice people. There is not too much of him there—a plaque of the 1968 All-Star team, one of five with C. Flood in CF; two very good portraits he painted, one of Lou Brock when they were young Cardinal teammates, the other one of his five children, now with their mother, the woman he married twice. He said again that he was fine, that he owned a little property, that he'd like to get back to painting. He came home because it was home—his ninety-two-year-old mother lives nearby, his children are in Los Angeles, and in the local bars he frequents he is still treated, loved a little, as the hometown boy who made good. "What can you do?" he said. "You sit in Alameda and think about all the things you should have done."

"He's the most sensitive man you'll ever meet, he's like an exposed nerve," said Richard Carter, who helped Flood write a book in 1971. And the monolith that runs baseball had an unerring instinct for how to hurt Curt Flood. The owners and all their tame sportswriters said over and over again that it was Flood who was trying to hurt people, that this greedy little guy was trying to take baseball away from children of all ages. That got him—he is by nature almost embarrassingly anxious to make other people comfortable, to make sure the people with him aren't upset. When I asked him about being black, about whether that had anything to do with what he did, he thought awhile and said, "Being black is always having people being cautious about what they call you"—the thing about being black, he was saying, was that it made other people uncomfortable.

Institutions with interests to protect or secrets to keep are very good at whipping up pressures or building up public opinion against the individual by questioning his motives, credibility, sanity, or sexual preferences. The isolation is usually enough, and if not, violence comes next: Frank Johnson's mother's house was bombed in 1967, and like a couple of others, he receives death threats that come like Christmas cards. When Ernest Fitzgerald's C-5A testimony was publicly supported by a production controller named Henry Durham in the Marietta, Georgia, plant where Lockheed was constructing the big planes, signs began to appear around the town with two words: KILL DURHAM. Durham's job was eliminated and the mood got so rough in Marietta—the local paper began calling him a public enemy, an ignorant nod to Henrik Ibsen—that federal marshals were called in to guard the former executive before he left town. The telephoned threat that finally did it was a promise to throw acid in his young daughter's face. Mrs. Durham, a religious woman, was removed as a Sunday-school teacher—a Christian penance that had been applied to Frank Johnson years earlier in Montgomery. When Nan Durham wrote about that to Billy Graham, asking for help and guidance, the evangelist's office sent her an envelope full of Bible pamphlets.

When I told that story to Gail Sheehy, the author of *Passages*, she said, "Do you know why they really crucified Christ?" Why? "Because he was such an embarrassment to other men. They had to get him out of their sight, like the people you're writing about."

Henry Durham's sin was the same as the transgression of Ibsen's Dr. Thomas Stockmann, the public enemy who warned that the town baths were polluted. In American terms, Durham was not a team player. That was the charge jabbed at Fitzgerald when the new Nixon Administration decided to keep up the pressure first applied on the air force bureaucrat in the Johnson years. A confidential memo to Nixon's chief of staff, H.R. Haldeman, spelled out the reasoning:

"Fitzgerald is no doubt a top-notch cost expert, but he must be given very low marks in loyalty; and after all, loyalty is the name of the game. Only a basic no-goodnik would take his official business grievances so far from normal channels. We should let him bleed for a while at least. . . ."

The memo was written on January 20, 1970, by a Haldeman assistant named Alexander Butterfield. Within four years, he was bleeding for disloyalty, having trouble getting work after he testified that President Nixon was tape-recording Oval Office conversations.

There is a poster, the gift of a friend four years ago, in the bathroom of John Hanrahan's house. It's from Jamaica and states part of the lore of the Rastafari Brethren: "If every man, black and white, yellow and red, does not make significant steps in their personal lives toward the Freedom of Man, then they shall all suffer at the hands of their own reluctance."

Reluctance seems to be the code of the land. News-magazines trumpet a new individualism in the land, but it emerges as a very old egocentricity, a self-centeredness. When my father told me to be an individual, to "act like a man," he didn't mean going along, covering my ass. There are so few men, so many asses. Why?

One of the people with whom I wanted to talk about that was Charles Peters, the publisher and editor of the feisty little *Washington Monthly*. He's not the last one, and he has not faced crushing opposition, but he is unbending, an angry man. He has a message much like my father's, and if he did not have a magazine to spread the word, Peters would go door to door saying, "We need risk takers. . . . We need people who are willing to shed their institutional cocoons and stand or fall on the basis of their actual performance. . . . What we have is everybody protecting everybody else's feather bed. You do it because you want yours protected in return. That's why they had to protect the Lockheed secret and go after poor Ernie Fitzgerald."

Peters walked out of his feather bed in 1968, leaving a protected $25,800-a-year GS-18 job as director of evaluation of the Peace Corps to start his little magazine to slash at feather beds, usually with thoughtful exposes of the doings of the federal bureaucracy. Since then he has been paying himself $20,000 a year, keeping the magazine going by mortgaging and remortgaging his home. The rising Washington real-estate market has been his biggest backer and currently he's into the banks for $43,000.

Charlie Peters sees the energy of a nation going down the drain as people become more mobile and have to identify one another with badges—badges that are usually flashed in answer to the second question, "Who are you with?" "That's what's most depressing of all," he said, "the compulsion of men to seek their identities in the gaudier identity of someone or something they perceive to be greater than they are. . . . The classic example is the beautiful-girl problem at a New York cocktail party. If you want to get anything going, when she says hello you've got ten seconds to make your move before her eyes start wandering. You can hold her if you say you're with the *New York Times*, or Jimmy Carter, or Hitler."

If anyone is searching for other reasons to stick with the team, there's always "the wife and kids." That was laughed at by most of the people I found. John Hanrahan, who has four-year-old twins, said he and his wife never even talked about giving in to the *Post*: "We know each other too well for that." Ernest Fitzgerald said: "I found out that families are the easy excuse. Families are usually stronger than the men."

There were a thousand reasons not to stand alone at the *Washington Post*, and I think I heard most of them. "It was very complicated." . . . "You don't understand—you have to put things in perspective." . . . "We have nothing in common with the cretins in the shop, and they make a good buck already." . . . "Because I knew that anyone who bucked management was never going anywhere around here." . . . "They're not so bad here. They're very good on the little things—the publisher says hello on the elevator, they know your name."

On February 15, 1976, the mailers' union accepted the *Post*'s "final" offer—a "bad" offer, union leaders said, but the alternative was probably losing their jobs to strikebreakers—then the pressmen and a few supporters like Hanrahan were left outside the building. There was a real attempt to persuade the assistant Maryland editor to come back. Some of it was infuriating: editors calling Debby Hanrahan and saying, "Look, tell John we'll forgive him." Some of it was tempting: Hanrahan's onetime boss, Barry Sussman, called and said, "John, you were right. But don't make a mistake now. Come back." In April, Donald Graham, the publisher's thirty-one-year-old son and the paper's assistant general manager, took Hanrahan to dinner, but they had trouble understanding each other. They shook hands and Donnie Graham said, "Good luck, John. I mean it." The termination letter came on June 20, 1976.

"Part of me said, 'Yeah, go back,' " Hanrahan said. "But I kept thinking that if this had happened someplace else, the *Post* would be denouncing it. They'd be saying, 'OK, the union made a mistake, but there are principles involved here.' In my whole life I'd never been tested. I was a reporter, I could sit back in judgment of other people. Now there was a principle involved. . . . What happened seemed unfair to me. . . . I knew one person wasn't going to make a difference. But he can try. I tried."

Why? Why John Hanrahan? Or Fitzgerald or Flood? Frank Johnson? Their backgrounds were quite different and only Johnson's suggested that he was born and raised to be what he is today. The judge is a true son of "the Free State of Winston," Winston County, Alabama—stunningly rugged northern Alabama hill country that hid the fiercely independent mountain men who fought with the Union in the Civil War. Winston has not changed that much since a local named Curtis spent the ten years after the war tracking down the Confederate soldiers involved in the torturous deaths of his three brothers—he killed each of the surviving rebels. Beneath the robes he wears only occasionally on the bench, Judge Johnson is that kind of man even if his vision of justice is more modern. He is rigid, certain in his convictions, among them that real men always drink their coffee black, smoke unfiltered cigarettes, chew good-tasting Red Man, and stick with Schlitz, "the only decent beer for a man to drink."

John Hanrahan is from Fort Dodge, Iowa. He always wanted to be a newspaperman and began working for the local paper when he was a teenager. That work took him into the back shop and he put in time around presses and linotype machines—an experience, he found, that gave him a somewhat different attitude toward blue-collar workers than that of his colleagues at the *Post*. After earning a journalism degree at the University of Iowa, he went to the *Davenport Daily Times* as a sportswriter, eventually took off for Washington and worked his way up from the *Montgomery County* (Maryland) *Sentinel* to the *Washington Star* and, finally, the *Post* in 1968. The Davenport paper was nonunion, so he knew what it was to work for $90 a week when Guild papers were paying in the $150-to-$200 range. The people he worked with tended to describe him in the same way: solid, unusually diligent. He was no star and probably never would be, but a *Post* editor offered him the chance to carve out his own investigative beat on the metropolitan staff a couple of months before the strike began.

"Diligent" was a word I also heard a few times about Fitzgerald and Johnson—sometimes "too diligent" was used for both. The

245

same could once have been said about Flood, who went a long way with what he jokingly calls "just this little body."

But "simple" was the word that fascinated me. It was as close as I could come to figuring them out, to understanding why they are heroes—and to me they are the real heroes of my time. They were not crusaders—Fitzgerald has become one, a frustrated one—they did not go forth looking for a battle, for dragons, arenas, and crowds. They are different from Ralph Nader and Daniel Ellsberg, who are not simple men. I don't think Frank Johnson would have taken on the whole South unless the civil-rights cases were brought to his court, his home. Curt Flood may have wanted nothing more than to stay out of Philadelphia—he would not have been the first to feel that way. John Hanrahan never intended to give up a good job for a principle he had barely thought of over the years.

"John's everything he seems to be," said Elizabeth Becker, a *Post* reporter who worked with Hanrahan during the strike and then went back. "How many people can you say that of in a lifetime? John is a simple man, and I mean that in the best sense of the word. He is a clear man. He sees clearly."

In Ernest Fitzgerald's case, the air force's special investigation cleared him of conflicts of interest and interesting sexual behavior, but it did quote one informant as having said: "Mr. Fitzgerald was sincere and dedicated but things were either 'black or white,' 'right or wrong,' and usually his own ideas were the ones he considered right." Fitzgerald doesn't argue with that: "I didn't do anything I didn't do my whole life, only it was public this time." And this time Fitzgerald's ideas were the ones that were right.

So what? So, as John Hanrahan said, they tried. Frank Johnson made a big difference in this country. The others doubt that they have. "Most people think I'm an asshole," said Fitzgerald, who now owes $400,000 in the legal fees it took to get his job back with no work to do in it. "The main frustration is that it doesn't seem to do that much good. . . . Maybe there's a cumulative public impact. People may be getting an idea of how the defense industry really works."

Maybe. Maybe he's just one angry man—alone. Like Samuel Abelman, M.D. Dr. Abelman, the hero of Gerald Green's 1977 novel, *The Last Angry Man*. The foulmouthed old nut who was stuck in a Brooklyn slum cursing and curing a humanity he was sure wasn't worth the effort. I loved that book, loved Dr. Abelman. How did the young television hotshot from Greenwich describe the old doctor. . . .

"The disappointments had been many, the moments of triumph too few, and his sixty-eight years had been, to a great extent, a succession of losing battles. Yet he was not a man to pity, or to shed tears over, or to offer charity. Far from having been beaten, he was ascendant. . . . he was still in the race, conceding nothing, compromising nothing, challenging everything . . . cursing the crap artists who knew the arts of control.

"There aren't enough people left who get mad, plain mad. Not mad for a cause or a purpose, but generally mad at all the bitchery and fraud. We take fraud for granted. We accept it. We like it. We want to be had. That's where he was different. He knew he was being cheated and he didn't like it one tiny bit. . . . He was the last angry man."

No. Abelman was not the last. Neither is Fitzgerald. If he was, then who are the people who keep slipping Defense Department documents under his door? At home and in his Pentagon office Fitzgerald finds unmarked envelopes containing memoranda and calculations documenting big and small outrages in defense spending. As soon as he gets those papers and figures them out, they find their way into print—in Jack Anderson's column, in Charlie Peters' magazine. Part of the cumulative effect. Some people in there care enough to get those things to Fitzgerald, and someday more people out there may care enough to do something about it. That would be only fair, because men like Ernest Fitzgerald have done a lot for the rest of us. Power—the crap artists who know the arts of control— does have to take into account that anyone could be the next angry man. They can stomp on Ernie Fitzgerald, but because of him Henry Durham pops up to plague them. They can beat Curt Flood, but because of him they have to live with Reggie Jackson and a lot of talented kids they haven't heard of yet. Men like Flood and Fitzgerald did it for all of us and we scorn them, maybe because we're ashamed of ourselves. Maybe because we're too embarrassed to admit that they're what keep us going.

"Please," Debby Hanrahan said, "don't say that this is sad, that we're sad. John has never been happier. I've never been happier. He's a free man."

Yes, he is. After the last pickets from the pressmen's union finally gave up in March 1977, John Hanrahan walked into the Post Pub, the *Washington Post*'s drinking place. A woman at the bar, a woman he did not know who took classified ads on the telephone, got up and hugged him. She began to cry and said, "John, someday you'll be able to tell your kids what you did. I don't know what the rest of us are going to say."

I called Ernie Fitzgerald and John Hanrahan as I finished putting together this book. "I'm doing fine," said Fitzgerald, whose legal fees have now reached $800,000. "I'm still suing, they're still stalling. But one of these days I'm going to force them to take a real look at where all this money is going."

"I started my own business," Hanrahan said. "We're legal investigators. I do my reporting now for law firms instead of newspapers. We're doing pretty well. I learned a lot—about myself and about other people. There were hard times. Very hard, you know that. But I have no regrets."

My own times were not as hard. Jet lag is hardly permanent. But I thought I learned a lot, too. The lag that stuck with me was between governed and government. That may be permanent, a product of the speed of modern communications and the inevitably delayed reactions of government. Again and again, traveling between coasts, I thought I was seeing a frustrating, sometimes dangerous, sometimes comical gap between what was happening in Woodland Hills, California, or Cincinnati, Ohio, and what was happening in Washington, D.C. The people I was learning about and from seemed to be struggling to build a new country or, at least new lives for themselves.

They, those people "out there," had, for all practical purposes, the same information as their governors in Washington—that was what the communications revolution was all about. But they were acting on it more quickly than any government could, particularly a federal government that sometimes seemed to be trying to see whether it can strangle itself in webs of functions and functionaries. That lag, it seemed to me, showed itself in different perceptions of war and peace, and in simmering revolts over taxation or over crime. The underground economy, after all, more significantly than political actions like tax-cutting propositions, was a direct assault on Washington. But Washington had trouble keeping up—perhaps, through the federal courts and the Congress, it was a government condemned to deal with the rights of criminals while its citizens organized neighborhood patrols to fight crime.

That American lag—government concerned with the issues and problems of the immediate past while people were wrestling in a newer world—could be with us for a long time. At least until that future when each of us is connected electronically to the government by some sort of communication miracle. Then there will be a whole new set of problems for Americans.

Democracy, after all, is a lot of trouble. The more we have, the more trouble it causes. But if I had to go back to one paragraph I wrote while living out of airplanes these few years, it would be from the essay I did on leadership for *Esquire* at the end of 1979: "The United States is more democratic and more open than it was in the good old days of 'leadership.' It is a better, if more confusing, place to live in now but a harder place to govern, populated by a people almost impossible to lead."

Terrific people—on both coasts, and in-between. As for me, after the wonders of living in the West, I moved back East in January of 1981. We traded our view of Santa Monica Bay for an equally spectacular one of Central Park. I only wish there was some way you could put a hot tub in a New York apartment.

Acknowledgments

Because the work in this book was done from many places over a period of three years, the list of people to whom I owe thanks is very long. But its very length reminds me of the good times we had.

In New York: Ken Auletta and Amanda Urban, Clay Felker, Gail Sheehy, Elizabeth and Byron Dobell, Lynn Nesbit, Michelle Evans and Tully Plesser, Mary and Roger Mulvihill, Amy Peck, Susan Parker, Dominique Browning, Sara Maltz, Peter Kaplan, William Shawn, Pat Crow, Shirley and Milton Glaser, Jill Krementz and Kurt Vonnegut, Bina and Walter Bernard, Pam Hill and Tom Wicker, Ann Black, Tom Priestly, Kiki von Fraunhofer and Jerzy Kosinski, Jane O'Reilly, Julienne and John Scanlon, Richard Wald, Betty Friedan, Don Singleton, Peggy Barber.

In Los Angeles: Jean Vallely, Mary Murphy, Ciji Ware and Tony Cook, Millie Harmon and Steve Meyers, Marcia and Paul Herman, Susan and Alan Friedman, Carol and Frank Lalli, Diane Wayne and Ira Reiner, Fran and Roger Diamond, Jean Brooks and Mickey Kantor, Carol and Peter Wallen, Mimi and Wally Baer, Alice and David Clement, Susan and Don Rice, Aimee and Monroe Price, Sherry and Steve Stockwell, John Phillips and Linda Douglass, David Freeman, Gerry Chaleff, Phyllis Kirk Busch, Tony Richardson, Kathleen Brown and Van Sauter, Kevin and Jim Bellows, Penny and Phil Tracy, Jan and Phil Barnouw, Harriett and John Weaver, Frances and Norman Lear, Margery Schwartz, Ed Salzman.

In Washington: Felicity Barringer and Phil Taubman, Brooke Shearer and Strobe Talbott, Steve Weisman, Lesley Stahl and Aaron Latham, Barbara and Richard Cohen, Prudy and Bob Squier, Cokie and Steve Roberts, Emily Friedrich, Alan Katz, Marie and Greg Schneiders, Charlie Peters.

In different places: Ned Whelan, Chris Isidore, Laura and Barry Seaman, Dolly and Tom Corcoran, Clark Hoyt, Roger Youman, David Sendler.

Universal Press Syndicate: Tom Drape, Lee Salem, Alan McDermott, John McMeel, the Andrews family.

And to Cathy O'Neill, who took me to many places I'd never been.

About the author

Richard Reeves was born in New York and grew up in Jersey City, New Jersey. A graduate of Stevens Institute of Technology, he began a newspaper career as the first editor of the *Phillipsburg* (N.J.) *Free Press*. He was a reporter for the *Newark* (N.J.) *Evening News*, the *New York Herald Tribune*, and the *New York Times*. His syndicated column appears in more than one hundred fifty newspapers nationwide. His work has appeared in virtually every national magazine and he has been the political editor of *New York* magazine and the national editor of *Esquire*. He has written and hosted two nationally televised films, including "Lights, Camera . . . Politics," for ABC News, winner of the 1980 Emmy for documentaries. He is the author of four books.